Paedophiles and Sexual Offences Against Children

Wiley Series in

The Psychology of Crime, Policing and Law

Series Editors

Graham Davies
University of Leicester, UK
and
Clive R. Hollin
University of Birmingham, UK

The Psychology of Interrogations, Confessions and Testimony
Gisli Gudjonsson

Children as Witnesses
Edited by Helen Dent and Rhona Flin

Paedophiles and Sexual Offences Against Children
Dennis Howitt

Paedophiles and Sexual Offences Against Children

Dennis Howitt
Loughborough University, UK

JOHN WILEY & SONS
Chichester · New York · Brisbane · Toronto · Singapore

Baffins Lane, Chichester,
West Sussex PO19 1UD, England

National 01243 779777
International (+44) 1243 779777

Other Wiley Editorial Offices

John Wiley & Sons, Inc., 605 Third Avenue,
New York, NY 10158-0012, USA

Jacaranda Wiley Ltd, 33 Park Road, Milton,
Queensland 4064, Australia

John Wiley & Sons (Canada) Ltd, 22 Worcester Road,
Rexdale, Ontario M9W 1L1, Canada

John Wiley & Sons (SEA) Pte Ltd, 37 Jalan Pemimpin #05-04,
Block B, Union Industrial Building, Singapore 2057

Library of Congress Cataloging-in-Publication Data

Howitt, Dennis.
Paedophiles and sexual offences against children / Dennis Howitt.
p. cm — (Wiley series in the psychology of crime, policing, and law)
Includes bibliographical references and index.
ISBN 0-471-93939-0 (cased) — ISBN 0-471-95591-4 (paper)
1. Child molesters—Great Britain. 2. Pedophilia—Great Britain.
3. Child sexual abuse—Great Britain, I. Title. II. Title:
Pedophiles and sexual offenses against children. III. Series: Wiley series in psychology of crime, policing, and law.
HV6570.4.G7H685 1995
364.1′536—dc20 94-23099
CIP

British Library Catologuing in Publication Data

A catalogue record for this book is available from the British Library

ISBN 0-471-93939-0 (cased)
ISBN 0-471-95591-4 (paper)

Typeset in 10/12½pt Century Schoolbook from the author's disks by Mackreth Media Services, Hemel Hempstead.
Printed and bound in Great Britain by Biddles Ltd, Guildford, Surrey

Contents

About the Author

Dennis Howitt is Senior Lecturer in Social Psychology at the Department of Social Sciences at Loughborough University. Formerly he was Research Officer at Leicester University's Centre for Mass Communication Research. He has a long-standing research interest in applying psychology to social issues and has written a number of books in this area, including the Home Office published report *Pornography: Impacts and Influences* (1990) and *Child Abuse Errors: When Good Intentions Go Wrong* (1992), which dealt with the mistakes of professionals in child protection work.

Series Preface

The Wiley Series in the Psychology of Crime, Policing and Law will publish concise and integrative reviews in this important, emerging area of contemporary research. The purpose of the series is not merely to present research findings in a clear and readable form, but also to bring out their implications for both practice and policy. In this way it is hoped that the series will not only be useful to psychologists but also to all those concerned with crime detection and prevention, policing, and the judicial process.

If one wished to pick a topic on which everyone has a view, tinged with a strong emotional overtone, there is little doubt that sexual offences against children would rightly figure high on the list. Alongside much media coverage, the topic of child sexual abuse has attracted the attention of many academic disciplines—including criminology, psychology, and sociology—while being of direct concern to many practitioners—including social workers, probation officers, forensic and clinical psychologists, psychiatrists, police, and forensic nurses. With so many vested interests and concerns it is perhaps inevitable that a myriad of different views, even myths, have been constructed about the perpetrators of sexual offences against children. It is all too easy to lose sight of the fact that many of our views on the perpetrators of sexual offences are based on anecdote and theoretical speculation, rather than research evidence. The drift from myth and stereotype to socially constructed reality is easy to make but often difficult to question.

Those who query orthodox beliefs face a difficult task as their questions can raise many anxieties. Awkward questions can cast doubts over academic research and theories; can cause policy makers and practitioners to wonder about their role; and make educators worry about the messages they pass on to their students. Dennis

Howitt has a fine history of asking awkward questions about sensitive topics that other might well prefer to avoid. His review, with Guy Cumberbatch, of the effects of pornography contributed significantly to that debate. Moreover, he has published regularly on institutional racism, generating a fierce controversy within the British Psychological Society. His book, *Child Abuse Errors: When Good Intentions Go Wrong*, took a long, hard look at the world of child protection; asking fundamental questions about policy, research, and practice.

With a trenchant discussion of paedophilia, this book continues his tradition of tackling the hard issues. In an across-the-board sweep of theory, research, and practice, Howitt simply refuses to accept the core assumptions and methods that are often "taken as given" by workers in this difficult and demanding field. It is certain that some of what Howitt has to say will generate controversy, and it is highly unlikely that anyone will agree with everything he has to say. If that is the case, as we suspect that it will be, then, in our view, this text will have helped to achieve the aim of this series in generating constructive debate. A truly useful contribution to knowledge should make us pause, and look, and consider, and question: academics and practitioners alike should read on with interest and perhaps a little trepidation.

CLIVE HOLLIN

GRAHAM DAVIES

Acknowledgements

I am grateful to Peter Beaman for some of the transcriptions, Guy Cumberbatch for ideas and some interviews and Rosalie Shute for checking the manuscript and ideas. Ray Wyre and Charles Forte in the UK and Leo Cotter and Sharon McAvoy in the USA were of enormous help in providing offenders for the research.

CHAPTER 1

Introducing the Paedophile

"It has to be recognized that studies of sexual behaviour, the *scientia sexualis*, tend either to reinforce the normative order, which is predominantly the case in studies on identified deviance, or to provide a reinforcement for self-gratification fantasies, predominantly in studies of 'normal' sexual behaviour, which ignore the social location and grounding of sexuality. The question is not whether we can understand the varieties of sexual behaviours in and by themselves—this is meaningless—but whether the study of the varieties of sexual behaviour can yield answers to the uncertainty of the moral order."

(Mohr, 1981, pp. 51—52)

Being face-to-face with a paedophile is not a comfortable situation. Most of us harbour a catalogue of beliefs and emotions about such people, which structures our perceptions of what to say, think and do. Rarely are our feelings built entirely on factual knowledge. They are as likely to be based on newspaper headlines, the attitudes of professional colleagues and notions picked up from books and articles on sexual abuse. Images such as satanic abuse, paedophile rings, bogus social workers, dirty old men in raincoats and sadomasochistic or perverted child sex killers may dominate. While these may not be typical of offenders, this is probably less important than the extent to which such images structure our understanding. Doing research on paedophiles causes hardened research colleagues to shudder, "how could you?" or to question the point of doing so. But understanding paedophilia involves far more than why some people grope children. It strays into questions about the nature of childhood, the nature of sexuality, the social construction of moral issues and the knowledge base on which professionals build their therapeutic and assessment work.

No list of research findings about paedophiles encapsulates knowledge fixed for all time. Researchers create theories and research to serve a purpose, to meet a social demand. This is not to imply some sort of gigantic fraud in which researchers, in the name of science, provide deliberate distortions. Nevertheless, it does mean that knowledge is created in a context that is inevitably morally loaded. Furthermore, researchers are constrained by circumstances to adopt a particular style of research to take place in a narrow range of contexts. There is no concerted, worldwide programme to study sexual abusers, only piecemeal contributions by individuals and groups, especially in North America, including Canada. A great deal of the research comes from a small number of researchers at a small number of treatment centres. Consequently, not only are there substantial gaps in our knowledge but also relatively few perspectives dominate. Unlike much psychological research, most of the research on sex offenders is done by practising clinicians alongside their day-to-day therapeutic work. This encourages the focus of research onto treatment and assessment issues. We need to explore more widely.

GRAHAM'S STORY

It is important to get close to our subject matter. A case study can illustrate much of the complexity of the paedophile lifestyle. Graham's account of his long history of offending and his strong erotic orientation to boys is disturbing. In some respects, we should feel no sympathy towards him. His extensive involvement in sexual and other crimes should be inexcusable. But, much like his own victims, he suffered harsh experiences of childhood abuse. Elements in his story are surprising. In particular, note the way in which his adult offending retains features of his childhood abuse, despite new elements entering his offending pattern. Graham, when interviewed, was attending the former Gracewell Clinic in Birmingham, UK.

> "I'm 36 years old. My whole life has been revolving around sexual abuse from the age of four. I was abused from the age of 8 by multiple abusers through until 16. I started abusing children myself when I was 14. I've lived in a fantasy world since I was four, I suppose really, ...

predominantly sexual fantasy ... I've offended and been caught three times. Once was against my 10-year-old cousin, for which I got a six months' prison sentence suspended for two years. At the time I wasn't really bothered and worried about what I'd done because I didn't see anything wrong with it. [I was 19 then.]

"So I carried the relationship on with my cousin and met him outside the court after I got sentenced. Then I got caught again ... still didn't see anything wrong with what I was doing. Then I got caught again [five years later] and I got a seven-year prison sentence this time. But my fantasies had become so bizarre by then that I'd started to live the fantasies out by subjecting children to multiple abuse, videoing it for my own gratification at a later date. Fantasy was definitely taking control of my life ... I wanted to live the fantasy in reality.

"I'd actually been sexually abused before ... the concept of sexual abuse didn't mean anything to me. I didn't really understand what was going on. It was my father—although my perception of that was I was abusing him, because he never actually touched me. It was me who was touching my father ... My interpretation of it was that I was abusing him ... It was when me and my father used to have a bath together. I ... masturbated him off. I mean, I didn't know what I was doing at the time, obviously. I just knew he was enjoying it. It was bringing smiles to his face and making him happy. So all that was going for me, as far as I can remember, was that he makes me happy by looking after me and taking me out, spending all his time with me. So that was my way of paying him back. I can't really remember clearly ... all I can remember was that I didn't mind doing it. This didn't happen every time we had a bath.

"That stopped after I told my mother about it ... I didn't know what I was saying really. I didn't understand what was happening. [M]y mother wanted me in the bath ... [but I was] waiting for my dad coming back and she was angry about that ... I said I wanted to play with his willy ... She gave me a good slapping, gave me a bath and sent me to bed. Then I can remember when he came in there were a lot of arguments ... My father rejected me for a few years ... I used to sit with him all the time. On his lap, watching TV. I spent loads of time with him. After that he just kept on pushing me away. I couldn't understand why it stopped me and my father having baths together or him having any contact with me at all ...

"Then I met another guy called Andy, who was a friend of my father, and he started abusing me ... I decided ... there's no way I was going to tell on this guy because I don't want to destroy this relationship ... I used to pick men up, that was part of my fantasy. It was me that was in control and I used to go and pick men up from public toilets and places like that, at 9 or 10 years old. So, I've always looked on myself as the abuser—all the way through.

"The fantasy, it was a different type of fantasy then. You see, I'd lost my father through what was my fault. I didn't really understand at the time, I didn't understand what was going on and what I'd said was wrong. My fantasy then was to win my dad back and for him to acknowledge and be my father, you know, be close to me. But after I said about it he never had anything to do with me at all, he kept on pushing me away. So my fantasy predominantly then was father—I want my father back ... I was fascinated by the excitement that men had when they were with me. They were interested in me sexually. I was really aroused by other people's excitement ... It gave me a sort of feeling of ... power I suppose. I wasn't mixing with other children, I wasn't interested in other children. My pure fantasy was to be ... with a man who was my father. And all I wanted was my dad back ...

"I was very choosy about the type of men that I selected. Stupid when you think about it but I was. It had [to be] a certain type in a certain way, was like my father's age group. ... [It was men who looked like him.] I didn't like hairy men ... hairy chests ... exceptionally hairy bodies, or fat men or anything like that. But what was so special about me that excited these men, especially when they ejaculated and that, the looks on their faces ... I used to enjoy looking at all that and used to wonder what they were actually seeing and doing, what was going on for them from me, you know ... I met an eight-year-old boy called Colin who kept at me and at me to masturbate me and kept on touching me ... I wasn't interested at all, because all I was interested in was men and then one day he touched me and I felt really good and stopped him ... a few days later I met him downstairs where you had your bikes and all that, the lock-ups ... I said well you can watch and after a few seconds he just put his hand there and took over. And after about two or three seconds I just come everywhere and it was the most fantastic thrill that I'd ever had. And it was then that I realized what men were getting out of doing things like that to me ... I'm 14.

"And from that point on it was every single day abusing the boy for 18 months. I was superimposing myself on him, you see, my fantasy was that I was ... I didn't exist any more. The boy was me ... my fantasy was that I wanted to be the boy ... It went from that to oral sex, to me between his legs, up in between his legs. Never buggery ... I was projecting myself on him and taking on his excitement ... I think there'd be a feeling that I'd lost something because I was getting older ... I saw him as a way of holding onto what I'd lost. I mean, I've done this with older children that I've abused throughout my whole life. They've never really existed. I've become the child in the fantasy ... I just have to look at the child and I'm the child who's being abused ... I'm the child, so I'm abusing the adult.

"As time went on [my plan] would be to share the victim with other people, so that would heighten the feeling and the strength of the fantasy because the fantasy is multiple abuse, like for the child to be abused by three, four, ten, fifteen, twenty adults, that type of thing, you know. It's really bizarre.

"There was a boy at a later stage called Raj who actually videoed sexual acts with me and another guy ... as well. There were times when there was three of us abusing at once and I don't know whether that was my corrupting influence because he was only 9 years old and coming on for 10 ... But I don't know how much that was me ...

corrupting him into thinking that way, because I convinced him that it was good for him and he agreed with me, you see, so I suppose in a way you could say it was fulfilling his fantasy to be abused by as many men as—you see he was like me, he would choose the men. There's times when I'd take a guy there and [Raj was] not interested in him. And that is why Raj turned me on so much because it reminded me so much of myself, although he was an Indian boy. That was the way that I operated, so I really get into Raj. So I was using him to fulfil my fantasies really ... because I mean, eight years old, nine years old that's, fantasies like that ... they've got to be put there by other people, you don't just create a fantasy like that yourself.

"... All my fantasies were put there by other people, a corruptive influence of Andy, because that's what he was into, you know, he was into dressing me up in cop's shirt uniforms ... And he was into underwear, doing things with underwear and children's underwear and all that sort of carry-on, and that always rubbed off on me as well. So you take on other people's kinks, I suppose. Because at that age you can be corrupted easy, see, and lose total control of everything that's going on for you because other people control you.

"I'd actually had orgasms before that [at about 11½ to 12 years of age]. But not semen or anything coming out, it was just a good feeling as, the feeling as if you are ejaculating but nothing's coming out ... [I masturbated] all the time. Fantasizing about men. There was a lot of it happening in reality ... fantasizing about what had been done to me, and getting sexual pleasure out of it. As I say, although there was no orgasms, as you would interpret an orgasm, semen, fluid and things like that coming out, there was still intense sexual pleasure and feelings there from the masturbation that I was doing ... Thinking, even as a nine year old, ... what I can do with men. Not what men can do with me, but what I can do, what I do with men. I don't know whether it was a way of me getting back at my father or not. There's a lot of confusion there like trying to find something I've lost.

"... There's only two points in my whole life where my mother actually comes in ... there was once when I told her about my dad and the second time when I was about six or seven when I had my father because after that there was nothing but arguments in the family, my father started drinking heavy and totally changed the whole family life, the atmosphere in the house. My mother had had enough one day, I've never got on with my mother anyway. I've never really spoke with her, not that I can remember anyway or sat down and spent time with her. I've got two sisters as well, you see, so [I] suppose most of her time was devoted to them ... She was gonna leave us with dad. Now that for me would have been my dream come true. That was what I would have wanted. I can remember I'd put my arms around her legs and grabbed them and said, 'Don't go, don't go', and went hysterical, crying, really upset ... that she was leaving us alone with my dad, so I can't understand where that's come from, other than that there's no other memories at all ... relating to my mother, or my sisters ... Most of my life was spent outside the house from eight years old. And all I can remember before that was trying to get my father's attention back, win that back. You know, the fantasy of having a proper father ... It stopped once I met Andy, but I can remember when I was about 11 playing for the school football team in the cup final and my father said he'd come and watch and I was really over the moon about that ... he never turned up for the game, but Andy did—the main bloke that was abusing—and that really upset me, that did, when he didn't turn up. I played terrible in the game, because I'd really cheered myself up for him to be there and that shattered me totally relating to my father. The other time was when I was about seven and he took me out with him and he just left me sitting outside a pub for about three hours and then come out. But during all that time it was a continuous thing trying to win him back. I would have done anything, anything at all.

"The important thing for me is fulfilling the fantasy whether it was adults abusing me even as an adult, or me abusing children projecting myself onto them. I was always a helpless little boy who had power over everybody, who made everybody happy, made everybody excited, and everybody got enjoyment. So when I was 18/19ish I used to go to places and public toilets which I'd been doing since I was nine and met men ... three, four, five men at a time and I would always become the little boy, see my fantasy was to be the 8-, 9-, 10-, 11-year-old boy who's making everybody happy. And at the same time I'm happy because I've become 8, 9 or 10. But when I'm abusing an actual child the fantasy is that I don't exist any more as the abuser, I'm the child who's being abused, and I'm giving everybody else happiness and pleasure. Everybody's enjoying themselves, everybody's happy, including me as a child, because I'm getting enjoyment out of it as well.

"When I'm with adults I've got to imagine, I've got to become the child, but when there's an actual child there it's a lot easier to project yourself onto the child, because you, you actually become the child. Because there's a victim there, see. There's no real difference in the content whatsoever ... the feelings are the same and the orgasm's basically the same, as well.

"It wouldn't work [without the fantasy]. Even when I'm having sex with women, I've had two women in my life who I've lived with. I've got my wife and I've got kids of my own. Even when I'm having sex with her, she's nothing to do with it, I'm nothing to do with it—the whole thing's projecting back to the fantasy—me being a little boy and being abused. So it doesn't matter what sexual act I'm in, whether it's a group with men or one man on his own or a child on their own or a woman, ... it's revolving round the same fantasy.

"I wouldn't think about women, wouldn't turn me on at all. This is why here I'm frightened to let go, you see, because I don't know what I'm going to replace it with, because I've never had any other fantasies. There's never been any real other strong fantasy in my life.

"There's all different moods [which encourage the fantasy] depression, stress I know does come in here. I don't know whether I use [fantasy] to escape from reality or as a comfort to make me feel good or whatever. A classic example was when I was in Dartmoor jail ... I had to spend the whole time looking behind my back just in case somebody would attack with a knife or something like that. So I was under stress, pressure, I was depressed ... and I noticed at that particular stage that I was masturbating 10, 12 times a day over my fantasy whether because it was to do with the fact that I was under pressure and everybody was noticing me and I was becoming like a victim I suppose. And that was giving me feelings of being good ... I was going back to my cell and masturbating 10 times a day over the same fantasy of me being abused and projecting myself back to my childhood and that carried on ... until I left the place.

"If ever I saw a child with two or three men that would trigger it off because my major thing would be 'oh, they're taking the body of a child to abuse him' ... That would link me into my fantasy just seeing that out in the outside world ... All sorts of things kept my fantasy going ... Once I was at Victoria Station and there was a man come down with a small child to take it into the toilet. It was probably just an ordinary thing that a father would do, but to me that took me straight into fantasy, you know, because with me being abused in a toilet on quite a regular basis as a child.

"My view of all children [was that they're quite precocious and worldly wise]. But what particularly pleased me were children [who] just needed somebody to talk to. A classic example was my cousin. I met him at a ... wedding. He reminded me of myself a hell of a lot and we struck it off straight away ... They all were basically similar to myself in looks, build, except with the exception of Raj who was an Asian.

"I was watching a programme the other day called *Age Seven in the USSR* where there was clips of children in their underwear, as soon as I saw that [it] threw me into a fantasy straight ways. It's just ordinary things like that get me going. I mean when I was in jail I had a pile of magazine cuttings, a really thick pile, collecting them, all of children and just children that attracted used for fantasy ... Newspapers and magazines. In fact, you can pick up more pornographics, or what you could term as pornographic stuff, from ordinary newspapers and magazines.

"Child porn, any type of porn, child porn, adult porn, it doesn't matter what you look at, you can always pick out something that suits your fantasy. I've even used adult pornography to satisfy my child's sex actions. I've taken letters from soft porn magazines where it's been an adult that's been abused by four or five men and changed the women, only being a little girl or a little boy or myself being abused by all these men, you know, so it doesn't matter where you go. In fact I find it more of a turn-on to have a magazine where there's a boy sitting just in a position that would be perfectly natural, where you can see up his shorts and see his underwear. That would turn me on and send me in a fantasy just as quick as watching, or if not quicker, than watching a pornographic film.

"I did have [my own video camera]. It was a way of feeding my fantasies. I would take a child, corrupt a child, convince a child that that was a good thing to do, although I only actually done it with one boy and there was three of us abusing him. There was only two on the video actually doing it. The heads and that were cut off, there was two adult males and a young boy, it was Raj, and I would watch that after it was done and imagine that I was Raj being abused by the men ... But what I wanted to do was get another three or four men in there with a boy, so although at that point it was purely fantasy, it was something that I was bringing into reality. Because if I hadn't have been caught it would definitely have, the fantasy would have been realized, but using Raj to do it.

"I had a relationship with another boy called Mark ... he lived with me for two years, we lived together for two years as father and son. I left my wife and kids and I brought him to live with me from when he was 12 to when he was 14 and his fantasy [was being] multiply abused. And he'd been getting abused since he was 6 and I carried that abuse on until 12 and there was times when he actually asked me to get my mates round and set [it] up. I videoed him as well, just him and myself together and videoed him. There's another part of my fantasies—cub scout stuff, the boy dressing as a cub scout. I'm dressing as a cub scout, getting him into various poses, that type of carry-on. So I actually put that on video with Mark, but he actually wanted to live the fantasy with me and there was the perfect opportunity to do it. But I just couldn't do it ... I don't know what stopped me, but something overpowered my sexual urge to fulfil the fantasy because it was Mark. But with Raj it was a completely different thing, I was just using and abusing him, there it was just pure sexual gratification. There was something different with Mark, you see, when the actual opportunity was presented I turned it down flat ... jealous really about other people being with him. Because I was madly in love with him. That's what I felt at the time. It was a very close relationship. A very close relationship with Mark ... he was the spitting image of me. He reminded me so much of myself.

"Mark knew my fantasy as well as his own. He used to talk about things that had happened to another boy that he knew with seven, eight men abusing all at one time while I was having sex with him. You see, so he would be talking about multiple abuse while I was abusing him. And for me that was a fantastic turn-on. That really heightened my fantasy that was going on—because he's talking about something that really happened to another boy that he knows ... [The other men were friends that I met through public toilets and places like that ...]

"[When asked if Andy was a paedophile.] There was a definitely a group of them, a group of men involved with Andy who after I got known to a few men started introducing all the others then. We'd go away for weekends. I'd spend weekends with them. Well I'd be telling my mother and father that I'd be down my mate's house, camping in the back garden. So I'd become very devious at an early age.

"It wasn't actually marriage, it was common law. I was in sort of my 20s. [This was the first woman I'd had a relationship with.] There was another woman ... who I met through her son who I was planning to abuse. It was just part of the process, the grooming process ... getting to know the mother and ended up having a relationship with the mother.

"[I fathered] a son and a daughter. [Why did you choose to live with your common law wife?] I don't know, to be honest with you. It totally confuses me. She was more male orientated than female orientated. I met her and went back to her place and had a good time and had sex with her. I really, really enjoyed it, but then again, it wasn't sex because she was a woman, it was my fantasy. You see I'd never been in a woman's vagina before and I knew what I was doing like, and got in there, and it just felt really, really great ... It was a fantastic feeling, it really boosted the fantasy, and I thought to myself then 'you've really been missing out for years, all this, this is lovely, a woman's vagina.'

"[On fantasy about female children] That's only been over the last few years. That's been a new thing for me over the past six years—changing a woman into a little girl, it's something that I never would have done before and to actually abuse my own stepdaughter. I've never been interested in girls at all ... There'd been fantasies there before I abused by stepdaughter, that basically started, because I'd never been interested in girls at all. I'd been back home, Anthea had reached the age of six/seven, seven and she started sitting round like little girls do, showing her knickers and things like that and that really turned me on, I don't know why ... It was as if I was [taking] her to say 'Look, I want you to have sex with me'. She was making herself available for me, which is a totally ridiculous thing, I know, but that was what was going on in my head. So, for me, it was a beautiful thing because when I was little I used to wear shorts all the time and I used to do that with men deliberately. To suss out the type of man they were. Sit with my legs open and let them see up there and see my pants and everything like, because I knew that my father liked that when I was little. Andy loved that, some of the men that Andy was involved with loved it, because he took photographs of me in those positions as well ... Because it was something I'd done as a child, so the fantasy got really strong and I started changing myself into a little girl. Not just a little boy, because I saw that as being more powerful. The fact that as a little boy you can only show part of your underwear because you've shorts on but as a little girl you can show the whole lot, and for me that was something that was really personal. So I found myself ... projecting myself into a little girl. So I'd become a little girl instead of a little boy.

"I actually used my wife to dress up as a little girl on her own, because then [I] started going from an interest in little girls ... to the power that little girls have as opposed to little boys you see. I thought the effect was more powerful ... because ... it was easy for a girl to show what she had, if you understand what I'm saying, it's not so easy for a boy. And for a period ... I was totally preoccupied by being a little girl.

"[What about a woman having sex with her daughter?] I wouldn't say anything about that at all, as long as both people were consenting, then there's no problem. I always believed that a child can give consent, but at the same time, I've always believed ... if a child doesn't want to have sex with you, then a child will say no ... you can't pressurize children. This has happened to me on two or three occasions, the child has turned round and said, 'No, I don't want to get involved in this', so I just stopped and accepted what he said.

"What had actually happened was, this Mark ... was living with me for two years. I went back to live with my wife and kids and he was coming weekends. I was still abusing him when I was back with my wife. I let him stay in the house, he used to share a room with Matthew, my son, now because of my thinking and me projecting myself into Mark, I couldn't perceive any other thoughts in his head that he would like children—all I was thinking about was he was interested in me and other men. The last thing that come into my mind was that he would be abusing my son and for that matter he was abusing my two stepdaughters as well ... I didn't know anything about it until I got arrested. They questioned Matthew with dolls, although he was only five years old, and he'd shown them what's been happening to him and they've asked him who's been doing this and it turned out to be Mark. Mark had told him that if he ever told anybody he'd be taken away, the bogey man would get him ... When I found out about it, I was raging, I really wanted to kill him because he'd abused my son ... he was only 14 when he abused my son ... I realized what I'd done ... shattered my fantasies, for over a month I didn't fantasize at all. I was so guilty about what I'd done to my son because that's exactly what happened to me, what I was trying to avoid happening to my son, because I wanted to give him a proper life, so that he could get what I never had and instead of doing that I'd actually set him up to be abused like I had been abused as a child and when that struck home it really hurt me bad ... it was from that I realized that I've got some serious problems ...

"I was involved in criminal activities for long periods. In the West End of London I was involved in drug dealing. I was involved in illegal pirate videos, all the latest films coming out, collecting money off prostitutes. I was working for a guy called Bill Alderton in the 70s, he was running the West End, all the gangsters and that. I used to go round with some of his guys collecting the money from prostitutes. He had lots of different houses that he owned, and they'd have a room for a hundred pounds a night and you'd go in and collect the money the following day. I was involved in sex shops and, when I was younger, I was involved in making pornographic videos in Denmark, being in them, and magazines. I've been in different, various different magazines. I've never seen anything wrong with doing what I was doing.

"I was at one time doing a bit of stealing, the first time I stole was when I was 10 years old. Andy had gone on holiday for two or three weeks and I broke into the house next door and the meter and things like that, and got caught. Since then I've never ever been caught again. I've done a hell of a lot of break-ins, robberies, all the way through.

"I've got myself a boyfriend now. From the jail. He's 25 years old and I've realized now that relationships are not purely sexual. For me, everything's been sexual ... what I work on now is to build relationships. Barry's the man for me now, although he dresses up as a little boy for me. Whereas before I abused male adults and families, they don't actually know what's going on for me. But with this relationship I know it's still wrong and it's bad because it's still fuelling the fantasy, but Barry shares the fantasy with me, he knows what's going on for me, he knows what I want, he doesn't mind doing it because he enjoys it himself and that's not abuse any more as far as I'm concerned ... if it was real that he was a little boy [it] would be illegal."

Graham, by virtually any definition is a paedophile. His biography includes many themes that are common in the debate on paedophilia: intergenerational abuse, paedophile rings, pornography, early sexualization experiences, fantasy, a need for mastery and control, poor relationship with mother and distorted family background. His story also introduces rarer ideas uncommonly found in discussions of paedophilia. For example, he describes graphically his sexual activities with women and girls, neither of which were erotically arousing in themselves and departed markedly from his early exclusive sexual orientation to boys and men. But Graham is not a typical paedophile; there is no such person. Nor should one imagine that conversations with offenders will always produce such a flurry of insight. Graham had undergone intensive therapy at a specialist residential unit for sex offenders; his frankness was partly a result of this. During the normal course of events, according to Graham, little would have been revealed. In prison, for example, to reveal so explicitly the nature and extent of his fantasy life, he believes, would have left him languishing there longer than he did.

WHAT IS A PAEDOPHILE?

Paedophilia is, within limits, a flexible concept. It can be normal behaviour or a perversion; it can be a boon or a crime; it can be universal or a peculiarity; and it can be legal or illegal. Some definitions are fairly technical. In the first place, paedophilia's definition is primary an issue of theory, not merely classification, since classification implies a theory, no matter how rudimentary. Freund *et al.* (1984) used Latinesque words to classify sexual attraction along the dimensions of sex and age:

Gynephilia. Sexual interest in physically adult women

Androphilia. Sexual interest in physically adult males

Heterosexuality. "[T]he sustained erotic preference for persons of the opposite sex, when there is a free choice of partner as to sex and other attributes which may co-determine erotic attractiveness" (Freund *et al.*, 1984, p. 194)

Paedophilia. A long-term sexual interest in children with the typical body shape of an under 11-year-old

Paedohebephilia. Sexual interest in persons with the body shape of under 11-year-olds as well as pubescent persons between 11 and 14 years for females and 11–16 years for males

According to Levin and Stava (1987), "Pedophilic behavior is any sexual contact, forced or nonforced, between an adult and a minor" (p. 58), and they regard child molestation as a synonym for paedophilia. The term "child molester" is more usually regarded as a generic term for all who offend against underage persons:

> "Child molestation is defined as any sexual contact between an offender and a victim who, due to age and/or immaturity, is incapable either legally or realistically (because of lack of a true appreciation of the significance or consequence of the act) of giving consent. The specific sexual acts may range from mutual touching and fondling to actual intercourse, but access to the victim is achieved through pressure, coercion, or deception."
>
> (Hobson, Boland and Jamieson, 1985, p. 104)

Inherent in the child molester/paedophile distinction is the belief that while some men are sexually/erotically fixated on underage people, there are others who, through force of circumstances, uncharacteristically or intermittently engage in some form of sexual activity with children rather than with their usually preferred adult partners. Superficially, this may seem reasonable but may not bear close examination. Stylized case studies illustrate aspects of the problem:

> "Al is a 35-year-old man with a fantasy triggered by seeing a young girl with long blonde hair or by a magazine or television characterization of the same. He then imagines himself disrobing the girl and touching her hairless pubic area and nipple buds. He may masturbate to this fantasy or use it to become aroused enough to have intercourse with his wife. Acting out the fantasy with his stepdaughter led to his arrest."
>
> (Rowan, 1988a, p. 91)

> "Carl is a 40-year-old man with a history of alcoholism and conflicts with his alcoholic wife. His oldest daughter had taken over care of the younger siblings and was his confidante. On one occasion, when drunk, Carl fondled his daughter."
>
> (Rowan, 1988a, p. 91)

For Rowan, both of these men are clearly child molesters in that they had sexually assaulted a child. In question is whether both are truly paedophiles. Al is the archetypal paedophile of the two. His sexual fantasies centre around the physical characteristics of an underage female and, just as in Graham's case, sex with an adult woman is facilitated by fantasies of sex with a child. Carl is a doubtful case of paedophilia, according to Rowan. His scenario suggests that drink and his wife's inadequacies caused his single sexual assault on an underage child. While it is not beyond the bounds of possibility that Carl is a child molester rather than a paedophile, caution is appropriate. For example, if Carl, in similar circumstances, had fondled his friend George's penis, would we argue that he has no homosexual leanings? We know too little about Carl—has he offended against any children outside of his family? Has he masturbated to thoughts of intercourse with an underage girl? Carl may be keen to present his crime as the result of the pressures of unfortunate circumstances.

The problems of definition are even more difficult when we take Rowan's discussion of incest:

> "The socially unskilled or 'lazy' man need not look beyond his own home especially in the context of family and/or community acceptance of such behavior. A man may feel entitled to sex and dominant enough to demand that he need not go beyond the family for gratification. Typically, those men who are aroused by the seduction process rather than the sex itself will not often find that challenge in the family setting. Study of children at risk suggests that the adult male's lack of bonding to the young child because of absence through military service, work, travel, or incarceration might predispose that particular child to assault."
>
> (Rowan, 1988a, p. 93)

To suggest that men do not have sex with children because of social bonding is palpable nonsense. If this were the case every man would have intercourse with any child with the exception of those with whom he has bonded. Relatively few men, as far as we can tell, have an erotic interest in children. In the light of this, it is probably safe to assume that this incestuous offender has an erotic interest in underage children which motivates incestuous acts, rather than a bonding failure.

In psychiatric classification, paedophilia is regarded as one of the sexual paraphilias alongside fetishes and sexual activity with animals. Homosexuality was, until relatively recently, regarded as a mental disorder in the standard American Psychiatric Association diagnostic manual. Gay Liberation not only had a significant impact on the decriminalization of much homosexual behaviour but also helped to define homosexuality as a lifestyle rather than a pathology. In the second *Diagnostic and Statistical Manual* of the American Psychiatric Association (DSM-II), homosexuality was classified as a sexual disorder but this changed with the third manual (DSM-III). Suppe (1991) suggests:

> "There is, in fact, good reason to suspect that the classification of sexual paraphilias as mental disorders is the codification of social mores. The historical record clearly shows that in issues such as masturbation, abortion and contraception, venereal disease, and the inferiority of women and blacks, physicians have generally supported the prevailing mores, presenting research that gave credence and medico-scientific legitimacy to social prejudices."
>
> (Suppe, 1991, p. 10)

Support for these assertions can be found in Howitt (1992) and Howitt and Owusu-Bempah (1994) for child abuse and racism, respectively.

Other curiosities abound in the *Diagnostic and Statistical Manual*. For example, the diagnoses of zoophilia (sexual attraction to animals) and paedophilia are based on either overt activities or private fantasy. In contrast, fetishes, exhibitionism, voyeurism and masochism/sadism are recognized solely from overt activities. Thus, the person who can only be aroused sexually by thinking of sex with their next-door-neighbour's goat but never touches the animal may be suffering from the mental illness zoophilia. Apparently, someone who can only get sexually aroused by imagining that he is whipping his next door neighbour's naked body is normal! This reasoning appears to be quite arbitrary. The value of a psychiatric theory that classifies the fantasy-only paedophile as mentally disordered but not the fantasy-only exhibitionist is very much in doubt.

The way in which paedophilia is described has changed with fashions or developments in psychiatric thinking. In the first edition of the *Diagnostic and Statistical Manual of Mental Disorders* (DSM-I)

(American Psychiatric Association, 1952), it was listed as one of several "sexual deviations". Paedophilia was held to be sociopathic since the paedophile was at odds with society's mores, not just other individuals. Despite still being described as a "sexual deviation" in DSM-II, the notion of sociopathic disorder was abandoned and the categorization "nonpsychotic mental disorder" used instead (American Psychiatric Association, 1968). Later, paedophilia was listed as a member of the category "paraphilias" in DSM-III (American Psychiatric Association, 1980). Paedophilia was restricted to sexual activities between adults and *pre-pubescent* children or fantasy on this theme. Thus, adult sexual activity involving early adolescents is not classified as paedophilia:

> "Many would find DSM-III's classification unduly narrow by virtue of excluding contact with pubescents and early adolescents and would disagree that '[i]solated sexual acts with children do not warrant the diagnosis of Pedophilia' (p. 271), and would further reject the idea that the acts must be 'a repeatedly preferred to exclusive method of achieving sexual excitement' (p. 272) in order to qualify them as a sexual disorder."
>
> (Suppe, 1991, p. 24)

The revision, DSM-III-R (American Psychiatric Association, 1987), abandoned the requirement "repeatedly preferred". A categorization of paedophilia was allowed even when the men showed sexual arousal to other stimuli, e.g. other paraphilias or adult–adult homosexual or heterosexual intercourse. This change accompanied a growing awareness that paedophilia is often associated with other sexual crimes and activities.

Also contentious is the extent to which paedophilia actually results in psychological disability:

> "This investigation of the so-called 'sexual paraphilias' in DSM has reinforced the suspicion that they are not, *per se*, mental disorders, but rather constitute conflicts between an individual and society. Their inclusion in DSM-III is unwarranted, unscientific, and only serves to strengthen the conclusion that psychiatry has resorted to the codification of social mores while masquerading as an objective science. Indeed, even if this suspicion is incorrect, the burden of proof rests with psychiatry."
>
> (Suppe, 1991, p. 26)

But it needs to be stressed that Suppe wrote this in the context of a rare publication broadly favourable towards paedophile activity.

Describing paedophilia as a *paraphilia* means that it is classified with sadism, masochism, exhibitionism, voyeurism and other sexual practices that many regard as perversions. The key characteristics of paraphilia, starting with the most diagnostic, are:

(1) A highly sexually arousing, long-term and unusual erotic preoccupation or fantasy;
(2) A pressure to act out this preoccupation;
(3) Sexual dysfunction during conventional sexual behaviour with a partner, such as problems of desire, arousal or orgasm (Levine, Risen and Althof, 1990).

The fantasy of paraphiliacs has its origins in childhood and adolescence. Ageing paraphiliacs frequently describe how certain erotic imagery has stayed with them for most of their lives. While some men have periodic episodes of paraphiliac fantasy, they usually claim that this started prior to or during adolescence. The sense of pressure to act out these erotic fantasies in real life varies greatly. Masturbation is commonly used to discharge the physical arousal caused by fantasy. Frequent masturbation can, in some individuals, severely interfere with normal daily life. Many paraphiliacs experience this sexual arousal as intrusive, occurring when not desired. They are rapidly aroused when imagery relevant to their fantasy is encountered in magazines, videos and elsewhere (Levine, Risen and Althof, 1990).

Despite paedophilia being classified as a paraphilia, nothing should be assumed about its relationship with other paraphilias. Levine, Risen and Althof suggest that although changes from sadism to masochism, for example, are typical in the work experience of clinicians, switches from paedophilia to other paraphilias are uncommon. A study of adolescent offenders found that about half of them had committed two or more offences. Nevertheless, under a quarter of such multiple offenders offended in more than one category of sexual offences (Saunders, Awad and White, 1986). Switching between paedophilia, rape and exhibitionism was rare. About two-thirds of recidivists repeated exactly the same type of offence.

Substantial differences are found between the legal, social and biological definitions of paedophilia. In Western society, definitions of childhood have been based largely on arbitrary dates, milestones marking progress into adulthood. Biological changes may not correspond closely to these, and are insignificant in social and legal definitions. Childhood has been extended to leave a limbo time when the young person may be physically but not socially ready for reproduction:

> "At this point in our history, a very real conundrum exists for the researchers of adult/child sex ... what truly marks the point beyond which sexual interaction with a child is pathological and not just criminal?"
>
> (Ames and Houston, 1990, p. 339)

It may be more appropriate or meaningful to classify paedophiles in terms of the biological characteristics of the child. Perhaps if the offender consistently opts for children who lack secondary sexual characteristics such as breasts or pubic hair then he should be classified as a paedophile; there is a distinction to be drawn between *biological* and *socio-legal* children. In girls, biological children have not started their periods (but the age of menarche varies between cultures, individuals and historical period). Similarly, boys undergo changes from the flat and slim boy-type to a maturer shape:

> "Laws governing child molestation reflect this sociolegal childhood, regardless of its discrepancy with biological childhood. This discrepancy has served to cloud what should be a natural distinction between offender types, between child molestation and rape. By making this distinction, important differences between these populations will perhaps be found and the etiology of pedophilia will become more apparent."
>
> (Ames and Houston, 1990, pp. 340–341)

For the purposes of this book, the word "paedophile" will be used as a generic name for sexual offenders against underage persons. At the same time it is acknowledged that this covers a multitude of sinners, perhaps not all of whom will have strong sexual desires towards underage persons. The advantages of using the term "paedophile" include its brevity compared to phrasal nouns such as "child sexual molester". It also adroitly avoids the conventional wisdom that there are types of sexual offenders against children who are not erotically orientated towards children. For example, incest offenders are commonly held to be different to "true" paedophiles, although this has not been proven and is in considerable doubt. One disadvantage is the connotations of child *love*, which may be anything but the truth. At times the terminology of other writers has to be adopted for stylistic reasons, despite reservations about their choice of language. Doubtless, Okami and Goldberg (1992) would describe the proposed use of the term "paedophile" in their phrase "slippage"—meaning that different researchers apply the term to vastly different phenomena such that it becomes very difficult to make meaningful comparisons between studies, or even to know what is meant by the term. This may be regarded as sloppiness; it can also be seen as one of the central things to understand in research and writings on child abuse—how ideas can change to suit different purposes (Howitt, 1992).

TAXONOMIES OF OFFENDERS

One way of simplifying the maze of information about offenders is to categorize them into broad types sharing common characteristics. Among the most significant taxonomies is *fixation* versus *regression* (Groth and Birnbaum, 1978). They had investigated convicted child sexual assaulters in Massachusetts in the 1970s. In every case there had been physical contact with the child. On the basis of this, two categories—*fixated* and *regressed*—were proposed:

> "'Fixation' is defined as a temporary or permanent arrestment of psychological maturation resulting from unresolved formative issues which persist and underlie the organization of subsequent phases of development. A fixated offender has from adolescence been sexually attracted primarily or exclusively to significantly younger persons. Sexual involvement with peer-age or older persons, where this has occurred, has been situational in nature and has never replaced the primary sexual attraction to and preference for underage persons."
>
> (Groth and Birnbaum, 1978, p. 176)

> "'Regression' is defined as a temporary or permanent appearance of primitive behavior after more mature forms of expression had been attained, regardless of whether the immature behavior was actually manifested earlier in the individual's development. A regressed offender has not exhibited any predominant sexual attraction to significantly younger persons during his sexual development—if any such involvement did occur during adolescence, it was situational or experimental in nature. Instead, this individual's sociosexual interests have focused on peer-age or adult persons primarily or exclusively."
>
> (Groth and Birnbaum, 1978, p. 177)

While this may make good sense, it holds a convenient subtext for offenders. In Groth and Birnbaum's sample there were clear life experience differences between the two types. Marriage, for instance, was rare among fixated offenders (only 12%), but common in the regressed type (75%). Strangers or acquaintances were the most frequent victims of fixated offenders (83% of cases); for regressed offenders, victims were more often friends or relatives (53% of cases). The two types perpetrated much the same sorts of sexual acts; penetration was equally common and the *modus operandi* were similar (i.e. the rates of seduction and enticement, intimidation and threat, and force or attack were much the same).

The description of the regressed type portrays them as "normal" heterosexual men who, under the pressures of adult or family life, turn to underage people for sexual "comfort". In other words, responsibility is deflected away from the offender. Once a man has adopted "an adult sexual relationship" then any deviation from this is the responsibility of his situation—which needs to be dealt with, rather than his sexual orientation towards children. This might appear reasonable since such men can apparently function sexually as adults. After all, they are frequently married. But this does not prove that the other requirement of "regression" is met—the absence of a concurrent, continuing sexual orientation to children. In Graham's case, knowing the full details it is hard to describe him as "regressed". Interviewed in other circumstances, he might have blamed his offences on his wife's lack of sexual interest in him or on stress.

So what of married offenders within the family? How could they be classified as anything other than regressed? Clearly information is needed about their sexuality and fantasy—but their honesty is a prerequisite for this. Take the man who abuses his stepchildren. If his wife dresses as a child when they have intercourse, if he fantasizes that she is an 11-year-old and if his offending is not limited to his stepchildren, would we say that he is a regressed heterosexual? Presumably not, but this pertinent information may not be known to us. Given the underreporting of abuse, case records may lack information about other relevant offences. His therapist may not seek this information, believing that regression accounts for his case.

A number of other issues can be raised about the fixation/regression typology:

(1) It is based on clinical experience with incarcerated offenders, which may limit its usefulness when applied to the general community;

(2) It lacks validation by research.

Conte (1985) stresses the inadequacy of its underlying theory:

> "The typology assumes that sexual contact with children is largely a function of the failure of normal developmental processes whereby an adult sees himself primarily as a child and, therefore, seeks sexual contact with children or a maladaptive response to stress. In fact, no such connection has been demonstrated. For example, the onset of sexual contact with children in many cases cannot be tied to any stress in the adult's life. As many professionals talk about the typology, they indicate the belief that *fixated* offenders are untreatable and *regressed* treatable. This is an observation that follows more from studies of incarcerated offenders ... At present there are no descriptions of community-based offenders supporting the utility of the *fixated* and *regressed* typology nor suggesting that community treatment of one group is more effective than treatment of the other."
>
> (Conte, 1985, p. 343)

Reservations are also appropriate about the view that incest is different from extrafamilial abuse, which is based on three untenable assumptions (Conte, 1985):

1. "Incestuous fathers do not abuse outside the family". This is undermined by evidence that incest offenders may well be offending outside the family or raping adult women (Abel *et al.*, 1983). Similarly, nearly half of offenders who had offended inside the home against girls had also molested females outside the home, and one in ten of them had offended against boys outside the home (Becker and Coleman, 1988).

2. "Incest is the sexual expression of nonsexual needs". However, all human sexuality involves non-sexual needs like love and anger. Furthermore, physiological evidence that incest offenders are sexually aroused by children also invalidates this assumption. Research shows that incestuous offenders often have erections to nude depictions of underage children (see Chapter 4). Rather than incestuous offenders being forced by family circumstances towards abuse, at least some have the same sexual arousal patterns to children as extrafamilial offenders.

3. "Every member of the family makes a psychological contribution to the development and maintenance of sexual abuse". Empirical evidence that incestuous families are different from others is unimpressive and largely anecdotal.

Significantly, regressed paedophiles are never homosexuals (Groth and Birnbaum, 1978). But why cannot stress or sexual deprivation drive homosexuals to turn to children? The concept of regression seems to be the problem, not the nature of heterosexuality.

INCESTUOUS AND NON-INCESTUOUS OFFENDERS

> "Mr A. is a 38-year-old white male, employed as a certified public accountant in a large corporation, who was involved in incestuous relationships with his now 11- and 14-year-old natural daughters over a period of several years. His deviant behavior began when he was under considerable job-related and marital stress. It coincided with his changing jobs to a more demanding one and having persisting doubts about his performance. He had few friends and his wife did not provide emotional support. In fact, they had become increasingly emotionally distant and less sexually active with each other. Since he came from a conservative background and had a strict sense of morality, he did not consider having an extra-marital relationship. He felt particularly fond of and close to his eldest daughter who was then 9 years old. Initially, he had her sit on his lap for long periods of time while he fondled her genital area. About two months later the sexual involvement progressed to oral–genital sex and then to penile–vaginal intercourse. He always felt guilty afterward, but managed to rationalize that whatever he did was out of love for her. Also, he falsely interpreted her lack of physical resistance to mean enjoyment of the sexual activities ... Initial laboratory assessment indicated high arousal to adult consenting sex, adolescent girls and young girls."
>
> (Travin *et al.*, 1985a, pp. 94–95)

Obviously this man is an incestuous father. Despite the excuses that are made for his behaviour throughout the case study, he persists with sexually abusing his daughters over a lengthy period of time. It is a drawn-out process, not a brief "mistake". The case study suggests that he cannot resolve the inadequacies of his marriage by having an affair or, by implication, buying sex—he is too high-mindedly moral for that. On the other hand, he is resilient enough to cope with the guilt he feels at incestuous sexual intercourse! But it is easy to see why he turned to his daughters for sex—he gets sexually aroused by underage girls in general. Little more evidence is needed to confirm that he is a paedophile. Just what do his sexual fantasies concern?

Girls? In truth, has he also been abusing outside of his family?

It is conventional to regard the dynamics of sexual abuse within the family as different from those outside of the family. The evidence for this is far from convincing, as in Mr A.'s case. While it might be possible to imagine brief sexual episodes that may not be paedophiliac in nature, one would need to know a case in far greater detail than is usually possible before rejecting the possibility of paedophilia. It is traditional to regard incest as a sort of non-sexual sideshow to family pathology, caused by the problems of the wife and mother as much as by the offender himself:

> "In terms of pattern, it is the same: the emotionally dependent man, the domineering or managing wife; withdrawal of the wife from an increasingly frustrating relationship, usually including the refusal to continue sexual relations. The husband then begins drinking and sexually molests an accessible little girl, usually someone over whom he exercises authority and who is not likely to reject him. The child usually feels her father, and most authority figures, can do no wrong and accepts the attentions as a favor. She may, in fact, feel flattered. The aggressive component commonly seen in the rape of adult victims is not usually evident in child rapes. Consequently, the child does not see the happenings as an assault, and she will be unlikely to report it to her mother unless they have an especially trusting relationship."
>
> (Peters, 1976, p. 411)

With good cause, feminists have taken exception to this sort of women-blaming scenario (MacLeod and Saraga, 1988). The offender is held hardly to blame—but his wife is. It goes without saying that numerous acceptable ways exist for dealing with unsatisfactory wives—putting up with them is just one of many. Sexually abusing her children, needless to say, is not one, and makes no sense unless the man is already sexually attracted to underage children. If he is, then this may account for the fact that his wife rapidly loses sexual interest in him. Furthermore, if his interpersonal needs are satisfied by relations with children, we should not be surprised that his wife domineers—or that is the way she appears to him. Some offenders express variants on this theme:

> "Well, 15 or 16 years ago, my wife committed adultery and I caught her and gave her a damn good hiding ... didn't I? Well, instead of me going out and finding another woman and chucking her out, I was thinking of the kids, you know, and I stuck it for the kiddies' sakes ... [A]bout two or three years after that ... me mum and dad died, both within three months of each other, and I was left on my own ... I started drinking

> heavy ... I got as I wouldn't work. I turned to my daughters ... just fondling them. No sexual intercourse ... just pushed my hand up their jumper ... and sometimes down their knickers ... My second eldest says I did try it [sexual intercourse] on with her once but I were drunk, she said I was absolutely drunk ... but my eldest and my youngest they tried to feel me, didn't they?"
>
> (Howitt, 1992, pp. 178—179)

If there is anything in the view that incestuous offending has different causes from other sexual abuse then signs of paedophilia in incest offenders should be weak. In addition, incestuous men should be less likely to demonstrate the inadequacies in social and sexual functioning often held to underlie sexual deviance in general. Pawlak, Boulet and Brandford (1991) compared intrafamilial and extrafamilial offenders using self-report measures of current sexual functioning (the Deogatis Sexual Inventory). This assesses:

- Sexual information or knowledge;
- Sexual experience;
- Drive;
- Psychological symptoms;
- Affects;
- Gender role definition;
- Sexual fantasy;
- Body image;
- Sexual attitudes; and
- Sexual satisfaction.

Important components of effective sexual behaviour should differentiate extrafamilial from intrafamilial sex abusers if the theory is sound.

Male inpatients and outpatients of an Ottawa sexual behaviour clinic were studied. Most of them had not been tried in court at the time of assessment. A quarter maintained their innocence of the charges and so could not be included in the research. Two samples were formed from the viable remainder. The *intrafamilial* sample had offended against their son/daughter, stepson/stepdaughter, niece/nephew or grandchild; the *extrafamilial* sample was made up of the rest. There were some differences between the two groups. For example, incest offenders were significantly older (averaging 37 years compared with 34 years). Not surprisingly, the incest group was likely to be married; the majority of extrafamilial offenders were not. The average age of their youngest victims was the same for both groups (about 9 or 10 years). Usually, the incest group offended against females (84%), compared to only 47% of the extrafamilial abusers. Only 5% of the incest offenders molested both sexes, compared with 18% of the extrafamilial sample.

A complex statistical technique (discriminant function analysis) identified the major differences between the two types of offender in terms of a range of possible criteria. Only three things contributed significantly to distinguishing between them:

1. Satisfaction. Incest offenders had greater satisfaction with their sex lives, including frequency of sexual contact, sexual drive and variation in sexual activities.

2. Fantasy. Incest offenders reported fewer fantasy themes.

3. Experience. Extrafamilial offenders had less varied experiences.

Although each of these indicated that both incest and extrafamilial offenders had inadequacies, they discriminated only poorly between the two types of offender. The authors point out that some of the significant measures merely reflect what one might expect—people with a partner showed greater sexual satisfaction and experience. One drawback should be mentioned: the questionnaire did not deal with deviant fantasy, perhaps a crucial test of whether or not incestuous offenders differ from non-family offenders. To this might be added evidence that the empirically based paedophilia scale of Toobert, Bartelme and Jones (1958) for the Minnesota Multiphasic Personality Inventory (MMPI) appears to be poor at distinguishing between incest and extrafamilial abusers, despite being regarded as one of the better questionnaire methods for assessing paedophilia. Furthermore, Panton (1979) found no differences on the paedophilia scale although social introversion was higher in the incest offenders. (Note that the paedophilia scale of Toobert, Bartelme and Jones (1958) may not be very good at distinguishing paedophiles from other men, according to recent research by Johnston *et al.*, 1992).

Despite the paucity of objective evidence that differentiates incestuous from extrafamilial offenders, some commentators, although aware of this situation, believe that there are at least some incestuous offenders who have no true sexual interest in children. For example, Salter (1988) argues:

> "In my practice I have seen incest offenders who, I believe, had no prior history of sexual assault prior to the incest, although they frequently had strange practices, beliefs, and opinions regarding sexuality. The incest was, in some cases, a conversion of nonsexual problems into sexual behavior rather than the result of a long standing sexual interest in children."
>
> (Salter, 1988, p. 51)

A therapist's failure to elicit accurate information about prior sexual orientation towards children may lead to the mistaken view that no such interest exists. Disclosure by offenders may only occur well into therapy, if ever. An offender who (erroneously) blames his offending on stress may create the impression that he does not require intensive therapy for his offending but for his circumstances. In short, caution is required over denials of erotic interest in children in those who offend against children. The validity of a theory of different types of offender based on offenders' claims is questionable.

A more promising approach is the taxonomic analysis offered by Knight (1988, 1992). He describes seven different extant typologies of paedophilia, mainly variants of the *true paedophile* versus the *regressive/frustrated* types. Some include a *sociopathic* paedophile (which includes violent/aggressive paedophiles), others a *pathological* type who may be senile or mentally defective. Based on such typologies and the general clinical literature, four different paedophile types (fixated, exploitative, sadistic and regressed) seemed possibilities. It proved difficult to separate these different types empirically on the basis of clinical or questionnaire studies using known samples of men believed to represent these different types. A final typology was developed using a statistical technique that "objectively" creates types and specifies the criteria to be used to identify members of a type. This is statistically rather complex, although the resulting six types are easily understood. The fixation and social competence aspects of paedophilia were not the opposite ends of a continuum as in Groth and Birnbaum's typology, but were totally independent factors. Thus it is possible to have a fixated but socially competent offender. The six types were:

1. Interpersonal. High contact with children (this is the object-related offender who seek a general relationship with children).

2. Narcissistic. High contact with children but the motivation for contact is exclusively sex. Usually genital activity is high in this type.

3. *Exploitative.* Low contact with children, low physical harm.

4. *Muted sadistic.* Again, low contact with children, low physical harm.

5. *Non-sadistic aggressive.* Low contact, high physical damage—clumsiness and the like might account for the damage.

6. *Sadistic.* Low contact, high physical damage.

Such a typology is highly dependent upon the sample on which it was based, so clearly a lot of further work is needed to establish it as reliable and workable.

Inevitably, sexual politics influences the classification of adult sexual activities with children. Sandfort, Brongersma and van Naerssen (1991) argue that the typical "science of sex" approach misrepresents the truth in important respects. The failure to differentiate between *paedophilia* and what is called *man–boy love* leaves all adult–child relationships overshadowed by the psychiatric term "paedophilia", with its connotations of pathology. Rather than describing the *nature* of the adult–child relationship, the usual nomenclature neglects that sex is not the essence of, but merely part of, the relationship. Furthermore, the wants and motives of the boys are discounted:

> "In *man/boy* love the unproblematic affectional side of the phenomenon is stressed, suggesting reciprocity or even symmetry between the parties involved; it is understandable that boy-lovers in the United States adopted this term to further their goals. The choice of labels is never without political grounds or consequences. These labels also have consequences for the people who use them for their own self-understanding and influence the way they deal with their desires and express feelings."
>
> (Sandfort, Brongersma and van Naerssen, 1991, p. 8)

The age characteristics of paedophiles provide some insight into the nature of offending (Mohr, 1981). Normal involvement with children in economically highly developed societies is confined to the child's family, teachers and other professionals involved in the welfare of children. The lifespaces of children and adults overlap little apart from these exceptions: "There is hardly a sphere of intimacy left, except where adults appear in a legitimated caretaking role" (Mohr, 1981, p. 43). Apparently the peak age group of children sexually involved with adults is in the 7 to 12 years range, according to earlier studies. The distribution of *offenders'* ages demonstrates three peaks:

1. The adolescent group. These are largely characterized by an immaturity of psychosexual maturation, which results in a sexual interest in younger people. As they mature and become attracted to older females, the socially unacceptable aspects of their sexual interests disappear. The age difference between these adolescents and their child partners indicates their lack of psychosexual development as well as the cause of society's disapproval. Children who become sexually involved with this group of offenders average 6.5 years of age. Probably most of these offenders will move on to age-appropriate sexual partners but others will retain their interest in inappropriate age groups.

2. The middle-aged group. Most people's involvement with children decreases after adolescence. Siblings, and attendance at school and recreational facilities ensure that adolescents have high contact with children. There is a decline in contact with children that continues up to and through the third decade of life. During one's 30s children begin to feature more in the life cycle, so that the middle-aged group are socially involved with their own and friends' children. This group is involved with children averaging 11 years of age.

3. The old-age group. Despite the grandparent role, this age group has no special proximity to children. Many may have ceased sexual activity and become increasingly socially withdrawn. Mohr suggests that this age group may be inclined towards children other than through proximity. Gross organic defects due to senility and so forth were insufficient to explain the pattern. A large proportion of the sexual incidents happen during play and games: "... many of these people were more comfortable with children than adults" (Mohr, 1981, p. 50).

Attempts to classify offenders have proven to be of very limited worth and validity. Nevertheless, they help to highlight the problematic nature of some of the conventional notions about offenders. Menard and Johnson (1992) argue that, despite such problems, typologies are not so much about classifying people than the problems they suffer. That is, the pure types identified by the typology do not have to correspond to any real-life cases.

THE PREVALENCE OF PAEDOPHILIA

"What, though, of those adults who experience a sustained preference for children as sexual partners, but who never—whether from fear or

> moral scruple—touch a child with erotic intent, finding more or less satisfying outlets in fantasy, or in 'substitute' activities varying from masturbation to marriage? It is impossible to know how many adults fall into this category, but on the speculative assumption that they constitute no more than 1% of the population, their total numbers would approach half a million ... I am taking it for granted that feelings of sexual attraction in adults towards at least some young people from about 15 upwards are so common as to be virtually universal, and that similar feelings for boys or girls in the years immediately following puberty are experienced by rather more adults than most of them are prepared to acknowledge."
>
> (Righton, 1981, pp. 24–25)

There is no doubt that substantial numbers of underage people are exposed to unwanted or unwarranted sexual experiences with adults. The only uncertainty is in specifying the exact number. The precise figures depend on decisions, such as whether non-contact abuse is included and how and where the research is carried out. Nevertheless, tentative but useful data is available (La Fontaine, 1990). In contrast, little is known about paedophilia in the community rather than in institutional settings. Simple information such as the numbers of active paedophiles in the general population is unavailable. More complex questions such as the number of men with unexpressed paedophile leanings are impossible to discuss knowledgeably.

Research by Templeman and Stinnett (1991) would be dismissed as trivial were more substantial data available. Nevertheless, it gives some indication of the extent of sexual interest in underage people. Undergraduate volunteers averaging 22 years of age from largely white rural areas or small towns took part. Their sexual histories were assessed using the *Clarke Sexual History Questionnaire* supplemented by additional questions. Illegal sexual behaviour was fairly common: 3% had arrests for sexual offences, 3% had been in trouble with others for their sexual behaviour, 3% had had sexual contact with girls under 12 years of age, 2% with girls between 13 and 15 years of age, 42% had behaved voyeuristically (window peeping), 8% had made obscene phone calls, 35% had engaged in frottage, 5% had been involved in coercive sex and 2% had been exhibitionist. In all, *two-thirds* of the sample had done at least one of these things and over *half* had committed an arrestable offence. Very few of them, just 3%, reported being a victim of sexual abuse as a child.

Their sexual arousal to different types of sex and age group was measured using the *Farrenkopf Arousal Portfolio and Cardsort*. The *portfolio* consists of separate pictorial collages of 0–6-year-olds, 6–12-year-olds, 12–18-year-olds and adults, as well as violence towards women, exhibitionism, voyeurism, dressing in female underwear and bestiality. Sexual arousal to each collage was rated by the men on a scale from 0 to 100. The *cardsort* involves a set of cards describing sexually explicit activities with a third person: rape, exhibitionism, voyeurism, frottage, obscene phone calls, and sex with boys, girls, adolescents and adults. Although fairly low levels of arousability were found on average to child stimuli, sexual arousal to depictions of teenagers was considerably higher and to adult women very high. While this is significant, other data are more revealing: 5% of the sample reported desire for sex with girls under 12 years of age, and 12% desired sex with girls in the 13- to 15-year-old age range.

Such data are at best suggestive because of the poor sampling methods employed. Finkelhor and Lewis's (1988) epidemiological study of child molestation ought to have provided far better evidence. They used a sample of 2500 Americans over 18 years of age contacted by random telephone dialling. Because of the strong risk that people would be unwilling to disclose over the telephone that they had sexually abused a child, Finkelhor and Lewis used a variation of the *Randomized Response Technique*. This involved putting *pairs* of questions to the respondent. For example, some were asked to answer "yes" or "no" to either member of the following pair, but not both:

(1) *Have you ever sexually abused a child at any time in your life?*
(2) Do you rent the place where you live?

The respondent chooses which one of the pair to answer at random (e.g. by tossing a coin). Since the interviewer does not know which of the two questions the respondent is answering, the respondent may feel free to answer truthfully. This is not the pointless exercise that it would at first appear, since so long as the researcher knows (i) the probability of picking question 1 or question 2 at random *and* (ii) the proportions of the general population who live in rented accommodation, statistical formulae can calculate the proportion of people who have sexually abused a child. Of course, this is based on probabilities, so it is never known whether a particular individual was an abuser or not.

This sounds fine in theory—though perhaps a little statistically complex. A difficulty arises because the sample was divided into two, and slightly different pairs of questions were asked. This was to enable the percentages answering "yes" to the "neutral" question when presented on its own to be found—each sample answered directly the other sample's "neutral" randomized question. So, the second half of the sample were posed the following pair of questions:

(1) *Have you ever sexually abused a child at any time in your life?*
(2) Are you a member of a labor union or a teacher's organization?

Within the margins of statistical variability, the two alternative pairings of the sexual abuse question should generate identical rates of abusing. In fact, radically different percentages of abusers were obtained—one estimate was 17% sexual abusers in the general population, the other 4%!

Finkelhor and Lewis rather implausibly explain this by suggesting that the so-called "neutral" question about union membership may have been rather more sensitive than had been intended compared with that about renting. Unfortunately, this *post hoc* argument is not convincing. For example, the two "neutral" questions showed equal rates of refusal to answer when asked as direct questions individually, and so do not appear to differ in sensitivity. Finkelhor and Lewis found no relationships between admission of abusing and family background or prior childhood victimization. Since previous research has found such relationships, this may cast more doubt on the method's validity. These problems notwithstanding, it is unclear what Finkelhor and Lewis mean by sexual abuse. Phrased as the abuse question is, possibly some respondents included their childhood sexual activities with other children.

Discussion of the issue of the non-sexually active paedophile similarly lacks relevant information. One commentator, Righton (1981), discussed 57 clients who were attracted to boys. About a third of them had never made any sexual contact with boys, although sometimes such thoughts filled their fantasy. It cannot be assumed from a clinical sample that a similar proportion of non-offending paedophiles could be found in the general population. The possibility of passive paedophilia is rarely raised other than in individual case studies (Hurry, 1990).

Some support, albeit rather tentative, for the view that paedophilia is relatively uncommon, can be found in research on the distribution of paedophilia related material available from pornography retailers. Although this cannot directly reveal the extent of paedophilia, it may indicate the relative interest in paedophiliac material compared with other types. Lebegue (1991) examined pornographic titles collected in the USA during the mid-1980s. Using the standard psychiatric diagnosis scheme (DSM-III-R), the titles were classified according to the paraphilias they indicated. Any references to schoolgirls were included in the paedophilia category. Partialism (i.e. an obsession with a particular body part such as breasts or bottoms) is not a diagnostic category in DSM-III-R. Over 13% of the titles dealt with a paraphilia and 4% with incest. Sadomasochism amounted to over 8% of the titles but paedophilia was less than 1% (roughly as infrequent as transvestism (2%), fetishism (1%) and zoophilia (1%)). Similar results were found in Australia (Lebegue, 1985); 12% were sadomasochism, 7% transvestism, 2% fetishism and 3% were teen/young sex. In this latter study the incest and paedophilia categories were combined but amounted to less than 4%.

Of course none of this is definitive proof of the small scale of active paedophiliac interest in the population; it merely suggests that such activity is relatively uncommon. Quite clearly, the question of the extent of paedophiliac interest in the population is a vexed one. It would be of considerably theoretical and practical interest to know how many men keep their paedophiliac urges under control and do not express them through offending. As it stands, virtually all that we know comes from offenders.

CHAPTER 2

What is Different about Child Abusers

> "Sexual offenders against children are not obviously different from other people. The most striking characteristic of the parents of abused children who came to the therapy groups at the hospital was that they were so ordinary. While waiting for the sessions to start they chatted about the difficulties of transport, of cars and the weather or helped each other to the coffee and biscuits that were provided."
>
> (La Fontaine, 1990, p. 102)

Common sense suggests that child abusers must be very different from "normal" people. Similar thinking leads to research into common factors among paedophiles that might give insight into the reasons why they offend. Several major contenders vie for consideration as the special "paedophile" ingredient. The list includes cycles of abuse, the homophobic view that these are rampant gays, inadequate family backgrounds, offenders' pathological (or pathetic) personalities and men doing what men are good at—abusing power. None of these simplistic views of paedophilia has any more than qualified support from research. That is not to say that there are not peculiar men who offend against children, merely that a single common denominator has yet to be found. It is necessary to assess how far such broad explanations provide an answer to the question, "why paedophilia?"; this chapter takes an especially close look at the childhood sexualization of paedophiles.

FAMILY BACKGROUND

The roots of paedophilia lie in childhood. Although few would contest this, precision about which aspects of childhood are involved is the difficulty. A number of studies, of varying quality, have looked into the parent–child relations and other family circumstances in the childhoods of offenders. Among the best is a study of the childhoods of girl-orientated paedophiles, boy-orientated paedophiles and incest offenders; all had admitted their offending (Lang and Langevin, 1991). A control group was drawn from men in the local community. Although the different groups were similar in age, the community controls were better educated than the offenders. Sexual and physical abuse were common in the childhoods of all groups except the controls. About half of the offenders had been sexually abused and at least a third of them physically abused, although this exceeded 50% for incest offenders. Double victimization involving both physical and sexual abuse was not unusual, at between one-fifth and two-fifths of offenders:

> "Collectively, sex offenders' fathers were considered more aggressive ... and stricter ..., but viewed as more affectionate to their sons ... The sex offender groups identified with their fathers ..., but homosexual pedophiles were less inclined to do so. Only one Mother Scale was significant: Aggression to Fathers ... There was a trend for mothers of sex offenders in general to be more aggressive to their husbands, but not to their sons."
>
> (Lang and Langevin, 1991, p. 65)

Exceptionally high (clinically deviant) scores were found for offenders' mothers being aggressive to their partners, especially in the boy-orientated paedophile group. Paedophiles' mothers also tended to be stricter. (In contrast, another study, Bass and Levant (1992), suggests that paedophiles perceive their parents as unaccepting, rejecting and controlling.)

The research sought the criteria that predicted the men most likely to use violence in the course of their offending. A statistical categorization technique (discriminant function analysis) was used to determine the best predictors to identify violent offenders. Only the offender's mother's strictness and the offender's aggression towards his father proved influential. Disappointingly, only half of the violent men were correctly classified by these criteria. Classification was best for heterosexual paedophiles and controls, and worst for the incest offenders. Only a third of these who used force were correctly identified, compared to 87% of non-violent offenders.

A similar attempt was made to differentiate between sex offenders and community controls using the variables father's strictness, mother's aggression against father, mother's aggression against son, son's aggression against mother, father identification, father affiliation, and father's aggression against mother. This met with little success:

> "Obviously, parent–child disturbances leave residual difficulties in sex offenders as adults, but they do not play the expected critical role in the sex offenders' own use of force on children."
>
> (Lang and Langevin, 1991, p. 70)

In exploring the childhood and adolescence characteristics of non-violent paedophiles (excluding incestuous fathers) and rapists, consecutive admissions to the North Florida Evaluation and Treatment Center were reviewed (Tingle *et al.*, 1986). Rapists were compared with perpetrators of non-violent sexual crimes against children (excluding incestuous fathers). Abusers were older than rapists and more likely to have an intact marriage. Domestic upheaval in childhood was common: rapists were more likely to come from broken homes (72%) than were abusers (44%); two-thirds of rapists and just under 50% of molesters ran away from home in their childhood; nearly 30% of rapists and 20% of molesters had spent part of their childhood being fostered or in an institution; roughly 40% of both groups were physically abused by their parents, although rapists were much more violent throughout their childhoods. The fathers of both groups were relatively insignificant in their domestic roles, and about half of both groups reported not being at all close to them. Despite about 83% of molesters claiming to be close and attached to their mother, only 23% said that she was someone with whom they could discuss personal problems. Emotional loneliness of this sort was also characteristic of peer relationships: three-quarters of molesters and even more rapists had few or no friends when they were growing up. A greater proportion of rapists showed this characteristic. It should not be forgotten that similar patterns of disruptive family life can be found in many offender groups.

Turning to adolescent sex offenders, Saunders, Awad and White (1986) took three different categories of offending: (i) the so-called courtship disorders such as exhibitionism, toucherism (brief touching of a woman's breasts or genitals) and obscene phone calls, (ii) sexual assaults such as indecent assaults, rape and attempted rape and (iii) paedophiliac offences against victims of either sex. About two-thirds of the paedophiles' victims were boys; the courtship disorder offences involved *older* females in two-thirds of cases; and for sexual assaulters, two-thirds of the victims were the same age as the offender. The offenders had been referred to the Toronto Court Clinic in the early 1980s and had either been convicted or had admitted their guilt. They and their parents were interviewed separately and as a family unit.

Demographic characteristics, including social class, family size and order of birth, were similar in all groups of offenders. Paedophiles (like assaulters) came from disorganized family systems; they had fewer legally married parents, more parental conflict and violence towards each other, and greater separation from their parents in adolescence. Violence between parents was commoner in paedophiles, as was sibling truancy from school. The sexual assaulters and the paedophiles were the least well adjusted at home, at school and in the community. Thus, only about 40% of the paedophiles were seen as "good" boys at home. Social isolation was common, with 60% of the courtship disorders, 32% of sexual assaulters and 72% of paedophiles having no close friends. A third of the paedophiles (and relatively few of the others) were seen by their parents as not being cuddly as infants.

In summary, more paedophiles:

> "had witnessed physical violence between their parents, were described as having been infants who did not enjoy being cuddled, and had siblings who were truant. Whether there are connections between the disorganized, violent nature of their family background, the perception of their not being cuddled as infants, and their seeking out sexual contact with young children is open for speculation. Clinically, this appears to be a very heterogeneous group which contains several subgroups. For example, there might be differences between the offenders who assault male as compared to female victims. The offenders against male children might also differ according to whether they are pedophiles or young homosexuals who are in the midst of an identity crisis and are experimenting in an attempt to clarify their gender identity. In other words, some might grow up to be homosexuals and not pedophiles."
>
> (Saunders, Awad and White, 1986, p. 548)

Birth order may have a bearing on the likelihood of paedophilia. Paedophiles and homosexual delinquents were more frequently the last of three or more children according to a study of Czechoslovakian offenders (Raboch and Raboch, 1986). The researchers do not provide an explanation. Bernard (1985) found that only 32% of his Belgian sample of paedophile club members had no older siblings. Perhaps sexual involvement with siblings is much more likely for the youngest child of the family, which leads to adult offending in the victim of the elder siblings. (But, as we have seen, other research does not support this finding about birth order (Saunders, Awad and White, 1986)).

Psychodynamically orientated theorists take a radically different view of the role of family background. The functions and maintenance of repetitive paedophile fantasies have concerned some of them (Protter and Travin, 1987). Fantasy is an organizing theme in the offender's life, which can provide an entry point into deeper conflicts. The case of "Mr D", a 42-year-old laboratory chemist, who had been arrested for masturbating his eight-year-old nephew, is illustrative:

> "He described his mother as an extremely distant and cold woman who sounded like she suffered from episodic periods of mild agitated depression. On occasion, however, she would become overtly seductive to the patient often complaining to him in a confidant-like manner concerning the inadequacies (sexual and otherwise) of her alcoholic and feared husband. Often in these instances he would spend time nursing his mother and felt he was used by her because she was lonely and frustrated. The patient during this period of his life felt isolated, depressed, and suffered from chronic nocturnal enuresis up until his late adolescence."
>
> (Protter and Travin, 1987, p. 289)

When he was nine he attended summer day camp where a male helper sexually interfered with him several times. Two years later he began to wear his mother's underwear while masturbating in front of the mirror when he felt lonely and helpless at the emotional demands of his mother and his father's prolonged absence. His attraction to young boys surfaced while babysitting a six-year-old; he rubbed the boy's back in the bath. Although initially distressed by his sexual arousal during this episode, 18 months later it became part of his masturbatory fantasy. He had few friends, and his wife, whom he met at college, was his first sexual partner. She appeared to him as fairly domineering, unaffectionate and little interested sexually. Their rare acts of sexual intercourse were accompanied by his paedophiliac sexual fantasy of sex with young boys. His fantasy was of a young boy with red-tinged hair, which he combed prior to removing the boy's clothing in fantasy in order to masturbate him. The boy's hair was just like his father's. Laboratory assessment showed that he had erections to slides of prepubescent males and to girls to a lesser extent.

The authors suggest a number of "heuristic" strategies for understanding the perversion:

> "a) the perversion as an oedipally-tinged castration anxiety related to triangular conflicts in the family [as represented by the fear he had of his father and the somewhat seductive approach of his mother]; b) the perversion as a collage of introjected part objects (or the transitional objects) as a way of dealing with various earlier preoedipal conflicts, traumata, and deficits; c) the perversion as a shoring up and reparative manoeuvre to buttress a faulty and fragmented self; d) the perversion as a defensive means of coping with nuclear separation–individuation struggles, often indicating both a desire and fear of merger with significant caretaking others; e) the perversion as an eroticized operation to express hostility as a reparative act by vindictive triumph [which is represented by his paedophile relationships which involved the young boy in the way in which he would like to have been treated and also the hostility towards the abuser in his childhood which perversely gets directed toward the child]."
>
> (Protter and Travin, 1987, p. 291)

While there is some evidence that the childhoods of paedophiles are frequently stressed in some way—relationships between and with parents are not always ideal, and often they seem isolated and lonely children—we have no great insights into how family dynamics might cause paedophiliac offending. Just what pathway leads from such family circumstances to offending? Perhaps a likely possibility is that these factors encourage the child to early sexual experiences. A child who is unhappy at home and lonely might be particularly prone to the sexual approaches of paedophiles or older children. Through this mechanism, family dynamics might lead to a cycle of abuse. In our case study of Graham (Chapter 1), for example, although he had been abused earlier, the trail of involvement with paedophiles really began with him seeking a replacement for his father. There is no direct evidence for this process. Knowledge of family dynamics alone leaves big gaps in our understanding of paedophilia's development.

PERSONALITY AND SEX ABUSE

> "A portrait of the paedophile? Perhaps this is an irrelevant question, because it seems on the whole that a paedophile is a person like you and me."
>
> (Bernard, 1985, p. 86)

> "Another common idea about sexual offenders one hears in community settings (especially in expert testimony in legal proceedings) is that there is a 'profile' which describes sexual offenders. Court testimony often includes the opinion: 'this man couldn't have done it, because he doesn't fit the profile' ... There is no currently verified profile of the typical adult who sexually abuses children. Indeed, all available information suggests that there is considerable variation in the characteristics of men who have sex with children. Virtually every characteristic has been found not to be present in at least some cases."
>
> (Conte, 1985, p. 345)

Wilson and Cox (1983) argue for a socio-biological explanation:

> "Paedophiles are variously shown to be timid, isolated, dependent, submissive, effeminate, sexually inhibited and generally not adequate to the task of competition with other men for adult heterosexual conquests."
>
> (Wilson and Cox, 1983, p. 323)

In this sentence lies a theory of paedophiles which holds that they are unable to become effectively involved with women. They are much like the animals who fail to succeed in the herd's sexual pecking order—who have to seek substitute activity with immature females and males. Wilson and Cox based their argument on data gathered in a postal survey of members of the Paedophile Information Exchange. Formed in 1977, this London-based organization sought to spread knowledge and understanding about paedophiles in order to alleviate the guilt and isolation that they experience. About half of those sent the questionnaire replied, and a number of these were also interviewed. Thirty-eight per cent were professionals, 34% were white-collar workers and 14% were blue-collar workers (the remainder were either unemployed or provided no pertinent information). Teachers made up an eighth of the men, which led the researchers to suggest gravitation towards jobs with high contact with children, although not necessarily for sexual reasons.

In general, there was no evidence that the paedophiles

demonstrated clinically abnormal levels on any of the measures. Nevertheless, as assessed by the Eysenck Personality Questionnaire (EPQ), paedophiles were *more* psychotic, introverted and neurotic than the general population. Some caution is needed because some of these differences were small, despite being statistically significant. Additional trends included:

(1) Higher psychoticism was associated with being exclusively paedophile and preferring younger ideal partners;
(2) Higher scores on extraversion were found in those who were sexually interested in both adults and children; and
(3) Higher levels of neuroticism were to be associated with unhappiness about being paedophile and a greater inclination to seek professional help.

It might be more useful to indicate the sorts of questions on which paedophiles were most *unlike* the general population:

Shyness. "Do you tend to keep in the background on social occasions?": 39% *more* paedophiles said "yes" than normals.

Sensitivity. "Are your feelings easily hurt?": 44% *more* paedophiles said "yes".

Loneliness. "Do you often feel lonely?": 83% *more* paedophiles said "yes".

Depression. "Have you ever wished you were dead?": 139% *more* paedophiles said "yes".

Obsessionality. "Do good manners and cleanliness matter much to you?": 19% *fewer* paedophiles said "yes".

Concern with looks. "Do you worry a lot about your looks?": 43% *fewer* paedophiles said "yes".

Sense of humour. "Do you like telling jokes and funny stories to your friends?": 28% *fewer* paedophiles said "yes".

Relationship with mother. "Is (was) your mother a good woman?": 10% *fewer* paedophiles said "yes".

Wilson and Cox argue that extraversion is partially inherited and that the paedophile's early experiences of isolation and inadequacy stemming from early childhood are constitutional in origin. They concede that some social anxiety and withdrawal might be caused by society's hostility to the paedophile; the personality characteristics may thus be an effect of, rather than a cause of, paedophilia. Nevertheless, they prefer the innatist argument:

> "Examination of the characteristics of children that the paedophiles found most attractive points to the conclusion that the ability to achieve social dominance over the child may be the key to understanding the paedophile's choice of sex target."
>
> (Wilson and Cox, 1983, p. 329)

Paedophiles most frequently mentioned naive innocence as the most attractive quality in children and "softness, simplicity, openness and willingness to learn". Male sexuality perhaps requires some measure of social dominance for satisfactory arousal and competent sexual performance. Paedophiles, lacking this competition and social competency, are more at home relating to children. Many of the paedophiles felt children were easier to approach than adults.

Paedophilia is seen as "adaptive", just one of several means of coping with failure to relate satisfactorily with women:

> "Ethologists have noted that the males of most mammalian species are thrown into strong Darwinian competition with one another; those that are most successful monopolize an unequal share of female resources, and the others have to make do with various substitute sexual outlets (Wilson, 1981). Following this model, we would not expect to find any direct genetic predisposition toward paedophilia *per se* ... paedophiles may inherit their submissive nature which in turn makes for difficulties in establishing normal male sexuality. A second stage, involving conditioning and social-learning experiences, would then have to be postulated to account for the focusing upon children as the alternative target."
>
> (Wilson and Cox, 1983, p. 329)

Whether this accounts for any truly paedophile activity is a moot point. It seems not to deal with the "true" paedophile, who shows a virtually exclusive sexual arousal pattern to children with no interest in adult women from childhood onwards.

> "Our results [show] no striking connection between paedophile preference and either thought disorder or aggressiveness. A few of the

paedophiles in our sample may have been bordering on clinically-significant levels of psychoticism, but by no means the majority."

(Wilson and Cox, 1983, p. 328)

So, although there are few signs of clinical abnormality in paedophiles, personality is partially responsible for their offending. The approach of Wilson and Cox is exceptional among psychometric approaches to paedophilia in that it attempts to postulate a theoretical account on the basis of psychological measurements. While considerable reservations have to be expressed about the thesis that paedophiles cannot relate to women, especially given their skill at, for example, infiltrating single-parent families, we cannot afford to be too cavalier towards the limited theories available.

Turning to the more purely empirical investigations of the paedophile's personality, Peters (1976) described the results of psychological tests given to a large sample of sexual offenders including (i) those who had committed assault (rape and statutory rape), (ii) paedophiles (corrupting the morals of a minor), (iii) exhibitionists and (iv) homosexuals. A variety of psychological measures were used. Concentrating on paedophiles, he reported a particularly large number of physical symptoms but fewer signs of emotional disturbance. Peters suggests that paedophiles turn emotional problems into physical ones, which means that they:

"feel unable to compete with other men in efforts to attract adult women because of this felt inferiority. Retaining normal heterosexual aims, they then turned to little girls for affection and sexual gratification."

(Peters, 1976, p. 409)

Paedophiles were also found to be immature, with strong dependency needs. They appeared to be less confused about their sex role identification but with a high level of anxiety about their physique and bodily functioning. Under stress, they were inclined to withdraw and become isolated, a tendency also indicated by their drawings:

"The Rorschach [the ink-blot test], like most of the other tests, shows the pedophiles to be significantly more passive than the rapists. It also indicates markedly diminished sensitivity to the needs of others, associated with repression of their own needs for affection and of their sensuous impulses. It is likely that this insensitivity permits them to be

> oblivious to the problems created by their seductive behavior toward their victims, victims who frequently are children to whom they are close and toward whom they consciously maintain feelings of fondness."
> (Peters, 1976, p. 410)

In contrast to the common view of paedophiles as inadequate, the offenders rated themselves above average in terms of physical characteristics, intellect, education, ability at work, and social and marital relationships:

> "We believe the high self-ratings made by the pedophiles, exhibitionists and rapists are due to, or at least consistent with, a use of denial as an ego defense mechanism, which was observed clinically in the psychiatric interviews and in the course of group therapy sessions."
> (Peters, 1976, pp. 410–411)

In general, there is a degree of inconsistency in the psychological test data on paedophiles. It is useful, then, to remember Levin and Stava's (1987) review, which sought psychometric differences between paedophiles and other men. A number of difficulties are inherent in much of this research—in particular, little effort is usually made to identify paedophiles as a "pure" category rather than a group of men who offend against children but who also have a history of other forms of offending. The Minnesota Multiphasic Personality Inventory (MMPI) is one of the more commonly used measures in this area. Primarily, it assesses psychopathology rather than personality. Although there are several empirically derived subscales of the inventory, generally speaking, research reveals few differences between paedophiles and others:

(1) Social introversion was highest in paedophiles, though not clearly more so than in other sexually deviant groups (Langevin *et al.*, 1978);

(2) Incest offenders tended to score higher on social introversion than the extrafamilial offenders (Panton, 1979); and

(3) No differences were found in the profiles of various types of offenders, including a group of molesters of 13-year-olds and younger (Quinsey, Arnold and Pruesse, 1980).

In other words, research using the MMPI provides no clear-cut, strong trends that might help us to understand paedophilia better.

Much the same sort of conclusion was reached by Okami and Goldberg (1992) in reviewing the research evidence on the social inadequacy of sexual offenders against minors using the MMPI.

Summarizing research using psychometric measures other than the MMPI, Levin and Stava (1987) tentatively suggest a way in which personality might be associated with paedophilia:

> "pedophiles may be fundamentally guilt-ridden individuals. Further ... heterosexual pedophiles, in addition to being self-abasing, may inhibit aggression, whereas homosexual pedophiles typically establish mutually dependent relations."
>
> (Levin and Stava, 1987, p. 75)

However, these characteristics might also be produced by the nature of the settings in which such research takes place, usually prison:

(1) Guilt and the inhibition of aggression might be a consequence of the hostility and derision directed against sex offenders by other prisoners;
(2) Impression management might encourage sex offenders to present themselves as reformed and sorry for what they had done.

The possibility of finding a simple personality profile that differentiates paedophiles from other men has appeared increasingly unrealistic as the research and clinical base has widened. Simplistic notions such as social inadequacy driving men to sex with children become unviable as highly socially skilled paedophiles are found. With few exceptions, personality studies of paedophiles have been empirically orientated, with scant attention paid to theory. Perhaps even less encouraging is the lack of power of personality tests to distinguish clearly among types of paedophile, let alone between paedophiles and other types of sex offenders.

PAEDOPHILIA AND HOMOSEXUALITY

> "In principle, it should not be difficult to design a study which would provide the information needed to show the relationship between homosexual behavior and child molestation. One might, for example, take a random sample of those men and women who are 'homosexual' and find the proportion of them who can be regarded as 'child

> molesters.' Alternatively, one might identify a random sample of those who are 'child molesters' and see what part of this sample can be classified as 'homosexuals.' Finally, appropriate comparisons with comparable groups of 'heterosexuals' would allow an investigator to determine the extent to which child molestation is an act characteristically related to homosexual behavior ... In fact, it appears that no such study has ever been conducted. And there are good reasons for believing that no such study ever could be conducted."
>
> (Newton, 1978, p. 31)

It is generally held to be a dubious proposition that homosexuality and paedophilia are linked. While some paedophiles are homosexually orientated towards both adults and children, this does not in itself demonstrate a causal association between the two. There are a number of issues:

(1) Uncertainty about the rates of paedophilia in heterosexual and homosexual men;
(2) Uncertainty about the rates of homosexuality among adult men;
(3) The apparent sexual preference of some heterosexual people for adult females while offending against boys.

Nevertheless, hostility towards homosexuals has meant that the general public has been antipathetic towards the employment of gay men as teachers of underage students. It is wrong to assume that homosexuality characterizes a fixed and identifiable proportion of the population: the situation is far more complex than this allows. Since the famous Kinsey reports (Kinsey, Pomeroy and Martin, 1948; Kinsey *et al.*, 1953) on human sexuality, it has been believed that homosexual experiences are common even in sectors of the population regarding themselves as heterosexual. For example, Kinsey, Pomeroy and Martin (1948) found only 50% of people to be exclusively heterosexual throughout their lives. Are the others to be deemed homosexual because of, say, their childhood sexual experiences? Such problems mean that casual questions about paedophilia and homosexuality are far more complex than first appearances suggest. The definition of and rates of homosexuality are politically sensitive matters. A British survey (Field *et al.*, 1994; Wellings *et al.*, 1994) claiming that the true rate of homosexuality in the general population is about 1% received considerable adverse public criticism (Wilby, 1994). One implication of such low rates, of course, is that homosexuals are more marginal than suggested by previous studies and less than a numerically substantial minority. Such low estimates also have implications for interpreting the high rates of boy-orientation among paedophiles.

An alternative approach would be to assess the rates of homosexuality among paedophiles themselves. This is unlikely to be very fruitful for obvious reasons. For example, there is no evidence or belief that female homosexuals are involved in the equivalent of the sort of "boy-love" movement that characterizes the more public aspects of paedophilia. The question could be refined:

> "to ask how the child molester's sexual orientation/preference is related to his 'attraction' (either on a short term or long term basis) to children. From this standpoint, however, there would seem to be no *a priori* reason for suspecting that knowing whether one is 'homosexual' or 'heterosexual' would enable one to be any better at predicting attraction to young children than knowing whether one is right- or left-handed, blue- or brown-eyed, ... or having any other specific characteristic."
>
> (Newton, 1978, p. 35)

It is important to distinguish homosexuality directed towards adults from that directed towards underage children. This allows us to see that adult-orientated homosexuals are no more likely to become sexually involved with children than are heterosexuals. Surveys have identified few paedophiles amongst homosexuals: Westwood (1960) found less than 3% claiming to be interested in young people sexually—which is not the same as actual sexual contacts. About 12% of Westwood's sample had had contact after 18 years of age with boys of 16 or younger. Seventy-six per cent of the men said they would not engage in homosexual activities with anybody under 17, and 6% said that they felt free to engage in sexual activities with a boy of any age. Another study showed that nearly half of the men convicted of sexually molesting boys were actually married at the time (Gebhard *et al.*, 1965); less than a third preferred children sexually to older people. Using measures of sexual arousal to different sets of pictures, it was discovered that although heterosexual men were sexually aroused by pictures of girls rather than by those of landscapes, homosexual men were no more aroused by pictures of boys than landscapes (Freund, 1963). In short, just knowing the nature of an adult's sexual involvement with children says little or nothing about their orientation to adult men or women.

But there is an anomaly that cannot be ignored. Offending against boys is considerably more common than expected given typical estimates of homosexual contacts between adults. For example, at the Clarke Institute of Psychiatry in Canada, it was found that over a third of the offenders targeted male children. This is far more than would be expected on the basis of estimates of the male adult-orientated homosexuality rate (Freund *et al.*, 1984). Interestingly, as many as 86% of a sample of offenders against boys described themselves as either homosexual or bisexual (Erickson, Walbek and Seely, 1988) although this may be a problem of self-definition rather than an accurate description of their adult sexuality. Furthermore, while surveys show that victims of child sexual abuse are more likely to be girls (La Fontaine, 1990), nevertheless boys are a large minority of victims. One of the few exceptions to this trend is Gebhard and Gagnon's (1964) finding that only 12% of victims under five years of age were males—closer to the generally accepted adult homosexuality rate. Significantly, a fifth of those who offended against such young children also had sexual contacts with animals, which led to the interpretation that such offenders were polymorphic—largely undifferentiating as to sexual object. In the light of this:

> "it is likely that the development of partner sex preference and age preference are not independent of each other and that sex preference in pedophilia is etiologically different from the sex preference of males who prefer physically mature partners of either sex."
>
> (Freund *et al.*, 1984, p. 198)

On the grounds that paedophilia is uncommon in women, they argue that the mechanism may be physiological in nature, but that is just one of the possibilities.

Some hold, with good reason, that adult homosexuality is a negative indicator of paedophilia. That is, unless a homosexual has a history of paedophile activity with children, he is unlikely to offend against children under any circumstances:

> "There were no peer-oriented homosexual males in our sample who regressed to children. Homosexuality and homosexual pedophilia are not synonymous. In fact, it may be that these two orientations are mutually exclusive, the reason being that the homosexual male is sexually attracted to masculine qualities whereas the heterosexual male is sexually attracted to feminine characteristics, and the sexually immature child's qualities are more feminine than

> masculine ... In any case, in over 12 years of clinical experience working with child molesters, we have yet to see any example of a regression from an adult homosexual orientation. The child offender who is also attracted to and engaged in adult sexual relationships is heterosexual. It appears, therefore, that the adult heterosexual male constitutes a greater sexual risk to underage children than does the adult homosexual male."
>
> (Groth and Birnbaum, 1978, pp. 180–181)

While one might have considerable doubts about Groth and Birnbaum's analysis of the nature of homosexual attraction, they are clearly unequivocal about the risks of adult homosexuals becoming diverted into paedophilia. Homosexuals committed to adult partners will not be forced by situational or personal pressures into even temporary paedophile episodes; heterosexual men apparently pose a far greater risk in this regard.

It is unclear the extent to which paedophiles can be classified as homosexual or heterosexual; it depends too much on what one means by these terms. Some paedophile men choose exclusively underage girls and others exclusively underage boys; others abuse both sexes. It is not uncommon for men who appear heterosexual in terms of their adult partners to choose boys as their illicit targets. Research at the sexology department of the Clarke Institute of Psychiatry looked at the characteristics of men who offended against boys compared with those against girls (Freund, Watson and Rienzo, 1987). Offenders against both sexes were excluded, as were intrafamilial offenders and those showing courtship disorders (e.g. exhibitionists). Offenders against girls usually had just one victim (59% compared with 33% of offenders against boys). This trend did not apply to men who had been teenage sex offenders against children. It is difficult to know precisely what these data imply. Freund, Watson and Rienzo suggest that offenders against girls are often not true paedophiles, otherwise they would exhibit more persistence in finding victims. Offenders against boys are more likely to repeat the offence. Of course, a simpler explanation is that offences against girls are more likely to lead to arrest. Freund, Watson and Rienzo argue that homosexual paedophilia accounts for offences against boys better than heterosexual paedophilia accounts for offences against girls. Unfortunately, this is conjecture since there is no independent evidence of erotic fixation on children other than the number of victims.

Homosexuality might impinge in other ways. Breer (1987), in his study of adolescent boys who offend sexually against other children, writes of "ego-distonic" homosexuality as a major cause of molestation by teenage boys. This involves conscious or unconscious homosexual feelings that are unacceptable to the boy himself. Some adolescent offenders cannot accept any homosexual adjustment but are unable to change successfully to heterosexuality. Deep conflicts about their personal sexuality are typical. Molesting a girl child may serve as a defence against such concerns.

FEMALE OFFENDERS

> "A bogus woman social worker who sexually attacked a baby boy was today being hunted by police. The trickster indecently assaulted the eight-month-old infant after conning her way into his family home."
>
> (*Leicester Mercury*, 9 March 1993, p. 3)

Female offenders remain a relatively rare phenomenon in the research and clinical press on sexual abuse. Does this mean that women rarely offend? Increasingly it is being argued that female offending has remained a hidden but extensive problem. Social attitudes to male and female sexuality may be partly responsible for this lack of visibility. The woman who initiates intercourse with a 14-year-old boy might be seen differently had she been a man. She might be seen as giving "a lesson in manhood" much desired by the boy. Another possibility is that the forms of sexual abuse by women are different. Sexual provocativeness and suggestiveness towards a boy may appear harmless compared with a molester fondling a girl's breasts, for example. But we have no knowledge of which is the more damaging other than our socially derived assumptions. Kasl (1990) suggests that abusive acts by females upon boys may be "covert" or may involve sexually intrusive behaviour:

> "such as bathing a male child when he is old enough to bathe himself, giving him enemas, commenting on his growth of pubic hair, or walking around seminude in the presence of the child and getting a sexual high from seeing him stare or become sexually aroused."
>
> (Kasl, 1990, p. 260)

Many boys may remember these incidents as shameful or repulsive but some may not calculate such events as abuse. This may also be the case with girls. For example, Evans and Schaefer (1987) found that only after psychological therapy could women identify sexual abuse by other women. While treated and untreated women did not differ in their recall of sexual abuse in childhood by men, a quarter of the treated group began to identify their abuse by women compared with none of the controls.

Most of the case histories of female offenders describe extremely disturbed individuals. A good example of this is Cooper *et al.*'s (1990) description of a female sex offender who exhibited several paraphilias:

> "Miss K was an unmarried Caucasian woman aged 20 who was referred for a pretrial examination having been charged with two counts of sexual assault on two sisters, aged four and five. Sexual contact had occurred repeatedly over several months, during babysitting. Abusive acts included slapping the children, inserting pencils and other objects into their vaginas and performing oral sex on them. During these activities she usually felt angry, although not always with the victims. She had become increasingly preoccupied with violent sexual fantasies involving the children and was becoming more apprehensive about possibly acting these out. Miss K also admitted that she had sexually molested several other young boys and girls over the previous two or three years, again while babysitting. However, these incidents had not come to police attention, and at the time of her assessment she had no known prior criminal record."
>
> (Cooper *et al.*, 1990, pp. 334—335)

No doubt, she would be regarded as dangerous were she a man. It is typical of the literature on female offenders that they are described as having been extensively abused as children. Miss K, for example, claimed that her uncle repeatedly assaulted her sexually when she was three—it is documented that he was eventually sent to prison for sexually abusing one of his own children. Miss K's brother initiated her into a number of sexual behaviours when he was 14 and she was 12 years of age. Mutual genital fondling, oral sex and penetrative intercourse were involved over a period of time. Conscious that this was abnormal, at the same time she took pleasure in the physical and emotional closeness involved. Later, when she was 14, a different older brother engaged her in sexual activities of a far more aggressive nature; they engaged in bondage and other sadomasochistic fantasies. These she found "exhilarating" and her sexual fantasies became more violent and sadomasochistic in nature. After leaving home at 17 she was subjected to unwanted sexual advances by older men on two occasions. She has an extensive psychiatric history and since adolescence has complained of frequent depression and suicide thoughts, and had often attended crisis centres. A deeper layer of perversity exists that does not appear in the above account:

> "During her childhood Miss K admitted initiating manual—genital and oral—genital stimulation with a dog and a cat, both male family pets. Sex with animals was and is a frequent fantasy for her."
>
> (Cooper *et al.*, 1990, p. 335)

Her sex hormone levels were normal but her laboratory sexual assessment using a vaginal photoplethysmograph revealed an unusually arousable woman. This enabled the measurement of her vaginal blood volume, vaginal pulse rate and vaginal pulse amplitude in response to explicit slides of girls, boys, women, men, adult heterosexual sex, adult sadomasochism, adult–child sadomasochism, adult lesbian and adult heterosexual oral sex. There was relatively little difference among the slides. Confirming the extremity of her response, it was noted that:

> "During the assessment, Miss K frequently responded to the point of orgasm."
>
> (Cooper *et al.*, 1990, p. 337)

Few researchers or clinicians discuss the impact of the female abuser in any great detail. An exception is Breer (1987), on adolescents who molest other children. He suggests that serious and multi-victimed paedophilia in later life is a likely outcome in boys who have been abused by *men*. They offend outside of their own home in an attempt to find young victims. When victimized by a *woman*, Breer claims that boys under five years do not recall the abuse, possibly because of the trauma it engenders. These boys do not go on to offend against other boys, but against girls instead. For Breer, this means that there is a conflict focusing on their relationships with females—they are literally afraid of approaching same-age or older females sexually since this would arouse a conflict between the fear of and wish to be engulfed by them. By abusing younger girls, they reproduce the trauma situation with themselves in control rather than as the victim; strong sexual feelings can be dealt with without them feeling out of their own control and they avoid concerns about homosexuality. Older boys abused by a woman may be less traumatized and may regard the abuse as a positive sexual opportunity, not as a major trauma. The main effect is that boys become sexualized early. (Breer stresses that these are his personal impressions, with no more force than this.)

This may be related to the "trauma control and mastery principle" observed in those soldiers who endlessly repeat the traumatic situations of war by recreating them in circumstances in which they can achieve control. Similarly, adolescent molesters recreate their trauma with a child, putting themselves back into the abusive situation but with the key difference of being in control, not the helpless victim.

There is a form of abuse that is perpetrated on adolescent offenders by their mothers. A high proportion of these mothers have themselves been victims of sexual abuse, inside or outside of the family, which leaves them angry and ambivalent in their relationships with males. Their sons may become the focus of their hatred for their own molesters. Boys are then put into situations that imply that they should molest without it ever being stated. For example, boys might be persistently encouraged to bathe with a younger female relative long after the age that both of them have become modest about nudity. Should they respond to this sort of situation by molesting, all hell can break loose and they may be thrown out of their homes. Breer describes the case of Ricky U., which illustrates the confusing sexual dynamics that can exist between boys and their mothers:

> "Ricky's mother had a history of extremely provocative behavior with him over a long period of time. He showered and slept with her until about age nine. She made a point of appearing around him in the nude. Ricky drilled a hole in the bathroom door and used to observe his mother in the shower for two years. On one occasion his mother told him that if he were not her son, she would have sex with him. She did the next best thing and introduced him to some of her friends who became involved with him sexually ... Ricky was placed in residential treatment after he battered and sexually abused a two year old child for a period of hours. At one point the victim stopped breathing ... it appears to be an example of a near homicide resulting from conflicts centering around maternal seduction."
>
> (Breer, 1987, p. 73)

Hurry (1990) describes "Kevin", who had been referred for therapy following self-mutilation around the age of 19. While he had apparently never sexually abused a child, nevertheless he had paedophiliac fantasies about touching young girls. Among these was the fear that his penis would become trapped if he penetrated a woman. Apparently this was partly based on an anal and oral view of vaginas stemming from a childhood incident in which he soiled himself and was washed by the nursery school teacher. He recalls the incident as one in which the excited woman put her face close to his penis as if she wanted to put it in her mouth. She penetrated him with her finger as she washed his bottom. After several years of therapy he became able to divulge his experience of abuse by his mother:

> "... the mutual touching between himself and his mother while he shared her room, and later on holidays. He remembered his excitement—and his fear. He could not see properly through Mum's nightie, and when he touched her there was 'nothing there' ... Mum touched him when he was little, sometimes she used to put her hand over 'it' and put 'it' down between his legs, and tell him how like a girl he was, and how she had wanted a girl."
>
> (Hurry, 1990, p. 15)

Some of these themes were repeated in terms of his relationship with his sister, six years older than him:

> "Kevin would fantasize about his sister, and with great shame he told me how he would try to watch her bathing. If she came into his room he would have an erection. He reacted with panic and rage when she jokingly slapped him on the bottom, saying she had touched him 'in the crack'. The analysis of his reaction to this incident brought memories of early sexual play, particularly when his sister washed him, and made clear Kevin's lack of differentiation between phallic and anal excitement. Kevin described both how his sister had penetrated him with her finger while washing him and how fascinated she had been by his penis."
>
> (Hurry, 1990, p. 16)

Kevin could not cope with his desire to be touched as if he were a girl. Consequently, in fantasy, he reversed the roles, so becoming the person doing the touching. Such fantasies and the thought of carrying them out terrified him.

One typology of female sex offenders differentiates them according to whether the offender acts alone or not (Mathews, Mathews and Speltz, 1990):

(1) Self-initiated offences:

a. Intergenerationally predisposed: in this, the commonest category, the women typically report extensive sexual and physical abuse in childhood. More than any of the other types, this is likely to select girl victims—generally their own children. The offending largely re-enacts their own abuse.

b. Experimenter/exploiter: normally an adolescent girl who victimizes a boy of six or under whom she babysits. She fondles him, gives him oral sex or has him touch her body parts or even attempt intercourse. Fear of sexuality may cause her interest in young children.

c. Teacher/lover: she is a woman who engages in what she portrays as a "love-affair" with a boy in the 11- to 16-year-old range. Often it happens during troubled periods in her romantic relationship with an adult man.

(2) Accompanied offences:

a. Male-coerced: these women, often in a multiple family incest situation, are made to abuse (usually their own) children by an important male partner, including older brothers.

b. Psychologically disturbed: a woman with strong dependency needs may indirectly abuse her children by setting up situations in which abuse can occur.

While female offenders may be the minority, there is a possibility that they have a disproportionately greater effect on their victim's later sexual offending. For example, although 70% of Tingle *et al.*'s (1986) sample of molesters had been abused by males only, 13% had been by females only, and 17% by both males and females. That is, nearly a third of the sex molesters had themselves been molested by a woman in childhood. Carlson (1991) found that nearly a third of men on a long-term sex offender programme had experienced legally chargeable abuse by a woman, such as oral sex, masturbation, fondling or intercourse. The figure reaches 50% if one includes less flagrant offences such as voyeurism, sexual kissing, extended weaning or flirting. It was difficult to find any men who had not been abused by a woman if invasion of privacy (e.g. enemas, obsessive cleaning of his foreskin, etc.) or inappropriate relationships (unloading emotional and sexual problems, sleeping with him or substituting him for the father) are added into the equation.

Such findings are difficult to equate with the rates of female offending in general since they are based on information gathered from samples of men who are offenders themselves. Nevertheless, they seem to demonstrate that where a boy is offended against, the offender may well be female. This is supported by other studies of male victims. One study found that over 40% of offenders against boys were female, often ones in caring roles such as babysitters, teachers and parents' friends (Risin and Koss, 1987). About 30% of a sample of undergraduate males had been abused by females (Urquiza, 1988).

There is a parallel in some forms of abuse by women with the boy-love aspect of some abuse claimed by paedophile activists. For example, Mathews, Mathews and Speltz (1990) relate how one woman described her abuse of one of her son's 14-year-old friends:

> "He came down and I met him and talked to him and all of this ... I knew I started feeling some kind of fondness ... He came back in the summertime. And I started getting to know him a little bit more ... it was something ... He was a big help—not financially. At night, when my kids were sleeping, when nobody was around, he started flirting, started giggling and things. And I made a pass at him. And he says 'nope.' And then he went back to school ... And he came at Christmas time and says, '[Ann], I'm a man. I'm ready.' ... We had sex. And then he went back to school and came home again in the summertime. And things started to progress off and on ... But we had an affair, a love affair."
>
> (Mathews, Mathews and Speltz, 1990, p. 285)

The one area in which abuse by females is well documented is in American day-care, providing care for six-year-olds and younger. Finkelhor and Williams (1988) studied cases of child sexual abuse in these settings for which substantiation could be provided by child protection agencies, the agency for licensing the day-care centre, the police or combinations of these. As few as a fifth of alleged cases might be substantiated. Females were common abusers in these settings. About a fifth of both the girl and boy victims had been abused by a female acting alone or with other females. About half of the female victims and two-fifths of the male victims had been abused by males acting singly or together. Female and male abusers accounted for the rest—more or less a third of victims. Notably, in contrast to the impression created of female offenders in general, the female offenders in these settings were less likely to be single and to be socially isolated from their peers compared to male offenders. They were also less likely to have histories of any of the following: school problems, alcohol problems, drug problems, psychiatric problems, isolation from peers or prior arrest, although these were not statistically significant. Furthermore, the victims of the women were younger and more numerous, the women were more likely to abuse with others, the women were more likely to threaten to harm the family, and the abuse was more likely to involve kissing, digital–anal penetration, insertion of objects into the vagina or anus, forced child–child activity or ritualistic aspects. So, it would appear that the characteristics of female offenders are dissimilar from those of male offenders in this context, and that penetration of orifices with fingers and objects is more commonly perpetrated by female offenders.

The evidence of abuse by females, especially in the biographies of paedophiles, leads to the more general question of whether sexual abuse by men or women tends to make the victim paedophile.

MOLESTATION THEORY: SEXUAL ABUSE CYCLES

It is a simple equation to suggest that sexual abuse in childhood is a cause of paedophilia. There could be a variety of reasons why this might occur:

(1) Identification with the aggressor, such that the child deals with their own abuse by becoming like their abuser;
(2) Anger concerning their abuse is acted out against other young people;
(3) There is a "career" progression from being a paedophile's victim to becoming a paedophile. This might be particularly the case in circumstances in which the child's involvement with paedophiles is a long-term matter;
(4) Abuse causes psychological fixation in childhood.

None of these is particularly convincing when assessed against the available research on childhood abuse among paedophiles. This is especially so in the light of the limited support coming from studies of the rates of abuse in the childhoods of paedophiles, in which no massive differences between abuse rates in paedophiles' and non-paedophiles' childhoods are found. A cycle of abuse is sufficient to explain only a small proportion of paedophile careers.

The available evidence may not be as robust as it appears. Frequently the recognition of abuse in childhood involves a slow unveiling of the truth; it is not usually something that could be assessed by ticks and crosses on a self-completion questionnaire. For example, one offender who was regularly sent as a seven-year-old to watch an adolescent female relative bathing found it difficult to see in this the possibility of abuse of himself and the girl. Some offenders describe how they see themselves as the initiator of the sexual activity rather than being abused.

Although Finkelhor (1984) argues that research shows relatively low reported frequencies of abuse in offenders' childhoods, and Hansen and Slater (1988), in a review, concluded that sex abusers did not differ from other sex offenders and non-sex offenders in respect to abuse, the data needs more careful examination before abandoning the possibility. Five types of non-psychotic males were obtained from the sexology department of Clarke Institute of Psychiatry in Toronto (Freund, Watson and Dickey, 1990). Sex offenders against *both* female and male minors were excluded. Using physiological measures of erection to various sorts of explicit sexual materials, as well as other procedures, Freund, Watson and Dickey also separated their offenders against children into what they describe as child molesters and true paedophiles (those with little response to adults). Their early experience revealed abuse by men and women as follows:

- Heterosexual pedophiles: 25% by a man, 7% a woman
- Homosexual pedophiles: 26% by a man, 6% a woman
- Child molesters: 18% by a man, 8% a woman
- Heterosexual controls: 9% by a man, 3% a woman
- Homosexual controls: 10% by a man, 2% a woman
- Heterosexual offenders: 8% by a man, 8% a woman

The major differences were thus between paedophiles' and controls' rates of abuse by adult males.

Others have obtained substantially higher levels of reported abuse in the childhoods of offenders. Comparing non-violent child molestation offenders with rapists, Tingle *et al.* (1986) noted that molesters (56%) were rather more likely to have been sexually abused as a child than rapists (38%). Despite the differences in incidence, the patterns of abuse were similar. About 60%, in both cases, involved oral sex, about 50% anal sex and about 45% fondling. The average age of first abuse was similar for both groups—for child molesters it was 8.5 years and for rapists 9.2 years. Lang and Langevin (1991) indicated that 50%, more or less, of heterosexual paedophiles, homosexual paedophiles and incest offenders reported having been sexually abused in childhood compare to 0% of their community control group. Breer (1987) reports data on a number of sexually abusive adolescents whom he had classified as pre-paedophiles (likely to become adult paedophiles against boys). Virtually all of them had been sexually molested by men. Only 1 out of 17 repeatedly denied abuse in childhood. In contrast, for the boys who were either incestuous abusers or only abused by females the findings are virtually reversed. Just a little over a quarter of them admitted being abused and half of these had been molested by females.

Many paedophiles may falsely claim to have been abused, so the molestation theory of paedophilia is essentially untenable (Freund, Watson and Dickey, 1990). There is some support for this point of view in Hindman's (1988) study of paroled adult male offenders. Those interviewed in the period 1980–1982 were compared with those interviewed between 1982 and 1988. In the later period she explained to them that they would undergo lie-detector tests to evaluate their claims. If their self-reports of abuse were proved false then they would immediately go back to prison. Without the threat of the test, claims of childhood abuse were made by 67% of the offenders, but this figure dropped to 29% when re-imprisonment for lying was threatened.

It is an open question as to why these differences occurred. While they might imply that offenders' claims of childhood abuse are simply self-serving excuses, this is clearly not the only explanation. Another possibility is that the tentative acceptance that they have of their childhood abuse is insufficiently strong to survive the threat of imprisonment. Furthermore, given that the lie-detector is a controversial instrument, it might well be that offenders calculated that denial was the safest course of action since no one would take action against them if they had denied their abuse despite it having occurred. Given the longitudinal nature of the research, the results could also be an artefact of other changes occurring over this period of time.

One might speculate about how paedophilia is transmitted intergenerationally in families. Are men with a paedophile in their family themselves more likely to offend? Like all studies of families, outcomes can be difficult to interpret—is paedophilia genetically transmitted or does abuse within the family affect several members of that family? A rare example of a study of family inheritance patterns of paedophilia compared those of diagnosed paedophiles with those of a sample of clinically depressed men (Gaffney, Lurie and Berlin, 1984). The clinical records of inpatients at the Johns Hopkins sexual deviance clinic over a 39-month period commencing in 1980 were examined. Those not meeting the standard psychiatric diagnostic criteria for paraphilia (DSM-III) were discarded from the research. Morbidity is the risk or probability that another member of the family will also show the same clinical syndrome. One finds out how many relatives are also paedophiles as a percentage of the total number of relatives the individual has. Thus, a morbidity rate of 2 means that one in fifty relatives of paedophiles are also paedophiles. The morbidity risk for *paedophiles* was 5 for paedophilia and 0 for any other paraphilia; for *non-paedophile paraphiliacs* the morbidity was 11.5 for paedophilia and 6.1 for non-paedophiliac paraphilia; and for the controls, 0 for paedophilia and 0.7 for other paraphilias.

The morbidity risks were stronger for male relatives than for females. So, for example, for the families of paedophiles there was a 10.3% chance that at least one *male* family member would be paedophile. In contrast, no females in these families had any paraphilia including paedophilia. For men in the families of other paraphiliacs, the morbidity rates were 3.7% for paedophilia and 14.8% for any other paraphilias. For the women there was a zero probability of paedophilia but a 3.2% chance of any other paraphilia.

> "pedophiles were not the middle-aged offenders of previous reports, their average age of onset being 27. We also found that 18.5 percent of the families of all patients with sexual deviancy had family members, mostly men, with a sexual deviancy. Families of those with pedophilia had members also having pedophilia. Families of those with nonpedophiliac paraphilia had members with a sexual deviancy not involving pedophilia. These data indicate that pedophilia is a familial disease, not associated with an increased familial risk of the other paraphilias. Further studies are needed to elucidate the manner of transmission."
>
> (Gaffney, Lurie and Berlin, 1984, p. 548)

The genesis of these family trends cannot be ascertained from morbidity data. The trends are compatible with genetic, family pathology and childhood molestation theories of paedophilia. The authors note that 27% of their sample of paedophiles were on record as having been molested in childhood against 14% of the other paraphiliacs but this was not statistically reliable.

Others have suggested that aspects of paedophiliac leanings emerge relatively early in the development of a child, but this is for gender preference rather than age preference. Freund and Kuban (1993) asked male paedophiles, homosexuals and heterosexual adults about their curiosity concerning the bodies of other people when they were children aged between 7 and 11 years. They regarded this as a measure of erotic interest. In the heterosexual males' childhoods, erotic interest in other children, especially girls, seemed very common, and relatively few had their erotic interest solely in adults. For heterosexual paedophiles, the data suggest that the commonest form of childhood interest was in adult females. In the case of homosexual paedophiles, the commonest sexual interest was indiscriminate as to age and sex. Freund and Kuban suggest that erotic sex fixation comes earlier in life than does age fixation. The authors regard this as being compatible with the view that for some paedophiles, paedophilia is laid down early in life since some men remember erotic interest in children but not adults at this age. Nevertheless, the data seem better able to support the view that erotic age fixation occurs largely in late childhood.

RE-ENACTMENT THEORY

There are problems with the proposition that sexual abuse in childhood leads to paedophilia in adulthood. In particular, the mechanism by which it might do so has been left to conjecture rather than systematically investigated. While, as yet, it has not been explored in relation to paedophiles, re-enactment theory does have implications for understanding the aetiology of paedophilia. Burgess *et al.* (1988) studied serial rapists, each of whom had attacked a minimum of ten women. Notably, when asked whether they had ever been sexually abused in childhood they overwhelmingly denied it. However, their self-reported earliest sexual experiences were assessed for abuse without relying on their own perceptions. Three-quarters of the serial rapists reported episodes that were coded as sexually abusive by the researchers. Fifty-five per cent had been sexually abused in either a forced or exploitative manner; the remaining 20% reported witnessing a sexually disturbing event. "Force" was apparently widely interpreted—Burgess *et al.*'s example was that of a child who had oral sex repeatedly for money. While forced sex mostly involved male perpetrators, it was also commonly employed by female abusers. Although nearly half of the aggressors were males acting on their own, nearly a third were lone females. One in eight episodes involved a man and a woman together.

These serial rapists frequently re-enacted their own abuse on their victims although it is unclear whether re-enactment was carried out on men. Re-enactment means the "direct replication" of the abuse that offenders suffered themselves: "Reenactment was a behavioral match or a clear symbolic reference to the abuse. If either or both were present, reenactment was affirmed" (Burgess *et al.*, 1988, p. 282). Over half of the serial rapists seem to have re-enacted before adolescence. Nevertheless, offenders themselves had not made the connection in their own minds. Comparing their abuse with their earliest self-initiated sexual activity reveals re-enactments involving family members, acquaintances and also strangers. One fairly detailed illustration is provided by the following:

> "Consider the following case, coded as reenactment. One rapist described memories he regarded as sexual, in which an aunt, while bathing him in a tub, would fondle his penis. This occurred several times. He recounts going to the home of a male school friend at around age 11 or 12 and finding his friend's mother (who was in her 30s) 'drunk and nude, lying on a couch.' His young friend ran from the scene, leaving the offender, who found himself intrigued by what he saw and highly excited. He states that she called him over to her and, when he approached, took hold of his hand, moved it across her body, and thrust it between her legs. He reported that he found this exciting and inserted his fingers into her. He thought that it was wrong and that he should leave, but then he leaned over and kissed her on the buttocks. With that, she 'popped me in the ears.' This action startled and frightened him, and he ran from the house feeling 'scared to death,' fearful that his mother and father would be informed, realizing he had done something wrong but feeling he did it because he wanted to. He remembers being upset, confused, and scared. He knows that these are the same feelings he has every time he rapes."
>
> (Burgess *et al.*, 1988, p. 289)

The re-enactment process is an attempt to deal with the "confusion and stress" generated by the sexual aspects of the abuse. Re-enactment may well be either ignored or punished by the family or community, neither of which deals effectively with the trauma. The child becomes unable to control his own arousal and becomes preoccupied with sex and sexually arousing aggressive thoughts:

> "To reduce victimization, serial rapists need to be identified early and stopped. This means acknowledging and reporting boy sexual abuse. This includes being sensitive to the reenactment behaviors noted in the initiated activities of abused children, which in turn need to be differentiated from peer play."
>
> (Burgess *et al.*, 1988, p. 293)

It has been suggested that the age of an offender's own sexual victimization may be an important factor in determining his choice of victims (Greenberg, Bradford and Curry, 1993). Although there did not seem to be any difference between men who erotically preferred children under 11 years of age and those who preferred pubescents (hebephiles) in terms of their recall of abuse in childhood (under 40% recollection in both cases), those who preferred older children were themselves first abused later in childhood. Recollection of abuse was higher in boy-orientated hebephiles than girl-orientated ones.

VICTIMIZATION AND SEXUAL BEHAVIOUR

Olson (1990) studied men in private or community mental health settings. All were undergoing psychotherapy and nearly two-thirds said that they had experienced sexual abuse. Where the abuse was incestuous the mother was responsible in over 60% of the cases and the father in over 50%. For non-incestuous abuse, the most likely perpetrators were neighbours. According to a problems checklist, victims and non-victims were most different on rage, compulsive spending and compulsive sexual behaviour. There were other differences, all of which revealed more problems in the abused, including school sexual behaviour and substance abuse. Less reliable differences included violence in a relationship and hiring prostitutes. Compulsive behaviours such as compulsive relationships, compulsive shop-lifting, compulsive overeating and compulsive overworking were also found.

Sexual "disturbance" is the typical outcome of sexual abuse of boys according to one review of the empirical evidence (Urquiza and Capra, 1990). The effects are described as "inappropriate sexual behaviors (for example, confusion about sexual issues, compulsive sexual behaviors, and sexual acting out/offending)" (Urquiza and Capra, 1990, p. 113). Studies such as those by Friedrich and Luecke (1988) and McCauley *et al.* (1983), implicate the more severe forms of sexual abuse as "disinhibitors" of children's sexual behaviour. Furthermore, sexual crime in youth is common among those sexually abused in childhood (Fehrenbach *et al.*, 1986; Groth, 1979b; Longo, 1982). Similar effects of sexual abuse on sexual behaviour in adulthood have been claimed; for example, victimization by adult men (but not young males) tends to push boys towards homosexuality

(Finkelhor, 1979; Johnson and Shrier, 1985). The general difficulties encountered by men who were sexually abused as children were sexual adjustment, low sexual self-esteem and sexual identity (Urquiza and Capra, 1990).

ABUSE OR SEXUALIZATION?

Some conceptions of sexual abuse create a rigid dichotomy between adult–child and child–child sexual activities. Adult–child sexual contacts are regarded as problematic because of power differentials, whereas child–child contacts are seen as "just part of growing up", unlikely to be harmful so long as there are no obvious marked inequalities between the "participants". Usually, an age differential (of five years or so) is held to demarcate an abusive from a peer sexual experience. But, otherwise, the rationale for why adult–child sex is considered harmful and peer sex almost healthy is missing. It may well be a worthwhile dichotomy but one that cannot be taken for granted since this would be to disregard two major issues:

(1) Is adult–child sex necessarily harmful?
(2) Does child–child sex have no repercussions?

The answer to the first question is complex and requires a sweep through research history rather than a current summary of cumulative research findings (Howitt, 1992). There is no doubt that serious social and psychological harm can be caused to some children by sexual abuse in childhood. But this is not quite the same as saying that it is universally seriously harmful or that the physical acts alone were responsible rather than adult responses to them. There is a sense in which the research evidence creates an extreme picture of the harm done by abuse through concentrating on clinical samples of victims (Goodwin, Cheeves and Connell, 1990; Roth, Wayland and Woolsey, 1990; Schaeffer, Sobieraj and Hollyfield, 1988; Shearer *et al.*, 1990; Steiger and Zanko, 1990). These may well be very selected samples of people who have failed to deal effectively with their abuse or are suffering psychological problems that were not caused by their abuse. The rates of psychological problems, including ones requiring hospitalization, are high in the general population. It is not surprising, then, to find abuse in the childhoods of a high proportion of people requiring psychiatric or psychological treatment. Studies of samples of clinical patients have tended to be more common in the modern professional literature and associated with the greatly increased concern expressed by professionals during the 1980s about the severe effects of sexual abuse.

In earlier decades, evidence of great trauma tended not to be found (Bernard, 1979; Card, 1975; Constantine, 1979; Ingram, 1979; Kinsey *et al.*, 1953; Powell and Chalkley, 1981), and the hysterical responses of parents held to be largely responsible for the upset caused to the child (Bernard, 1979; Ingram, 1979). In many ways abuse was regarded as having essentially neutral outcomes or even to be of positive value for at least the lonely child. But much the same thesis is common among pro-paedophilia lobbyists. General population surveys of the victims of sexual abuse, as opposed to clinical samples, have not produced the devastating evidence of the harm done by abuse that might be expected (Alexander and Lupfer, 1987; Finkelhor, 1984; Finkelhor *et al.*, 1989; Roth, Wayland and Woolsey, 1990; Winfield *et al.*, 1990). This is partly because they produce somewhat inconsistent findings, but what trends there are may not be unequivocal evidence of the adverse effects of abuse (Howitt, 1992).

The Dutch research by Sandfort (1988, 1989) is important in so far as he is careful to examine the question of how adult–child sexual contact was experienced by the child. Thus, some experiences might be forced and undesired whereas others may have been what the child wanted or was happy to go along with. Non-consensual adult–child sexual activity was found to be associated with later problems in terms of sex with new partners and psychosomatic health problems. On the other hand, consensual sex simply predicted higher levels of sexual desire, increased sexual arousability and fewer anxieties about sex. In other words, consensual sex resulted in a positively sexualized adult. A study of boys involved sexually with adults suggested them to be overwhelmingly consensual, with little or no sign of an adverse influence on their general sense of well-being (Sandfort and Everaerd, 1990). Sandfort (1992) makes an important comment on the role of research:

> "In my view, social norms cannot simply be incorporated into the conceptualization of social scientists. Researchers must base their findings on what they observe, not what society tells them they ought to observe. Rather than accepting those social norms, it would be better to be critical of them ... "
>
> (Sandfort, 1992, p. 39)

It is interesting to note that some of Sandfort's findings are challenged by one major figure in sexual abuse research (Finkelhor, 1991) not on the grounds of their veracity, but on moral principles:

> "Ultimately, I do continue to believe that the prohibition on adult–child sexual contact is primarily a moral issue. While empirical findings have some relevance they are not the final arbiter ... Some types of social relationships violate deeply held values and principles in our culture about equality and self-determination. Sex between adults and children is one of them. Evidence that certain children have positive experiences does not challenge these values, which have deep roots in our worldview. This is the main reason that Sandfort's research has had relatively little attention, and has little relevance for policy."
>
> (Finkelhor, 1991, pp. 314–315)

To this we might add the research of Farrell, who suggests that the experience of incest is largely positive in two-thirds of the cases he obtained through newspaper advertisements. One category—adult male with pre-teenage female—seems rather more harmful. According to Farrell, writing of the incestuous relationships that were viewed as positive, over 50% were still continuing. These may be of twenty or so years' duration. Farrell claims that three previous studies had tended to support his contentions, although none of these had been published.

The answer to our second question, that of the consequences of sexual activity between children, is even more difficult. Theoretically, at least, child–child sexual activity is conducive to paedophilia since one might expect that a pleasurable activity is repeated on future occasions. When these early experiences are with underage partners, a preference for young sex might be established. Such a possibility is not normally raised. Sexual attractiveness is socially defined in terms of youthfulness; fantasy of a young, nubile sexual partner is not uncommon in literature and elsewhere. If socialization achieves this, why should not youthful sexual contacts produce at least a residue of life-long sexual orientation to underage partners? After all, there is no absolute distinction between the physical characteristics of age-legal partners and age-illegal partners.

Since the evidence of sexual abuse in the childhoods of offenders is fairly strong, but not enough to account for all subsequent offending by any means, the "cycle of abuse" explanation is an incomplete explanation of all sexual interest in underage children. Traumatic child abuse is almost certainly responsible for the sexualization of at least some offenders, as we have seen. The extent to which non-traumatic experiences and peer-sex might also be responsible for some of the early sexualization of paedophiles has not been explored. In other words, rather than dwell on the effects of sexual abuse, the question could be extended to include the influence of all aspects of early sexualization on the offender.

Two principles underlie the suggestion that sexualization in general should be studied:

(1) That this early sexualization has a strong influence on the sexual fantasy and behaviour of offenders. That is, there should be thematically close parallels between the two.
(2) That such sexualization should be common, if not universal in the lives of offenders, or, at a minimum, should account for more offenders than the cycle of sexual abuse perspective alone.

There is nothing in this to suggest that the age of the sexual "partner" is crucial in the process. Neither is it suggested that the experience has to be pleasurable; it may well be that unpleasurable experiences are equally influential, as "re-enactment" theory suggests. Of course, the age differentials may influence how the child experiences the sexual behaviour. Furthermore, psychological processes such as identification with the aggressor may be involved in some cases. In other words, there is likely to be considerable variation in how a particular sexual act is experienced due to factors such as the relationship with the other individual, the child's level of psychological and social maturity, and the pleasure or pain caused by the act. It may also be that there are considerable variations in terms of the child's capacity to generate fantasy for future masturbation based on these experiences. Furthermore, Yates (1990) suggests that this process of sexualization (he calls it eroticization) is more certain among younger children rather than adolescents. The latter may have a sort of phobic reaction to the self-same acts.

Howitt and Cumberbatch (in press) noted that if the concept of sexual abuse is replaced by one of sexualization, a much greater proportion of paedophiles appear to be distinctive in terms of their offending behaviour and their early sexualization. So, for example, Terry:

> "Right from the time when I was younger I was assaulted sexually by my brother from the age of 4 to 6 approximately ... [He was] 17 or 18. Oral sex he would have on me. He would try to make me do it with him,

> and just generally messing about, molesting that sort of thing. By my sister from the age of 7 to 10. I don't know the exact time, just when I was at school ... [S]he made me perform oral sex on her and simulated sex, with the age it was difficult but it was something I really enjoyed. I started sexually offending when I was about 4 although it wasn't termed as that ... I remember going down to the farm and trying to simulate sex on a young girl of 2 when I was 4 and this continued when I went to ... boarding school, where there was a young girl of 15 and I was 12 nearly 13 ... And then when she left I was coming up to 15 ... and I was assaulting a young girl of 10 ... So my sexual experience started at school where I fancied this girl who was in the same flat as me, and I went into her bedroom and told her to take her pyjama bottoms off and her top, she gave some kind of protest, sort of a huff, but there was no sort of verbal protest, and from then on I took it as my right to go in there and do so. While this was going on the 10-year-old who was a bit younger than that was watching in the next bed, and when the 15-year-old ... left the 10-year-old wanted me to actually do it to her, she came and asked me to do it to her as well."

There is a remarkable connection between how Terry describes aspects of his early sexual experiences and the context of his abuse of other children in adulthood:

> "I was fantasizing about Jenny and Helen, the girls at school, right the way through the rest of my school days, right through borstal and beyond that, until I first got married and beyond that, and they were still there, they are quite sort of vivid in my mind, because they were happy times, I suppose, and that's where my first sexual experience started for my own side of things ... the fantasy ... always revolved around what actually happened at school, where I would be in the bedroom having sex with either girl ... I would go into the bedroom, ask her to take her pyjama bottoms off and open her top and that would be the substance of the fantasy ... I started noticing the stepchildren as being of the same proportions [as the girls in the fantasies] and then the fantasies would be going on with the schoolgirls which I had actually had sex with and the stepdaughters would come in and take the place of, in the situation at school perhaps, which they had never been to but they would take the position and the role of the schoolchildren at school, and then eventually it became them in the home setting, and then the fantasy led to abuse."

Of course, there are aspects of his early abuse that do not seem to have been incorporated into his offending and fantasy. There is no easy answer to the important question of why this should be the case, other than in terms of the pleasure aroused.

The case of Adrian is another example of childhood sexual

experiences being paralleled very precisely by later offending. All of Adrian's offending was against boys—indeed, there are other parallels in that he spent part of his life as a school teacher, just as his early abuser was:

> "The first [sexual experiences] I can remember in reasonably good detail were the ones that I had at boarding school ... when I was about 11 or 12. But I know I'd had sex several times before that ... I was in a dormitory and in the next bed to me was a boy called Tim, and Tim and I used to sleep with each other, get erections and masturbate each other. He was two years older than me and he used to suck me and I used to suck him. I adored him ... I was about eight ... I think Tim initiated it. I know there was one occasion when I came in from having a bath or shower ... We had a housemaster about 20 years old. He was sucking Tim off on the bed ... Tim got up and came over to me and started playing with me and this housemaster then started playing with me which started something ... [He also remembered abuse at about the age of eight] I was in the park near home ... I remember being naked and that's all. I can remember a man being on me ... but I don't remember much else."

In brief, Adrian's convictions were for indecent assault. He describes his typical sexually activity as:

> "masturbating them on most occasions, on several occasions I have had oral sex with them and them with me."

It would be difficult to separate his adult abuse of children from what he was doing with his peers in his adolescence, in which sexual activity with other boys was more extensive than even the above suggests. Furthermore, Adrian describes how his offending took place within a family group of which he was a temporary member and in the school context—in other words, very much the same sort of communal situation in which he had first become sexualized. Another aspect of his offending concerns the nature of his fantasy during offending:

> "I am usually a little older [than the victim] but younger, much younger ... than myself ... I would say probably about 14 or 15 ... usually all the time ... Sometimes I am an adult, but I am 14 or 15."

This fantasy recreation of themselves in childhood is a common feature of paedophiles' fantasy. It is strongly indicative of the reincarnation of childhood experiences in sexual abuse.

Others have noted a connection between early sexual experiences and sexual offending. What is different is the idea that sexualization itself may be more important than abuse as such by adults. O'Brien (1986), in his case studies of paedophiles, points out that half of offenders had been sexually abused in childhood. It is not at all clear the extent to which he systematically explored early sexual experiences: the lack of direct statements about these other than abuse suggests that sexualization was dealt with on an *ad hoc* basis. It is worth taking one of O'Brien's positive associations, the case of Charlie:

> "CHARLIE: Well when I was 5, I was being baby-sat by some people. When the mother and father weren't there, their son would take care of me ... He was 19, a college student ... Well, he'd take me into the bedroom, take my pants down and play with my penis and make me play with him ... When I was probably in sixth or seventh grade, some people lived across the street. They had three kids and we more or less hung around ...
>
> SHIRLEY [O'BRIEN]: How old were you when that started?
>
> CHARLIE: Probably about seventh grade [12 years] ... [He] was probably a first grader [about six years] ...
>
> SHIRLEY: Did you fondle or rub him?
>
> CHARLIE: No, he did that to me."
>
> (O'Brien, 1986, pp. 5–6)

There is a close correspondence between the age of Charlie's victimization and the age of his victims; it is also clear that the types of activities involved were similar. His pattern with his later victims is very much the same irrespective of their sex. Indeed, other styles of abuse other than fondling were not central to his *modus operandi*. He did have one boy carry out oral sex on him but that was exceptional.

Similarly, Barnard *et al.* (1989) acknowledge that there may be sexually abusive experiences in the childhoods of many child abusers. Indeed, they present a variant of the usual theoretical connection:

> "This consideration has helped to substantiate the theory that a molester's habitual sexual abuse of children is a repeated and unsuccessful attempt to master his own early sexual trauma through a reenactment of the cruel experiences. Unable to overcome the anxiety, guilt, and pain of his childhood trauma, the molester identifies with the aggressor in order to project or displace the original conflict onto another victim."
>
> (Barnard *et al.*, 1989, p. 31)

They present a detailed history of a child molester, which leads them to stress that he was *not* sexually abused as a child. On hundreds of occasions, the offender had committed reciprocal oral sex with adolescent boys and a small number of girls. He reports numerous acts of sexual play with male and female cousins at the age of about seven, and sexual activity with his sister, which continued for several years, although this appears to be mutual masturbation. When he was 10, he was initiated into oral sex by a younger male cousin. He was caught at the age of 13 in apparently attempted sexual intercourse with his 11-year-old sister and scolded about the risks of getting her pregnant. His earliest sexual memory was of his mother threatening to cut off his penis for exposing it to his aunt. None of this is construed as sexual abuse by Barnard *et al.*!

It is significant that his offending "began" at 15 when he had oral sex with a 6-year-old boy, and that virtually all of the boys he offended against were prepubertal and 9 and 10 years old. These were key ages in his own sexualization. He even describes the physical characteristics of his targets in terms of similarity to particularly important figures in his childhood sexual experiences. His offending against boys involved oral sex but he did not engage in anal intercourse with them because his solitary childhood experience of this was very painful. In view of his father's discovery of his sexual activities with his sister, he justifies his lack of involvement with girls because of the fear of getting them pregnant—a comment redolent of his father's admonition. He describes that a dominant sexual fantasy when having sex with boys was of girls approximately 14 years old. The close links between his childhood mutual sexual experiences and aspects of his adult abuse of children seem obvious; his childhood sexualization is reflected in his offending style and preferences.

While it seems that sexual contacts are very common in the childhoods of sex offenders against children, they are also very common in the childhoods of people in general. So, for example, using a sample of US undergraduate students, Haugaard and Tilly (1988) were able to show that over 40% of them had had sexual experiences with other children. The main categories of this were kissing and hugging (26%), exhibitionism (33%), fondling (15%) and genital fondling (16%). There are really insufficient details available to judge whether these activities are comparable with the childhood experiences of paedophiles, though many of them seem more like courtship exploration than sexually directed acts. Thus we could not begin to answer questions about the role of subsequent fantasy and masturbation in these "normal" sexual histories. Do they simply quench the imagination of a sexually inquisitive child or are they reinforced by orgasm? What is it about the paedophile that fixes these childhood sexual activities into their sexualities? There are limits on the information that can be recalled in adulthood about childhood experiences which might help to answer such questions. Perhaps we should end by noting that three-quarters of paedophiles in Bernard's (1985) study claimed to have been first aware of being a paedophile by the age of 20. Only 2% became aware after 30 years of age.

CHAPTER 3

What Paedophiles Think and Do

> "We hypothesize that a deficiency of empathy for children would characterize many, if not most, child molesters. This concept might be thought of as having a number of components: (1) absence of protective feelings toward children; (2) denial that children occupy a special status and qualify for special treatment; (3) disdain for childlike emotional characteristics—neediness, spontaneity, ignorance; (4) lack of interest in children; (5) feeling of inadequacy in a caretaking role."
>
> (Finkelhor and Lewis, 1988, p. 76)

The nature of sexual abuse has encouraged the disregard of offenders as people. They are portrayed as sick monsters who lie, cheat and deceive to avoid their just punishments. Such a caricature inevitably ensures that sympathetic accounts of the meanings of relationships with children for paedophiles are in short supply; there is an extensive paedophile literature in novels, biographies and elsewhere, but not stemming from research. One exception to this trend is Li (1991), who describes the psychological motives for relationships with children. Men recruited from referrals by psychiatrists, paedophile organizations and magazine advertisements were interviewed in order to "understand how my pedophile informants have understood their sexual life as an *experiencing subject*" (p. 133).

Relationships with children were not replacements for their failures with adult men or women, nor a final resort of thwarted libidos:

> "Over half of the informants have mentioned specific characteristics in children which they find particularly attractive. Thus to them,

> relationships and sexual activities with children are experienced as more satisfying than those with adults. These relationships are their first choice, rather than a substitute when adult sex is lacking."
>
> (Li, 1991, p. 133)

Children were described in words implying gentleness, warmth, generosity, innocence, truthfulness, broad-mindedness, affectionateness and perceptiveness. These contrast markedly with perceptions of adults as selfish, narrow-minded, materialistic and shallow in their feelings; the child's world represents the finest aspects of life. Li suggests that sex is not the primary motive of paedophiles. Love and the feeling of being wanted are among the things that the paedophile wants but the adult world fails to provide. One 74-year-old paedophile said:

> "As a boy-lover ... I don't go out seeking boys for my pleasure. I only encourage boys who come to me and want me to have a bit of sex play with them, and that has always been my angle. I have never ever forced a boy."
>
> (Li, 1991, p. 136)

A 34-year-old paedophile had had a hundred or so boys sexually over the years but that is not what he wanted:

> "Most important thing I look for, I suppose, is a loving relationship with a boy ... I can only point to four or five true relationships over that time."
>
> (Li, 1991, p. 138)

A small proportion of the men described their relationships with children as if they were romantic love and courtship. Another man suggested that children lose their appeal the moment that they "learn the ways of the world and ask what's in it for me or what is it worth. When that happens they lose all their charm and enchantment" (Li, 1991, p. 135).

Unlike many writers, Li argues the case for taking such views as representing paedophiles' true feelings rather than dismissing them as lies, cognitive distortions and self-serving excuses:

> "The discrepancy between pedophiles' views and those of mainstream society has to be examined critically to see if there is any possibility of achieving an optimal balance between individual rights and collective responsibility. In dealing with this problem, it must be borne in mind that the viewpoint of mainstream society cannot simply be taken as

> correct and that of the pedophiles taken as suspect. Instead, each should be analyzed in terms of its historical and ideological roots. Only after such an exercise can we begin to address the more practical questions of ethics, the law, and social policies with regard to sexual contact between adults and children."
>
> (Li, 1991, p. 141)

WHAT DO SEX ABUSERS DO?

The criminal sexual activities of offenders against underage people are, of course, extremely varied, including murder with rape through to exhibitionism and other non-contact offences. While there is a remarkable range, this does not mean that either extreme is typical of offending. Indeed, the extent to which non-criminal sexual activities are more typical of those with a sexual interest in children has not been quantified. For example, masturbation might be the typical response to arousal towards children, even among those with criminal convictions. The numbers of people whose sexual actions towards children consist entirely of secret, private fantasy and masturbation is unknown.

The formal evidence of what offenders do comes from two main sources—victims and offenders. It can make tedious reading for a number of reasons. There is no standard way of categorizing abuse, for example, due to variations in legal definitions, which vary widely between different countries and regions. The inconsistency of definition makes it difficult to summarize the data. The settings in which information is collected, as well as the sampling techniques used, have a big influence on the outcome. This produces somewhat eccentric swings in the trends found from study to study. One can opt to "fudge" the issue by overgeneralizing or by presenting something of the variability found in research reports. Whichever, the topic is an object lesson in the problematic nature of studies of the incidence of offending.

Victim Studies

While the definition of sexual abuse can be problematic (Howitt, 1992), it would seem likely that the bulk of offences committed against underage girls are non-contact acts such as indecent exposure, public masturbation and solicitations for sex, or legally less serious contact offences such as fondling or rubbing one's genitals against the body of the victim. In a stratified sample of young women in Los Angeles, more than 40% of the childhood incidents recalled were non-contact (Wyatt, 1985). Genital fondling accounted for over half of the contact incidents, intercourse and attempted intercourse about a quarter, and oral sex was relatively rare. Another study of adult women, again in Los Angeles, produced somewhat different findings (Russell, 1983). Very serious abuse (defined as "completed and attempted vaginal, oral, anal intercourse, cunnilingus, anilingus, forced and unforced") occurred in about a quarter or less of the incidents involving family members, but in three-quarters, approximately, of the recorded acts of strangers, acquaintances, friends and friends of the family. It seems somewhat counterintuitive that such high proportions of extrafamilial abuse were serious.

This impression is reinforced by surveys in Britain. Nash and West (1985) studied a sample of women patients registered with a doctors' practice as well as a sample of female students. In general, the students reported substantially more experiences of the "less serious" forms of abuse in their childhoods (including verbal suggestion, obscene telephone calls, flashers, and sexual kisses). Attempted intercourse constituted 4% of incidents for both samples and intercourse between 2 and 3%. Fondling the girl's genitals occurred in 9% of the community sample and 16% of the student sample; adults caressing children's thighs and breasts occurred in 2% and 18% of the respective samples. Non-contact offences accounted for about half of the abuse of students but only about a fifth of that of the community sample. The variability between samples might be to do with how they construe abuse. Students, for example, might be more aware of the feminist view of non-contact offences.

One survey had nurses and doctors evaluate abuse cases treated in the emergency room of a Florida hospital. Not surprisingly, given the context in which the data was collected, most of the assaults involved penetrative sex (Cupoli and Sewell, 1988). In the case of boy victims, buggery accounted for most of the cases, followed by the composite category of fellatio on the child, the masturbation of the adult and fondling. For girls, penile penetration of the vagina dominated, followed by a mixed category of cunnilingus, masturbating the adult and fondling, and the penetration of the vagina with fingers. Because girls were more frequently victims than boys, the most frequent victims of anal sex were girls. At a Canadian hospital, Mian *et al.* (1986) found fondling the most common (40% of cases), although oral sex occurred in 15% of cases and "dry" intercourse (simulating penetrative intercourse by rubbing the penis between the victim's thighs without penetration) in 14%. The entire sample consisted of six-year-olds and under, which may have affected the characteristics of the sexual activities involved.

Cases of the sexual exploitation of children up to the age of 12 reported by the Netherlands State Police suggest that the commonest forms of sexual contact involved the perpetrator fondling the child, having the child fondle him and the child masturbating him (Wolters *et al.*, 1985). Intercourse and attempted intercourse occurred in about 13% of the cases. Sadistic behaviour was a feature of 6%. Although it was the opinion of the police officers concerned that a quarter of the sexual contact was voluntary, coercion played a part in about half.

Each of these institutionally-based sources is likely to be biased by being an extreme situation, likely to attract the worst cases. Relatively trivial episodes are probably less likely to be reported.

Offender Studies

There exist claims that, on average, child molesters offend against 150 male or 20 female or victims according to their paedophiliac orientation (Abel *et al.*, 1987), although this may be a selected sample biasing the trends. One of the most thorough of the studies of offenders reports data obtained from sex offenders at the Minnesota Security Hospital (Erickson, Walbek and Seely, 1988). Consecutive cases over a 10-year period involving offences against children under 14 years of age were examined. Over two-thirds offended against girls, about a quarter against boys and only 4% against both sexes. There were few age differences between the male and female victims: about a quarter of both were under 6 years, another quarter were between 6 and 10 years, and the majority between 11 and 13 years. The broad trends in the acts committed were:

1. For females under 10 years

    - 34% offender fondled child
    - 17% vaginal contact
    - 15% oral sex on victim
    - 12% oral sex on offender

Other behaviours, such as attempted vaginal intercourse, anal contact, attempted anal sex and victim fondle constituted 8% of acts or less.

2. For females between 11 and 13 years

   - 35% offender fondled child
   - 23% vaginal contact
   - 13% oral sex on offender
   - 10% oral sex on victim
   - 6% attempted vaginal intercourse

3. For males under 10 years

   - 28% anal contact on victim
   - 24% offender fondled child
   - 7% oral sex on victim
   - 4% oral sex on offender

4. For males between 11 and 13 years

   - 29% oral sex on offender
   - 27% offender fondled child
   - 14% anal contact on victim
   - 14% oral sex on victim

These do not exhaust the things done to children by offenders:

> "Some aspects of offender behavior are difficult to quantify but deserve comment, based on our clinical experience. Attempted insertion of offenders' fingers into vaginas was fairly common, but insertion of fingers into victims' rectums was quite uncommon. Insertion of foreign bodies into the rectum or vagina occurred very rarely. Penile rectal or

> vaginal contact with younger children usually consisted of touching the rectal or vaginal opening with the penis, and rubbing of the penis between the legs. In cases where more forcible efforts were made, bruising and laceration of the tissues between vagina and rectum occurred. Where rectal penetration actually occurred, the victims usually had to be held forcibly and their cries muffled. Some strategies [were] routinely necessary in order to conceal the cries from others in the household."
>
> (Erickson, Walbek and Seely, 1988, p. 42)

Bribery was the most frequent way of obtaining sex; threat was not so common. Size and age discrepancies between adults and children make the question of coercion rather problematic, of course. In terms of what the perpetrators said, physical injury was comparatively rare. Usually offenders remained clothed during the offences. Nudity, when it occurred, was more common in domestic offences. Mostly the victims were individual although offenders might have several contemporaneous victims. Group activity involving several victims in the same episode occurred only with adolescent males.

Methods that inmates at an Ohio correctional institute had employed in their abusing were reported by Budin and Johnson (1989). The median numbers of boy victims was 3.5, and that of girl victims 2. The men tended to prefer a particular type of child, although the attractive characteristics varied substantially from offender to offender. Nearly half of those who answered preferred their own children and/or ones they described as passive, quiet, troubled, lonely children from "broken" homes; two-fifths mentioned children from single-parent homes. A sort of "empathy" is demonstrated by the fact that 45% mentioned targeting children who reminded them of themselves. Victims were typically found in the close vicinity; over half of them near the offender's home, a third in the neighbourhood, a fifth at family get-togethers and an eighth in playgrounds. Only a fifth molested victims recruited far from the offender's own home.

The child's trust was established in the enticement process by being a friend in 90% of cases. Other aspects of enticement included playing games (55%), giving money (45%) and choosing children previously victimized by another perpetrator (45%). Tangible gifts such as toys, candy, cigarettes, beer and drugs were much less common. Perhaps "they would say this, wouldn't they" but less than a quarter claimed to have used threats to obtain the child's cooperation and silence. *Of those who had used threats*, the threat of hitting was commonest, although less than 50%; also mentioned were threats to hurt loved objects and family members, and threats with knifes or guns.

At a specialist sex offender treatment programme in Seattle, therapeutically "successful" clients provided information about the characteristics of their offending (Conte, Wolf and Smith, 1989). The men were mostly experienced offenders with an average of seven victims, although the range was from one to forty. They were asked to write a "manual" on how to sexually abuse a child. Among the examples they provided were:

> "(a) Some way to get a child living with you. If you have a repertoire of jokes that move from risky to pornographic, have porn magazines lying around. Talk about sex. Watch the kids' reactions. Stick your head in their bedrooms while they are in their bedclothes. Act like it's a natural thing. Be sympathetic. Try a lot of compliments. Have accidental contact with their breasts."
>
> "(b) Be in a position where you are a close friend with someone who is involved in alcohol and drugs and probably has the attitude that kids are like dogs, just around the house. Someone who has a tight control over kids and where if the kid does anything wrong he'll be severely punished. Being a molester, you can pick on that and start showing the kids extra attention. They'll thrive on it and will become easily manipulated to your control. You can also set it up when the parents trust you and use you as a babysitter. You'll be alone with the kid, and the kid doesn't like his parents."
>
> (Conte, Wolf and Smith, 1989, p. 298)

Most of these offenders also expressed a preference for certain physical or behavioural characteristics in their victims—generally smooth skin, long hair, dresses, or slim body, darker skinned, darker hair, a cute face. Behaviours such as the victims being friendly and open were also mentioned. After they had identified a potential victim, most of the offenders thought about getting caught and this fear caused them to modify when and how to abuse: "I selected victims that I thought wouldn't report me" (Conte, Wolf and Smith, 1989, p. 296). Although some claimed that there was no targeting involved (i.e. a process of becoming interpersonally engaged with the victim), this was unusual; an example would be a man who abused a sleeping victim. Most offenders described how they built up a relationship with the child prior to initiating sexual contact:

> "Play, talking, giving special attention, trying to get the child to initiate contact with me. Get the child to feel safe to talk with me. From here I

> would initiate different kinds of contact, such as touching the child's back, head. Testing the child to see how much she would take before she would pull away."
>
> (Conte, Wolf and Smith, 1989, p. 297)

The use of adult authority, adult physical presence and isolation of the victim from others were among the methods used to gain mastery of the victim. Very few admitted to the use of physical violence or its direct threat, which suggests that alternative methods were available, such as warning the child to be careful not to tell anyone or withdrawing affection.

Lang and Langevin (1991) claim that about one in five sexually victimized children is subject to gratuitous violence as part of the offence on the basis of a review of the research. Nevertheless, Okami and Goldberg (1992) suggest that some writers substantially overstress the level of violence by ignoring "the large bulk of the literature which demonstrates convincingly that violence and overt coercion are not generally characteristic of child sexual abuse" (p. 320). According to Bradford, Bloomberg and Boulet (1988), the use of violence depends on the age group of the offender. Of adolescent offenders, 17% used violence; for the middle-aged group, 11% used some violence, 5% used moderate amounts of violence and 5% used excessive violence; and for senile offenders there were no cases of violence at all. It is difficult to know precisely what is meant by violence, since the researchers offer no definitions of their categories. This may not be typical of younger offenders since Saunders, Awad and White (1986) found that about half of paedophile offences by adolescents involved violence or the threat of violence. Perhaps it is relevant that about a third of recorded rapes are perpetrated against children (La Fontaine, 1990). Given that older children may be fully physically mature, we should not assume that these rapes are necessarily dissimilar in motivation from rapes of adults. That is, perhaps they are better classified with rape than with sexual offences against children when considering their psychological implications rather than their legal ones.

Abuse takes place at characteristic times. Victimization takes place most frequently on Fridays and Mondays during daylight hours or dusk (noon to 8.00 p.m.) (Peters, 1976). About a third of offences were between 8 p.m. and midnight, although these were almost all offences where the child was left in the care of the offender. Over two-thirds of the offences took less than 15 minutes according to the child.

Adolescents report rather longer periods—half of offences taking more than an hour. The offender was known to the child in 80% of cases and the offences took place in the victim's or offender's home in over half of cases. Nearly 80% of cases involved just one offender. This research was done on victims at a general hospital in Philadelphia and at a private psychoanalytic practice.

Maturity and Age Characteristics of Victims

Chronological age and physical maturity do not perfectly correlate with each other although most psychological approaches to offenders follow legal age classifications. There are problems in that the age ranges used to define paedophilia may have an upper limit varying from 12 to 18 years, say, if European or American legal criteria are employed. Taking puberty as the distinguishing factor would mean that the upper limit could be anything from 9 to 18 years. There may be advantages in using an index of physical development such as Tanner Scores (Lang, Rouget and van Santen, 1988). The Tanner classification (Tanner, 1978) is a scale of 1 to 5: a score of 1 means that the child has infantile morphology in its breast and genital area; 2 means that the breasts are beginning to bud, hair is beginning to grow on the body and in the pubic area, and changes are beginning in the mucous membrane of the vagina and inner labia; 3 means that the breasts have enlarged further, the areolae have become more prominent, there is a darkening, coarsening and curling of the pubic hair and an increase in bodily hair; 4 means that the nipple area forms a clear mound above the level of the breasts, and pubic and bodily hair have become more adult in character; and, finally, 5 indicates that the distributions of pubic and bodily hair, as well as the breasts, are like those of the mature adult. Because these scores deal with actual physical maturity rather than age, they might have implications for understanding paedophiles' choices of victim. Some paedophiles, for example, say that hairless and smooth skin is what attracted them to a particular child.

A sample consisting mainly of girls in the age range of 1 to 18 years at the University of Alberta Hospital paediatric clinic was studied between 1980 and 1986 (Lang, Rouget and van Santen, 1988). All had been sexually abused, as confirmed by verbal disclosure or from police or social services investigations. A control sample of non-abused children attending the same clinic was used for comparisons. While there was a substantial correlation between Tanner

Classification and age in years, they shared only 50% of their variance in common. That is, age and physical development depart substantially from each other. It is of considerable interest to find that relatively few (11%) of the victims of abuse were fully sexually developed—that is, physically adults. Indeed, the great majority of the victims (66%) were at the lowest levels of sexual development (Tanner level 1). Victims tended to be small and light for their age. There was a bimodal age distribution of victims, with peaks at about 4 years and 11 years. On average, victims were 23 years younger than their abusers. There was no relationship between the age of the offender and the age gap with his victim. In other words, younger offenders did not have a smaller age gap from their victims.

The sexual acts involved depended somewhat on the child's physical maturity. Bribes were commonest at Tanner 3. Intimate kissing, masturbation by the child or both masturbating, cunnilingus and fellatio were commoner in Tanner 4 children. Vaginal intercourse was commonest in Tanner 4 and 5s. Threats and emotional coercion were commoner at Tanner 5 than earlier. "Dry" intercourse was roughly equally common throughout the Tanner scores range. In some instances, age predicted better than physical characteristics. For example, dry intercourse, anal intercourse and attempted intercourse rejected by the child were all better predicted by age. Finally, Tanner scores better predicted whether ejaculation took place. It might be that the initiation of the abuse process might be influenced by the child's age characteristics, but when it becomes apparent that the child is physically immature the offender abandons his quest for ejaculation.

GROOMING: THE MOLESTATION PROCESS

> "I could be grooming a boy and thinking how I have ... already groomed ... in my fantasy, and go along with it. Almost as using it like ... a step-to-step guide of grooming a boy ... instead of the text written in front of me, I had it in my mind ... so I would groom the boys this way and would do things I had already thought about, and then when it came to getting to the crunch, I could start off by sitting him on my lap and fondling him ... and to see if he then accepted that ... and [if] he didn't register anything in my fantasy I would know that I could go onto the next stage, which might be taking photographs of him in his swimming trunks. I could then fondle him a bit more and get an erection, and if that was alright, maybe I would wait 'til he was changing out of one pair of swimming trunks to another pair to take a couple of pictures."

The molestation process is described as a cycle of behaviour by Wyre (1987) which repeats for subsequent children. Wyre suggests that for the typical extrafamilial paedophile the process involves three major stages, which appear to be led by fantasy laced with skilful deceptive ploys. The sense in which they are typical of all offenders is unclear.

Stage 1. The offender begins this stage by masturbating and fantasizing to old sexual experiences, which leads to fantasies about possible future contacts. A boy is befriended, perhaps at a club or in the street, while an effort is made to meet his parents and develop their trust. Visits to the cinema, theatre or elsewhere ensure that a more intimate level of social contact is achieved. This trust-building process continues for a while.

Stage 2. Digging deeper, the offender finds out about the boy's home and school problems. This enables a "counselling" role to develop, which leads to "friendship".

Stage 3. By now the offender is being visited at home by the boy. The boy is encouraged to let his parents know about this. Physical contact of a seemingly non-sexual sort begins to take place, for example, playful wrestling. Watching television together allows an arm to be placed around the boy. Any resistance leads to immediate cessation of the physical contact, but only to be tried again in the future. The offender increasingly fantasizes and masturbates about his soon-to-be sexual conquest. Sexual touches start but fully clothed, and at a subsequent meeting the boy's genitals may be played with. Warnings are issued about not telling anyone. Mutual masturbation to ejaculation may follow. Later, oral sex, then buggery of the boy, and then buggery of the offender complete the sequence.

The stages overlap quite considerably and are not too distinct. They correspond roughly to an approach/trust building/physical contact cycle.

Wyre also describes the "seductive incest cycle", which may apply to a natural father or stepfather. The stages are (i) tickling the child, (ii) bathing, (iii) the man's sexual arousal and fantasy, (iv) the child going to his bed, (v) the man knows that the child enjoys being tickled, (vi) "sex education" lessons may be used as a pretext to move to a later stage in the abuse cycle, (vii) the tickling reaches the child's sexual parts, (viii) the man masturbates the child's genitals, (ix) the child is trapped into silence by threats or being told to keep their "secret" while the man begins to convince himself that the child enjoys the sexual activity, (x) sexual contact is increased, (xi) the man increasingly thinks in a distorted way about the child and his sexual abuse of it, (xii) it becomes increasingly difficult to end sexual contact now it has begun, and (xiii) by masturbating to his fantasies about the abuse, his offending behaviour is reinforced.

One of the difficulties with such accounts of the abuse cycle is that they make it appear a relatively short-term and repetitive process. This may be the case with some abusers, but others show a long-term deviant career pattern which may begin in childhood or adolescence. Take the following case of Garry, who was in his 40s at the time of interview. Ignoring at this point his childhood and adolescent sexual experiences, his adult life began with a lengthy period as a frequent indecent exposer, "flashing" at boy targets as his preferred victims, while he later began a rather different career as a contact molester of two young girls. The two careers are very different in terms of their method of operation. First of all, on the career as "flasher":

> "There's two different styles I used to do. One is I'd just drop my trousers and underpants and masturbated or didn't masturbate depending on circumstances, time was one of the key factors ... the other one was completely stripping off, and doing masturbating. It would be in wooded areas ... deserted areas, like old buildings ... that type of thing, because where I lived ... at that time, we had a lot of reorganizing ... knocking terraced houses down, so there was lots of abandoned houses where children used to go and play inside, or they would be out in the street ... I used to ... do quite a bit ... in the back garden at night with a torch ...
>
> "[Also] I would go and look round the area first, ... look round and see where children played on their own ... areas where they were vulnerable and I would do this over quite a long period of time ... and then I would go to different areas all over [the city] ... and also offend in other areas which are already reconnoitred so I would change all the time [to] different areas.
>
> "It varied a lot ... it fluctuated ... best to put it down to days, because it varied from day to day ... if I had a good night, it could be anything between 40 to 50, if it was bad night, 5, 6 actual offences ... per night ... so ... you are talking about a lot of offending ... a lot of them ... I was masturbating but I didn't come ... I would drop my trousers and get an erection ... and that would be the actual offence in front of the child ... [I didn't always have an orgasm] ... sometimes I did.
>
> "[The offence took] a matter of seconds ... I would most probably picked out ... say there was a boy at first ... or two boys or three boys

> sometimes ... I would quickly reconnoitre the area to make sure that there was no one around ... and I walk in there and do it ... sometimes they would watch ... sometimes they wouldn't ... they run away, it varied ... I would sometimes come ... and just pull my trousers and pants up and walk off, or run off and that would be the end of it.
>
> "When I moved up to [a new city] I used to go out for cycle rides at night ... I used to park my bike somewhere and then go into a field where the houses backed on ... with the torch which I carried in the saddle bag ... after a while I got to know which houses had children in and which didn't ... and obviously I knew which ones were the interesting ones I wanted to expose myself to. So I used to ... wait in the ... garden in the dark where they couldn't see me ... to watch what was going on upstairs ... when they go to bed and pull the curtains ... and the parents came down, or while they were on their way down ... and I used to flash a very strong torch into the window, which [the children] would be aware of ... the light would go into the room ... they would come up to the window and look out through the curtains and see what the light was. Then I would expose myself and shine the light on my penis. So that's how it used to be done."

This persistent cycle of abuse is clearly not totally in accord with Wyre's stages. Given that it is a no contact, no interaction offence, the stages of "seduction" or "grooming" are unnecessary. Neither is it necessary to secure the child's silence since after a few seconds Garry would leave the scene. There are clearly elements of the abuse cycle present. Most particularly, it is abundantly obvious that Garry's offending involved a substantial amount of planning; there was little really spontaneous about it. Even Garry had targets with physical characteristics that he preferred. Furthermore, the reinforcement involved in the cycle was also fairly instantaneous in so far as the offence sometimes brought him to ejaculation. The alternative was that it provided him with what were for him erotic stimuli. In some ways, then, it is curious that he began an apparently totally different type of offence "mid-career". The mystery recedes somewhat if one considers that the prime theme in his sexual history is one of exposure and public masturbation. Not only does this tend to dominate his offending, but his adolescent sexual pattern also demonstrated much the same preference. The following account illustrates his use of exposure but, in the present context, it even more graphically displays the complexities of the "enticement" or "grooming" process at work. Garry, interviewed when he was a resident of the former Gracewell Clinic for sex offenders in the UK, uses a good deal of exculpatory rhetoric, which might be considered "distorted" thinking by some:

"[Nickola and Trudy] are two girls that I knew on the estate ... and it's quite an unusual one because they ... I lived in the big tower block, 17 floors up ... they have got an intercom system with the private rooms ... to stop people from walking in anywhere ... and I got this ... call off these two girls asking if I was Garry ... I'd never seen them before in my life and I didn't know who they were ... I said yes ... and they chatted and told me they were Nickola and Trudy ... Trudy was 8 and Nickola was 6 ... We were chatting and they said we live locally ... we have been thrown out onto the streets by mum and dad—they had gone off to the pub ... We chatted for a few minutes and they asked me more about me and I asked about them and they said well, we will have to go now ... but if you look over the balcony ... you will see us go.

"So I looked over and I says ahh ... very interesting ... because ... my fantasy and my favourite type of girl is a blonde hair, fair skin, slender with blue eyes ... and they fitted the description beautifully ... they were blonde ... quite long and tall and slender for their age ... and of course it got me thinking then, that was on the Saturday I think ... but on the Sunday they came back and asked me if they could come up because they were wet and it was a very miserable day ... at the end of March and it was pouring with rain and miserable ... mum and dad had gone off to the pub again and left them out in the rain ... and they said they wanted to come up and I said no ... well we are getting very wet here and we want to come up ... so I gave in and let them come up ... and that is where it all started ... and it went from thereon.

"I think ... that they had already been abused ... that's why they were so OK on it ... I've come to the conclusion that they were after something as well. Mostly they thought ... if we know a little bit about him we can use him for sweets and things like this ... I don't honestly know how they got my name and I never really asked them, I thought, well the opportunity is here ... I have got an ideal [opportunity] to offend and I have got very little chance of being caught so I am not going to say too much. I am just going to keep it under my hat and use the situation.

"[A]fter 4 weeks I decided that I was going to [offend]. Nothing happened, they just come and they had drinks and tea and watched television. I bought them some sketch books and they watched telly for 4 weeks ... This is on the Saturdays and Sundays ... they used to come up on a regular basis then, 'cause the mum used to throw them out ... go off to the pub and then go off shopping somewhere and leave them out in all kinds of weathers, sunny weather, wet weather or what.

"So after ... the fifth week I decided that I have got an opportunity to start offending ... I'd been thinking about it and how to plan it ... all the grooming and everything. I had got them semi-groomed after 4 weeks ... they were fairly easy to groom. I started buying them sweets ... and I used to give them dinner and all this type of thing. I thought well I shall try and introduce them into ... my offending side ... the exposing by very subtle means. What I did was I run a bath on the Saturday morning and I purposely didn't get in it ... I was fully dressed when they came up ... they come up on the Saturday morning and I said 'look,

I want a bath because I was going out this Saturday somewhere'. I didn't tell them where ... just made up some excuse I was going out ... and I haven't got time this afternoon, you will have to go off fairly early anyway, about 2 o'clock instead of 3 ... I've got to have a bath ... I have got you a cup of tea and some biscuits ... sit yourself in front of the telly, while I go and have a bath. I don't want to be disturbed.

"So I put the input into them that Garry was going off for a bath and don't come in. Well, you know what kids are like. I worked on the principle that ... the kids would do the opposite ... and come in which they did. What happened was ... after about 5 minutes ... I put a very small amount of suds in ... so it was just a little bit ... on the water level ... I got a knock on the door from Trudy first and she came. She asked could I go to the toilet ... because the bathroom and toilet were these encased ones with no windows in ... so I didn't lock the door. I never lock the door, but that's is part of the ... because I was always frightened that if the lights go off and everything—I am stuck in there and can't see a damn thing ... and I can't get the door open ... But ... that wasn't part of the ... it was purposely done so ... I knew they would come in.

"She knocked on the door and I said 'no, I am in the bath, I don't want to be disturbed' ... she says I am going to wet my knickers if I don't go to the toilet. So after a little while of bickering I let her ... [S]he come in, took her knickers down facing her bum towards me ... sat on the seat and did her ablutions and watched me over the top. She was trying to see where my penis was ... so I kinda puts my hands over it at first ... and then I kinda gave up after a while ... She got up, turned round and wiped her bum facing me ... and then pulled the chain and went. Then Nickola did exactly the same coming in, same excuses ... and she went out and then they knocked on the door and said can we come in and sit on the side of the bath? So that's what they did in the end ... [T]his used to be a regular thing for about 2 months. Then they asked if they could come in the bath with me ... and I said no, that's it ... I am not pushing it any further ... if I did get caught ... [I'd] earn a lot of bird ... from all the other [convictions], I didn't want that.

"So, I said you could have a bath on your own ... for about 2 or 3 months ... I used to have a bath, come out, empty it ... put some fresh water and foam in and then they used to jump in ... sometimes I was dressed sometimes I wasn't ... [T]hey sometimes undressed and got in before I had finished ... about 8 or 9 weeks later that stopped and they started running around taking off their clothes and doing ballet dancing ... they'd play some records and they used to dance to it and that type of thing.

"I didn't have the bed in the bedroom, I had it in the lounge [because the bedroom was being decorated] in front of the telly. I used to lay in there with nothing on and watch telly ... [T]hey saw my penis enlarged and they saw me rubbing it ... so they wanted to know what that was ... they wanted to know how ... what I was doing ... so I showed them ... I sat on the toilet and masturbated and came while they watched. It got a regular thing—they used to watch all the time ... watch me do it.

"[I]t was all purposely done ... but what I did was actually train them

> ... Nickola was very insecure and wanted lots of cuddling and attention ... and Trudy was more ... self-assured but she liked being cuddled and that. So what happened was that I groomed them into a position where they got sweets and they watch me masturbate then they would get their cuddles ... so it was a kind of grooming that way, and that's all ... effectively over the weeks by subtle ways of doing it I managed to persuade them and they thought it was quite natural to do, to watch me masturbate.
>
> "... I feel if I had the opportunity I would have gone to oral sex and that was it. I tried with Trudy and Nickola ... I tried to ... not blackmail ... I tried to persuade them with money up to £20 that I could lick their vagina ... or they would masturbate me off. But they refused so I didn't push it any further, I let it drop ... because it was upsetting them and I didn't want them upset ... But I tried you know by little subtle drops every so often ... I would say I'll give you £10 and ... they would refuse it point blank and I'd leave it for a few weeks and then bring ... I'd said I'll give you £15 ... no ... £20. Do it bit by bit until [it] became obvious that they weren't going to do it for no money. If I offered them £100 they wouldn't do it. So I left it—stopped."

Garry's "grooming" methods in his latter form of offending correspond fairly well to Wyre's description of the process, although this appears to be rather too rigid to accommodate the nuances of the individual offender's ways of doing things. Garry seems more intentional in his targeting and grooming; prior fantasy does not appear to be so integral in his offending cycle as is the case with some offenders. But he also includes masturbation as part of his offending—either he exposes himself and masturbates to a virtual stranger or he gets himself into a situation in which he exposes himself and masturbates in front of children whom he has carefully encouraged to express a degree of sexual curiosity.

A somewhat more flexible approach to the cycle of offending is discussed by Nelson and Jackson (1989), in connection with methods of encouraging offenders to be able to recognize their personal high-risk situations through the use of cognitive–behavioral chains. High-risk elements of the chain are an "idiosyncratic constellation". Past failures to control one's sexual behaviour are important sources of information about the sequence of thoughts and behaviours that leads to offending. The client is asked to list the steps in the chain of events. The reasons for the steps are not required at this stage, merely a precise description of what happened in the order in which it happened. The time intervals between events are of no significance at all. A minimum of 7 and a maximum of 10 important elements in the abuse chain are required. This effectively constrains the offender to produce significant elements—any fewer and the risk is that they are minimizing the importance of events, many more and they overemphasize the importance of trivialities. It is important not to allow interpretations to be introduced, despite the fact that some offenders may wish to justify, excuse or explain their behaviour. They have to describe events as if they were detached observers. One child abuser showed several factors, which Nelson and Jackson identify as:

(1) A history of four divorces, signifying unsatisfactory relationships with women;
(2) A lost job and the support of a pregnant girlfriend provide situational stress factors;
(3) A potential victim is relatively easily accessible;
(4) He knows that the victim has been abused previously without it being reported to the authorities;
(5) Alcohol is present as a disinhibitor;
(6) He finds himself alone with his victim.

First of all, the "objective" situation is presented by the offender as a third party might view it. Secondly, the offender's cognitions are provided. In the cognitive–behavioural analysis, the offender then describes his interpretation of each of the stages in the offence cycle; he is required not to speak with hindsight but as it appeared to him at the time:

(1) Divorce from wife number four.
Offender's interpretation: "Women are always messing me over. Yet I've got to be in a relationship with somebody."
(2) A new girlfriend moves in who is already pregnant by another man and is otherwise homeless.
Offender's interpretation: "This isn't exactly what I want, but it's better than somebody else's throwaways. At least she needs me."
(3) He gets made redundant.
Offender's interpretation: "I keep getting the shaft! I deserve better than this."
(4) Girlfriend's 13-year-old daughter moves in.
Offender's interpretation: "I really don't like this, but there's nothing I can do about it."
(5) She tells the offender that she has already been sexually abused, but despite telling her mother and grandparents nothing had been done.

Offender's interpretation: "She's sexually experienced. I guess her family doesn't care if she has sex or not."

(6) The abuser sees the girl naked as she goes to the bathroom. He tells the new girlfriend, who does nothing.
Offender's interpretation: "What a ripe and ready body! She sure turns me on! I guess her mom doesn't care what she does."

(7) The 13-year-old walks naked into the bathroom while the offender is nude and drying himself after a shower. He says that she must leave.
Offender's interpretation: "I think she's trying to seduce me. Why else would she come in here like that? God, I can't get much more turned on! I can't stand it ... got to have her."

(8) The offender has a row with his girlfriend and gets drunk in the bar. He arrives back home late.
Offender's interpretation: "After all I've done for her. She treats me just like the rest. I can do better than this. I'll just stay out and get drunk. That'll teach her not to make me mad."

(9) His girlfriend is in bed but the girl is watching television. He lies by her.
Offender's interpretation: "Whew! She turns me on and I know she wants it. Since her mom doesn't appreciate me, maybe she will after I make her feel good. Screw it! I deserve some pleasure too."

(10) The sexual abuse takes place.

The cognitive–behavioural sequence is likened to a road map, on which every twist and turn leads to the offence. Many of the decisions appear in the offender's description to be almost accidental or incidental to the offence, but the truth is that the offender is making deliberate choices that lead to the offences. There are clear examples of this in the case history of Garry. He presents some of his behaviours as almost "incidental" despite them contributing to the offending or being in themselves surprising in an adult man in relation to two young girls. For example, his initial superficially innocent willingness to entertain two young girls in his flat is not in itself wrong; nevertheless, it is an exceptional thing for an adult man to do, and led to the offending. This is the sort of apparently or seemingly irrelevant decision that some therapists consider important in offending behaviour (Jenkins-Hall and Marlatt, 1989). More details are provided in Chapter 7, in the discussion of relapse prevention.

A study of sexually abused children (largely girls) reported their experiences of the abuse sequence. It is significant that the children reported patterns of behaviour towards them that signal aspects of the "grooming" process. The most common of these were:

> "Treat you different from other kids (78%)
> Tell not to tell mother about things that happen to you (74%)
> Accidentally on purpose come in bedroom/bathroom when undressed (70%)
> Look at you in funny or sexual way (65%)
> Want to spend time alone with you, make excuses (61%)"
>
> (Berliner and Conte, 1990, p. 55)

The children also reported that the offenders commonly made comments that essentially justified the sexual abuse, including the following most frequent ones:

> "You like it (70%)
> Nobody will find out (61%)
> I'm not really hurting you (57%)"

Berliner and Conte claim that threats are made in the majority of cases. They give no statistics but mention some cases of direct physical harm such as threats with a knife. Also among the threats, however, were abandonment and rejection by their parents on the child's disclosure or the adverse consequences to the offender (e.g. one threatened suicide if the "secret" was revealed).

DISTORTED THINKING

> "Four years after the unanimous guilty verdict of the jury, John Cannan continues to deny any responsibility for the series of crimes for which he was convicted—the murder of Shirley Banks from Bristol and the rape and attempted abduction of two other women. Sentencing Cannan, Mr Justice Drake expressed his horror of the crimes by saying Cannan should be jailed for the rest of his natural life. In doing so, the judge removed any possibility that Cannan would make a post-conviction admission to hasten his release or improve his conditions in prison. Among the convictions Cannan denies is the rape of a woman in Reading for which there was overwhelming DNA evidence."
>
> (Kirby, 1993, p. 5)

Distorted thoughts are regarded by some as the *sine qua non* of the paedophile. It is these distortions of thinking that are responsible for the offender offending. Distortions provide offenders with an interpretive framework that permits them to construe the behaviours and motives of their victims as sexual and allows them to justify and excuse to themselves (and others) their offending behaviour. Changing thought processes is seen as the central task of much therapy. At least superficially, there is a good deal to suggest that offenders manifest such abnormalities of thinking. The beliefs expressed by offenders differ by the type of offence. The following are among things said by intrafamilial sexual abusers:

> "It's better to molest your own child than to commit adultery."
> "I've taught her everything else, why not about sex?"
> (Jenkins-Hall, 1989, p. 209)

In the case of extrafamilial offenders:

> "Some little girls (boys) are very sexually seductive/promiscuous."
> "I'm not hurting the child, just showing love."
> (Jenkins-Hall, 1989, p. 209)

But, of course, the matter of distorted thinking is not a simple one. There are a number of possibilities that need to be taken into account:

(1) Sex offenders do think and believe differently;
(2) Sex offenders do think and believe differently but this has nothing to do with why they offend;
(3) The distorted thinking is post-event rationalization, not a direct factor in the offence itself;
(4) The distorted thinking is merely rationalization to the therapist and others in authority designed to serve the offender's purposes;
(5) The offender is telling the truth no matter how preposterous his claims might appear to be; and
(6) What appears to be distorted thinking is merely a different ideology from that of the therapist.

These are not mutually exclusive, and one offender may exhibit several of them. Underlying them is a range of issues, such as the contrast between manipulative lying and thinking differently, and distortion as a causal factor rather than a *post hoc* manipulation. As yet, these issues have been ignored largely in favour of portraying sex offenders as evil, deviant and manipulative in all respects.

There are dangers, of course, in promoting the view that all child abusers lie and distort. The obvious one is the problem of how to deal with an honest offender. Howitt (1992) describes how the dominance of the view of offenders as untrustworthy liars who will always deny and distort can make it difficult to shed this image when it becomes counterproductive in dealing with an offender. There seems to be a relationship between the amount of denial exhibited by an offender and blaming the offence on factors external to himself (Gudjonsson, 1990). This relationship was found despite all of the offenders admitting their crimes—denial is quite clearly multifaceted. Johnston *et al.* (1992) found that paedophiles tended to agree to statements that reflected cynical manipulativeness—"I think most people would lie to get ahead" and "Most people will use somewhat unfair means to gain profit or an advantage rather than to lose it"—more frequently than other men.

Denial

The problems of interpretation become most acute when we address the case of the offender who denies his offending. It comes as no surprise to find that some offenders deny the offences with which they have been charged. But the disposal of a denying burglar, for example, rarely involves the intensive therapy that some sex offenders receive. Since most forms of therapy for sex offenders require their cooperation, denial of the offence in the early stages of assessment makes the prognosis extremely difficult.

Bennie, interviewed while a member of an offender's group at a Florida rape crisis centre, is a good example of a denier. The extent of his admission is unclear in the sense that the dialogue takes us up to a point but no further. He was 45 years old at the time of interview. Originating from Hawaii, he describes himself as an ex-soldier—a hand-to-hand combat instructor. He was married for 12 years when he was in Hawaii and has four children from that relationship:

> "It wasn't my wife's fault, it was my fault. It's just that I didn't feel comfortable, I felt ... well she was working and I wasn't working, and I felt like ... she could find somebody better ... and then I just left ... [M]y wife brought up the kids, they all went to college, and I respect her for that. My first wife, you know, all my kids went to college, they have college degrees ... three of them have college degrees, the last one is just going to college now."

However, he has a back injury from his previous work as a swimming pool constructor. Bennie had settled in the southern USA a few years before the offences. He has been with his present wife for 13 years but had been married only for about a year before the interview:

BENNIE. "We have got one [a boy of our own], but I have two stepchildren, daughters, one is 13, one is 15 ... I brought them [both up] when her first husband kicked her out of the house ... My stepdaughter Teresa (... she'd just turned 13) ... made accusations that I sexually abused her ... [but] not having sex with her ... I didn't think it would have gone this long ... she would really come up and tell the truth ... 'cause I am a lovable person, I play with the kids a lot and they play with me ... I use to bathe them when they were babies until they were six years old, and when they got about six I realized they were too big for it ... I don't bathe them no more ... [L]ast year sometime, we were watching a television programme ... and I was laying down on the carpet and she was over there by me. [W]e sat playing around—I sat kissing her by her chest. [S]he says things that I did which I didn't do ... may God help strike me dead if I am lying."

INTERVIEWER. "And what you are saying is that you had some sort of physical contact?"

BENNIE. "Oh, wrestling around that's all, and then kissing her by her chest that's it."

INTERVIEWER. "What does that mean, kissing someone by their chest ... 'cause it could mean several different things?"

BENNIE. "In the report it says kissing her breasts ... you know it was for may be 10–15 seconds ... that we are just playing around and kissing, I was kissing her like the skunk [in the television programme], and that was it."

INTERVIEWER. "Did you kiss her on the breast?"

BENNIE. "May be I did may be I didn't ... [when you are arrested] they try to use psychology on you, they make you say you did ... so I am going to say I did."

INTERVIEWER. "... that's no use to me ... I don't want to know what they say, I want to know what it is ..."

BENNIE. "... maybe I probably did?"

INTERVIEWER. "Does that mean that her breasts were bare?" BENNIE. "She was using a loose tank top, one of my tank tops, and she is a small girl, and it exposed ... you know ..."

INTERVIEWER. "... her breasts ... would be exposed?"

BENNIE. "Yes ... in the report it says I yanked this shirt off her ... and I kissed her all over the breasts ... She had a loose tank top, one of the big tank tops, and every now and then she use to wear and I told her after that ... I say hey don't go wearing the things I got around the house ... you know after I moved back in ... I told her don't go wearing things like that."

INTERVIEWER. "... did you kiss her on the nipple?"

BENNIE. "No."

INTERVIEWER. "... did you see her nipples?"

BENNIE. "... yes ..."

INTERVIEWER. " ... so where did you kiss her?"

BENNIE. "On ... above it ..."

INTERVIEWER. "... above the nipples?"

BENNIE. "Yes ..."

INTERVIEWER. "... and when you say kiss you mean kiss not suck or anything?"

BENNIE. "No."

INTERVIEWER. "And you say that took about 15 seconds?"

BENNIE. "No I am talking about wrestling and kissing and it was about 15 seconds ..."

INTERVIEWER. "... and what do you mean by wrestling?"

BENNIE. "Just ... you know hugging and rolling around, just about 10–15 seconds that all happened ... laying down on the carpet ... watching TV me and her ... I was laying down and she came and laid down over there, we were watching the cartoon character and ... I guess we were kind of playing around, hitting each other, and she was bugging me ... I told her she better stop it then ... we were watching the TV then I see the squirrel, I don't know, the skunk and the squirrel or whatever ... and I grab her and 'cause she likes to aggravate me ... and then that's how we started. Then it didn't take more than 10, 15 seconds ... then it was a commercial I think ..."

INTERVIEWER. "Did you know what you were doing?"

BENNIE. "Yes I knew what I was doing."

INTERVIEWER. "And did you think it was wrong or risky ...?"

BENNIE. "... no I didn't think it was wrong ... but they say it's wrong and I respect that ... and believe me I hope I will never touch that kid again. I consider my daughter ... I brought her birth in the hospital ... ok ... when I was playing with her and kissing her by the neck like that ... then [inaudible] I went down and kissed ... her breasts ... I didn't have no intentions of raping her or ... I didn't have any bad intentions of pursuing any further ... it was just a split second thing that we were just kissing like that and that was it ..."

INTERVIEWER. "... and she was 13 ...?"

BENNIE. "... no ... she had just turned 13 ..."

INTERVIEWER. " ... but it sounds like you are saying ... it's not an unusual thing to do, it's not a strange thing to do."

BENNIE. "No, 'cause ... whenever they go some place, go to church or like that ... they sometimes kiss me on the lips, sometimes they kiss me on the cheek, or they come and hug me like that ... or they come and sit down and show me their homework, sit on my lap, show me their homework and help them with their problems ... then ... it wasn't ... I didn't find it ... anything unusual or aggressive ... but how HRS [child protection agency] put it I was wrong and hey if I am wrong I am wrong."

INTERVIEWER. "... you didn't think it was wrong what you did ... is that right?"

BENNIE. "Yes ... but now HRS say it's wrong and I accept that ... [L]et me put it this way ... you know if I grabbed her breasts like that ... and sucked on and for a while like that ... then started arousing myself, then I would think something is wrong, but just a kiss, I don't think that was really wrong, my honest opinion, I don't think it was wrong. As plain like that. If I prolonged it and when for half an hour like that, 15–20 minutes, then I can see hey wait a minute, that's not right, or even 5 minutes, hey that's not right, but not for that short period of time."

INTERVIEWER. "How would you explain doing it ... the incident?"

BENNIE. "Just showing affection as a father ... I mean ..."

INTERVIEWER. "... are you saying that is normal ... showing affection?"

BENNIE. "To me I say yes ... Another thing, ... they all use to wrestle against me ... and you know ... we use to just play around like that a lot of times, but we didn't think anything wrong ... and that's the case you know, I think they should set some kind of guidelines to [inaudible] people and say hey you cannot do this, 'cause I would say ... maybe 85 maybe 90% of all males are guilty of sexually abusing their child ... My oldest stepdaughter, she just got raped now ... just this past year ... but I wasn't there and I feel responsible for that ... 'cause ... in that predicament I would say you couldn't have gone ... you are too young to go out nightclubbing ... Do I see my wife ... I cannot have no contact with her, that's what is really eating me up ... No, she wants to but ... she says if I don't put a restraining order on you, they are going to try and take the kids away from her. So I say hey I'll do anything so that the kids be home, I don't want the family to be separated ... and you know it hurts me a lot ... every minute of the day, it's not easy going through a pain that I am going through, but I think that's ... it's worse a pain than being away from my wife and kids, than the pain in my back ..."

INTERVIEWER. "Do you have a criminal record at all?"

BENNIE. "... [T]he HRS said I had all kinds of record, I don't have no criminal record ... I once turned myself in because they said they had a warrant for my arrest."

Bennie did have a further report of sexual abuse made against him while he was still at home with the family. He was also convinced that several of his wife's girlfriends wanted to have him sexually. When questioned about how he knew her friends wanted sex with him he suggested:

> "... because you know how women are they talk about men, about their husbands, and I guess she did it too ... and then she said oh yea, I will have to ... she says my husband had ... we maybe do it once a month or something like that ... so ... I guess that's a reason why."

The denial processes manifest in this interview are quite subtle. The major one appears to be minimizing the event in terms of its time duration, since the whole episode, including the "wrestling" is described as happening in a few seconds. A further aspect is the way in which an unusual behaviour, although not apparently the worst act of abuse imaginable, is normalized. Not only does Bennie believe that there was nothing wrong with the act on the grounds that it is part and parcel of the growing up process, he also argues that virtually every father is equally likely to be unfairly accused of abuse. There is also a grudging acceptance of the "wrongness" of his activities when he sees the abuse through the eyes of the authorities. The slightest question as to his true beliefs reveals him not to accept the truth of his comments about the abusive nature of the act. Throughout the interview he inserts rhetoric about his truthfulness and, in the full interview, his concern about children and their well-being. Everything is presented as a spur of the moment innocuous bit of play. It is quite informative, then, when he mentions that he had previously expressed concern to his stepdaughter about the revealing nature of the tank top she was wearing at the time of the abuse.

In the final section of the interview he alludes to his belief that his wife's girlfriends want him sexually. His justification of this is as inarticulate as anything else in the interview. There seems no basis to the belief in anything his wife had putatively mentioned to him. Indeed, his wife had merely said that a particular friend liked him. He moves from this to forcibly arguing that under no circumstances would he have sex with this woman, who did not arouse him anyway! Had Bennie been more open about his thoughts about his stepdaughter, we might have detected signs of distorted thinking about her sexual desires for him.

Ramon presents another variant on the theme. A Texan of Mexican descent, he was 38 years old at the time of interview at a Florida rape crisis centre, which he was attending for group therapy. He had served in the armed forces and had been married twice. His first marriage lasted 10 years and he was in his 9th year of marriage when the interview took place. He lived in the marital household where stepdaughters were present:

> "Having problems with the wife ... problems at work ... I was at home ... I guess I had too much time on my hands and I guess ... she use to parade in front of me ... naked sometimes from room to room or just walk up to me ... and I didn't know how to handle it from the beginning ... and ... I had mentioned to my wife once or twice about her walking in on me ... she use to walk in to me in my bedroom, I would be taking a shower or sitting in the chair ... I guess it's just something that just happened without thinking ... I actually didn't sit there and plan it out ... it's been pretty painful the past couple of months ever since it happened ...
>
> "There were weeks maybe days ... [when my wife] she just wasn't interested [in sex] ... [S]he complained she had headaches or she wasn't interested ... and weeks went by ... my brother's and I of course all my kids were all pretty close ... we would ask her if she wanted to go to the beach or go bowling or do something ... but she just wanted to stay at the house. So we used to do our thing ... go and have some fun ... and we did a lot of things like that bowling, movies, go out to eat ... of course wife she didn't want to go, she had a headache or didn't feel like it, or she was on her monthly thing ... I guess I just grew that more attached other than normally ... I guess to my kids. My wife knows that we all love each other ... I am not exactly a person who sits there and studies the Bible all the time, but I was brought up in a Catholic background and I guess throughout the time ... my daughter and I actually got closer ... more closer than my wife, brother and daughter ... and ... that's probably how everything started.
>
> "Well my daughters were very young when I married ... the oldest ... when I first met my wife ... she was about 5 ... the other one was about 2 or 3 ... so I actually came into the marriage bringing them up ... the little one had a skin condition ... I don't know what you call it ... came out of the skin ... so [we] used to take turns putting lotion on her ... and there would be times that I told her to go and put it on herself ... I was too busy ... and then when she turned 9 or 10 around ... she started developing ... and of course I put lotion on her breasts ... or her legs, or her arms, shoulder and so on ... this continued on for a while and then ... sometime around when she was ... well actually when she was 9 years old ... I got after her because her and her friends use to get together and read ... not read but look at some magazines ... you know they have magazines for men ... magazines for women, I don't know how they got it, but they had a magazine ... [I] kind of let her have it ... and assumed at that time she was pretty

> interested in magazines and I myself had to admit I use to keep some male magazines ... and as soon as I knew that she was getting curious ... she would walk in ... I mean ... in the shower ... and I'd usually try not to react like get out of here ... I would just try to act normal ... and ... of course the lotions, putting the lotion on still ... went on ... and then one day one night I was watching TV she walked in naked and she asked me to put on some lotion, and that was when mum was asleep ... and I put lotion on her, of course down in her vagina and her breasts, her back her neck, completely covered her with oil ... and ... that went on for a little while ... and ... then one day ... the police came in ... I was doing it for so long that to me it seemed like it was natural to me ... I admit I wasn't taking it in I guess ... I didn't think it was wrong either ... I just wasn't thinking ... and ... err it bothered me ... but I just it was an impulse thing I just did it anyway."

The way in which Ramon accounts for his offending is largely to hold his wife responsible for the abuse of his stepdaughter; she was not always as sexually providing as he seemed to wish and also a let-down as a mother. He took over the caretaking role in his account and grew overly close to his daughter. Because he had rubbed lotion into the skin of his stepdaughter when she was small, he claims that it did not strike him as unnatural that he was rubbing lotion into the vagina of the girl when she had reached pubescence. His account creaks in a number of places. In particular, he was aware of the sexuality of the girl and disturbed by her appearing before him nude and he discovers her growing sexual interest but nevertheless still rubs lotion into her vagina.

Salter (1988) provides a rare attempt to systematize the concept of denial. She mentions an interesting situation in which denial featured in the misinterpretation of an offender's admission. Salter was asked to provide a second opinion:

> "... on a psychological evaluation of an offender in which the offender admitted some inappropriate touching, but denied the extent of the offense as stated by his adolescent victim. The psychologists writing the evaluation used the offender's admission that he had engaged in some sexually abusive behavior (pulling the adolescent girl's underwear down and pulling her pubic hair to 'tease' her) as proof that the offender had not engaged in oral sex and other more extensive activities with which the victim had charged him; this assertion was supported by the claim that sex offenders either deny everything or admit the whole truth."
>
> (Salter, 1988, p. 96)

According to Salter, this view is mistaken, and offenders initially reveal only the tip of the problem. Denial is seen by Salter as a spectrum with all sorts of hues. It includes denial of the events, denial of fantasy and planning, denial of responsibility, denial of the seriousness of the acts, denial of feelings of guilt and denial of the difficulty of changing behaviour patterns. Several broad patterns can be identified:

(1) Physical denial with family denial. The offender denies that the sexual assault happened and has the backing of family and friends, who provide an alibi for his whereabouts at the time. Such offenders display "righteous indignation". The family support may make it difficult to treat such cases.
(2) Physical denial without family support. In this case, the offender merely denies the assault, although no family alibi is provided.
(3) Psychological denial. This is essentially contesting that he is the sort of person who does such a thing rather than focusing on the precise details of the time and place of the offence.
(4) Minimization of the extent of offending. This involves admitting part of the offending, but neglecting other aspects of offending.
(5) Denial of seriousness. This involves a failure to acknowledge the effects of the abuse on the child.
(6) Denial of the need for treatment. Some offenders make excuses for not needing treatment because, for example, they have become religious since the offence.
(7) Denial of responsibility for their behaviour. Blaming drink but having gone on the wagon may be used to explain the offending (i.e. it acts as a denial of personal responsibility for the offence). There is a variety of means of placing the blame on other people or other external factors rather than on oneself.

A therapeutic programme for dealing with deniers of the offence is described by O'Donohue and Letourneau (1993), together with some limited evidence of its effectiveness.

Ultimately, the extent to which the thoughts of paedophiles show them to be sick, manipulative and devious remains a vexed question. It is probably premature to assume too much. Believing them to be so may make it easy to construe everything that a paedophile says in these terms. What for some may appear to be distorted thinking may, at times, simply reflect radically different life experiences. If we wish to understand paedophilia better, and we have not been trying for long, it is probably better to be tentative about accepting any simplistic interpretation of what paedophiles say about what they think:

> "[I] thought it was just normal ... there was nothing wrong with it. The boys liked it, I liked it, the boys came back for more. I came back for more, they accepted it, I accepted it. I never saw any emotionally disturbed that were problems at school. I knew people who had befriended boys ... and ... their [school] grades had come up. They had had now somewhere they [were] loved ... they had had problems at home and they were doing good ... someone actually loved them ... someone actually cared for them. I had two or three boys that I knew who had come from sort of problem homes. I believed that I loved them, cared for them ..."

CHAPTER 4

Qualms over Technical Assessments

> "It is worth remembering that from ancient times Christian theologians, also, regarded the penis as evil and a shameful reminder of our animal natures. The fact that we call them private parts, which must never be exposed in public, adds to our fear and anxiety. The fear persists because, just as men in the Western world believe that the head is the seat of the soul, they are equally deluded in thinking that sexuality exists in the penis. This may explain our longstanding anxiety about its size and the current zeal to find causes of sexual aggression in the frequently measured but highly overrated appendage."
>
> (Greenland, 1988, pp. 377–378)

The idea that it is possible to gain insight into sexuality, even deviant sexuality, by investigating the penis is well established in work with sex offenders. Since the 1960s, a steady stream of research has described devices measuring changes in penis size and how to interpret these. These techniques, collectively known as either *phallometry* or *plethysmography*, are basically of two main types. The first, and earlier, type involves penis *volume*: a plastic ring is slipped along the penis and an inflatable cuff, made from a condom, is attached (Freund, 1963). The other end of the cuff connects with a glass cylinder which fits over the penis. The condom is inflated and changes in the size of the penis are transmitted through variations in air pressure within the condom to a meter (or electrical pen recorder, which makes a graph of the changes during assessment). The alternative procedure deals with changes in penis *circumference* (Fisher, Gross and Zuck, 1965). The penis stretches a flexible "tube" placed around the shaft of the penis, and this movement is converted into electrical signals. (Any device that turns physical changes into electrical information is called a transducer.) The original "strap" contained the liquid metal mercury, which was pushed up a glass tube by expansion of the penis, rather like a barometer that reacts to changes in penis pressure rather than atmospheric pressure. Increasingly, electrical pen recorders were substituted for their added flexibility and ease in recording change.

A different approach is taken when changes in the sexual arousal of women are measured. Vaginal *plethysmography* is usually based on changes in vaginal blood volume. The amplitude and rate of blood pulse in the vagina can also be measured (Cooper *et al.*, 1990). Sometimes changes in the temperature of the vagina are measured instead. The use of such devices on women is exceptional and is rarely discussed in professional publications.

There have been attempts to measure men's sexual interest in children under laboratory conditions using other measures. For example, Attwood and Howell (1971) measured the size of the pupil of the eye in response to pictures. (At the time, study of the dilation and constriction of the eye was popular as an indirect measure of attraction and repulsion to various stimuli (e.g. Hess, 1965). Slides of nude women produced dilation in nearly all controls but constriction in a group of child abusers. More-or-less the reverse pattern was produced in the response to pictures of underage girls. However, the data were rather more unclear than this suggests. For example, the greatest constriction to the nude women was found for one normal man. No further research on this vein seems to have been carried out. Pupillometry, as it was called, was probably too fraught with technical problems.

All of these procedures are limited to laboratory applications because of the bulkiness of the apparatus. No one has yet even attempted to produce a plethysmographic apparatus so unobtrusive that the day-to-day arousal of the paedophile can be continuously monitored. There is no alarm system that could warn of the genital arousal of a child molester—electronic tagging of the penis. In the usual context of a hospital assessment, a man is shown or hears material portraying one of several different sorts of sexual and non-sexual content. The age and sex of the people portrayed is varied, as well as aspects such as violence or coercion. Some studies use slides, some video, some tape-recorded descriptions and some mixtures of slide and tape. The material can be tailored to the sexual proclivities of the individual being assessed, and often the men generate their own fantasies for the research. This flexibility has enormous advantages since what is sexually arousing for one man may have no effect on another. The following is typical of the fantasy that can be used to accompany slides of pre-pubescent girls:

> "I really like little kids. They like me too. They always seem to want to climb on my knee or play horsie with me. I feel so good when I see them come running to me when I go into the room. They want to climb on my lap and wriggle around and cuddle up to me. They're so soft and cute. I hope she wants to sit on my lap today. She's the cutest one. It feels so good when I'm there. I just want to touch her a bit. Maybe we can do it in the other room. It feels good when she squirms around. Maybe she'll want to touch it. I could get her to do some things if we played some games. She seems to know all about it so it can't hurt her."
>
> (Farrall and Card, 1988, p. 268)

Some researchers and clinicians encourage the men to fantasize actively about the material, especially when slides alone are being used without any commentary.

It is a mistake to believe that phallometric methods constitute a simple and precise measure of sexual arousal (much as a barometer of passion). Volume and circumference measures can vary considerably. For example, in one study, the two types of measuring device were attached at the same time in order to compare their relative readings in identical circumstances (Freund, 1981). While the two measures correlate to a degree, penis volume was more effective than circumference at distinguishing between different types of erotic material. The two types of measure can even show opposite trends in research outcomes.

Penis circumference has not been shown to differentiate *rapists* from normals (Baxter, Barbaree and Marshall, 1986; Baxter *et al.*, 1984; Murphy *et al.*, 1986) although penis volume has (McConaghy, 1991). Similarly, although Quinsey *et al.* (1975) claimed that molesters of female children were likely to have their maximum penis circumference in response to pictures of nude female children, two other studies failed to demonstrate this (McConaghy, 1991).

There is no standard penis size against which to measure the amount of erection achieved. Penises fluctuate in flaccid size and shape at different times, so the question, "how big is a penis at full erection?" becomes important. The relative crudity of the measuring devices, partly caused by the variability of placing the apparatus on the shaft of the penis, means that absolute measures of arousal are impossible. Normally, measures are taken when the penis is limp and then when it is as erect as it gets in the laboratory; the man masturbates to full erection (alternatively, his greatest erection to any stimulus is used). In this way it is possible to express the amount of erection to a particular erotic slide as a percentage of the maximum size previously obtained. In other contexts, Abel *et al.* (1977) developed a rape index and Avery-Clark and Laws (1984) a dangerous child molester index. Both of these are dependent entirely on the relevant amount of arousal the man has to sexually violent slides compared with more neutral ones.

Some offenders fail to have any erection to the erotic material; about one in ten men is largely unresponsive (Travin *et al.*, 1985b). Many *clinicians* disregard data from such unresponsive men. Since the apparatus is relatively imprecise, there is a certain amount of variability in the readings which may swamp the effects of the erotic stimuli. Conventionally, cases are disregarded as uninterpretable when the apparent response to the erotic material is less than 10% of the man's maximum erection. Some *researchers* apply similar criteria, thus selecting participants who show the largest erections and eliminating those who do not respond much. This can sometimes equate to loading the dice.

There are other problems. One is the nonlinearity of measures of penis size. That is to say, the apparatus does not consistently show a uniform increase in reading for a given increase in circumference or volume of the penis. This, in general, would only be a difficulty for those inclined to regard the data obtained in such assessments as more finely honed than they actually are. Furthermore, Farrall and Card (1988) point out that in the USA federal and state anti-pornography laws prohibit the possession of or taking of nude pictures of children: "Thus, it is extremely difficult to obtain a set of visual stimulus materials that is both stimulating and legally obtained" (p. 264).

For illustrative purposes, we can take a study of phallometry's ability to differentiate between sexual offenders (Freund and Blanchard, 1989). Male outpatients (age range 18–55 years) attending the Clarke Institute of Psychiatry's Sexology Clinic in Canada were used. Some had offended against children, others against mature females. About one in eight offenders were excluded because they had offended against both age groups. Two items (from an unpublished questionnaire) were used to assess whether the offender denied that his strongest erotic feelings were for underage children:

> "1. When lying in bed and sexually aroused, do you imagine or fantasize about intimately touching a) boys or girls up to 10 years old, b) boys or girls 12–15 years old, c) boys or girls in both age ranges, *d) none of the above*?
>
> 2. When lying in bed and sexually aroused, do you imagine or fantasize about intimately touching females 17 and over more often than touching children or teenagers 15 years or younger? a) yes *b) no.*"

These questions were designed to distinguish between known offenders who admitted abusive thoughts and those who denied such feelings.

In the phallometric assessment, videos of nude people walking slowly towards the camera were shown. The images included physically mature women, early adolescent girls, 8–11-year-old girls and 5–8-year-old girls as well as males in these four age categories. Landscapes with no erotic significance served as non-erotic control stimuli. Using data on the relative amounts of erection to adults and children, and males and females, it was possible to form indices of both age and sex preference. A computer program chose cut-off points on these indices, which optimized the number of offenders against children classified as paedophiles or hebephiles, while at the same time minimizing the number of offenders against adults misclassified as offenders against children. This was done for part of the sample; the criteria developed on this basis were then tested on the rest. Fifty-five per cent of non-admitters were correctly categorized as attracted to children whereas 95% of the non-paedophile controls were correctly diagnosed as being sexually attracted to adult women.

This is, of course, somewhat disappointing. The panoply of physiological apparatus and computers did relatively badly at picking out the paedophiles from among those convicted of such offences but who did not admit to paedophiliac thoughts and fantasies. Furthermore, this was after eliminating a number of individuals from the research because of their low levels of erection to the stimuli and because there were signs of deliberate attempts to influence the phallometric test outcome. Additionally, since the phallometric test cannot differentiate between those who prefer adult women and those attracted to adolescent girls, men who had only approached 11- to 16-year-old girls had already been excluded from the study.

Of course, such findings place limitations on the use of phallometry in assessing the likelihood of paedophilia in individuals who deny their offending. Very little is known about the tests when applied to non-forensic cases (Freund and Blanchard, 1989). Even if the pattern on the assessment indicates paedophilia, this is not proof that the man has committed any particular offence that he may be charged with. Freund and Blanchard (1989) conclude that the complexity of interpretation of this phallometric data make it inappropriate for simplistic interpretation by casually trained staff:

> "The results of clinical diagnostic phallometric tests should be exclusively available to and interpreted by behavioral sexologists with medical or psychological degrees ... We do not condone the use of diagnostic phallometric tests by narrowly informed technical experts or their application in the same manner in which lie detector procedures are sometimes administered."
>
> (Freund and Blanchard, 1989, pp. 104–105)

Travin *et al.* (1985b) present a rather overly positive account of the use of laboratory assessment. Table 4.1 gives their data on the physical arousal of three sexual offenders prior to treatment. One was an incest offender against his daughter, the second was a paedophile who offended against the adolescent female age group and the third was a paedophile who offended against girls. The percentages are the average proportions of each man's maximum recorded erection produced by each of five different types of slides. The bigger the percentage, the greater his response. In general, all three offenders were aroused by adolescent females and all but the incest offender by young female children. The incest offender seems aroused by adult females, as was the paedophile who offended against female children. None responded to adult males. The incest offender showed moderate arousal to pictures of adolescent males.

Travin *et al.* recommend phallometric data as a means of confronting the offender with the actuality of his offending. So, for example, the *female incest offender* initially acknowledged only fondling his daughter but on confrontation with this data (which show high arousal to adolescent females) he admitted repeated oral sex with his 12-year-old daughter and having sex with an adolescent female outside of the family. The *offender against adolescent females* initially acknowledged sexually abusing an adolescent female but

Table 4.1. Amounts of erection (average proportions of maximum recorded erections) by offenders to different types of slide

Slide	Female incest	Female adolescent paedophile	Female paedophile
Adult female	51	7	80
Adolescent female	63	60	60
Young female	7	57	53
Adult male	9	0	12
Adolescent male	41	10	11

denied other paraphilias until his phallometric data became available, when he admitted abusing several young females and one adolescent male:

> "Many offenders flatly deny having a paraphiliac disorder or minimize the extent of the problem ... Confronting the offender with the laboratory results frequently elicits admissions of sexual deviation(s) or more detailed and accurate reports on the frequency and nature of the paraphilia. Resistance is an issue in any therapy, but with sex offenders therapy is unlikely to be beneficial until the offender is willing at least to admit to sexual deviation. Laboratory assessment via the penile transducer is effective in confronting this type of resistance."
>
> (Travin *et al.*, 1985b, p. 617)

There may be an element of wishful thinking in this (McConaghy, 1991). The particular measurement technique used lacks comparative data from normal, non-offending men. A study by Quinsey *et al.* (1975) found that normal men's erections to pictures of pubescent and younger girls averaged 70% and 50% of their responses to adult females! Furthermore, Travin *et al.*'s offender who admitted offending against an underage male following "confrontation" did not have his highest response to pictures of adolescent males. Given this, it may not be too tongue-in-cheek to suggest that if "confession" is the object, offenders could be shown fictitious laboratory results in the hope that these might elicit disclosure. The more serious point to this is that such tests are used in some parts of the world in the assessment of sex offence cases to serve law enforcement agencies. The problems associated with phallometry led Schouten and Simon (1992) to caution clinicians about their integrity and the rights of the accused. Nevertheless,

Farrall (1992) presents a detailed and thorough discussion of how to use phallometry. This is positive about the technique and rather underplays the broader implications of the limitations that others highlight.

Can Phallometry Differentiate Offender Groups?

Phallometry's usefulness resides partly in its potential to identify the sexual orientations of individuals. The less well it is shown to do this, the less we can trust it in clinical decision making. Hall, Proctor and Nelson (1988) took a group of otherwise mentally and intellectually normal sex offender males who were in the state hospital system for assessment for their offending. On the basis of both their sexual offence history and additional interviews, the men were classified as rapists of adult women, sex offenders against children up to 12 years old, and sex offenders against young people between 13 and 16 years. About a third of the original sample was lost because they only offended against underage males or their offences came under two or more categories. On average, the men had been arrested for only about one offence. Among the offenders against children, just over a quarter had used force.

The stimulus materials included various audio tapes depicting consenting intercourse with an adult female, rape of a female child, consenting intercourse with a female child and non-sexual assault against a female child. Penis *circumference* was measured (using a mercury-in-rubber strain gauge) while listening to these tapes. From most arousing to least, the erotic materials were consenting child, consenting adult, child sexual assault, and child non-sexual assault. While one might expect sex offenders against children to be aroused most by the child sexual activity, in fact the three types of offenders did not differ! Similarly, it might be assumed that the violent abusers would be more turned on by the sexually violent material. Against expectations, there were no differences between these violent and non-violent offenders in terms of how aroused they were by violent sexual materials. Interestingly, the immaturity of the victim did not seem to inhibit sexual arousal but the use of force did. There was a reasonable correlation between the paedophiles' arousal to both deviant and non-deviant sexual materials; those who showed the greatest erection to depictions of sex with children also showed the highest degree of erection to adult female depictions.

Another study compared physiological and verbal responses to a variety of slides including boys, girls, adult males, adult females and couples. The offender groups were male and female orientated paedophiles, rapists and non-sex offenders (Wormith, 1986). Using a statistical technique that produces optimum classifications of cases on the basis of the data collected (discriminant function analysis), it is possible to compare their known offender category with that predicted on the basis of their sexual arousal. The overall accuracy of classification based on penile circumference measures of arousal was 64%. Specifically, only 50% of paedophiles were classified correctly whereas 42% were classified as normal. About a third of non-sexual offenders were classified as rapists! Self-reported arousal to the slides was also effective at separating the paedophiles from the rest, largely on the basis of arousal to slides of male children. Nearly 60% of paedophiles were correctly classified but 17% were misclassified as normals! Finally, a content analysis of the verbal descriptions of the slides made by the offenders proved to be the most effective at discriminating. Paedophiles made more non-evaluative comments about the slides and avoided descriptions of the sexual features of the slides. Using this sort of comment, 83% of the paedophiles were correctly assigned to the paedophile category, although a quarter of the non-sex offenders were classified as paedophiles and a third of the rapists. While Wormith does not discuss this, it would appear that non-physiological measures of arousal were at least as effective in discriminating paedophiles from the rest. The fact that measures of penile circumference were used may explain the somewhat unsuccessful findings.

What about the value of penis *volume* for diagnosing paedophilia? In a preliminary assessment as part of a study of this, Freund and Watson (1991) compared offenders against adult women with community volunteers (believed not to be sexual offenders) in terms of their arousal to explicit slides (sometimes accompanied by an erotic commentary) of adults and children. Few of the offenders against women were actually diagnosed as having a preference for minors on the basis of the laboratory tests (only 3.1% of cases). In contrast, nearly one in five (19.4%) of the *normal* men were misclassified as having an erotic preference for minors. This has important implications for estimates of the prevalence of paedophiliac tendencies in the general population. For Freund and Watson, these findings imply that offenders against adult women may be a better control group for studies of paedophiles than so-called "normals"! The explanation of the findings, they argue, might lie in offenders having a vested interest in giving no signs of sexual interest in children!

In the study proper, sex offenders against female children (not adolescents) were compared with those against male minors (adolescents and younger children combined), because these were the only sizeable paedophile groups available for research. They excluded *admitters* of paedophiliac attraction using the two questions given on p. 107 (Freund and Blanchard, 1989), leaving just deniers in the final sample. Incestuous fathers and homosexuals were also excluded. The presentation of the data is complex. Essentially, the authors calculated the number of men with an erotic preference for underage children. A proportion of their sample was discounted on the basis that a percentage of offenders are not paedophiles at all and would not show the typical paedophile response to children. In other words, adjustment was made so that these non-paedophile molesters do not dilute estimates of the power of phallometry to identify paedophiles. Furthermore, apparently, those who were not sufficiently responsive on the phallometric apparatus and those judged to be faking were also excluded. The actual percentages based on the original (unadjusted) sample sizes who were correctly identified by phallometry as having a sexual interest in children are given in Table 4.2. Notice that the test was far better at identifying the preferences of those who admitted a sexual orientation towards children.

Table 4.2. Phallometrically correctly identified

Offence deniers	%	Offence admitters	%
Multi-offences against girls	58	Against girls	70
Multi-offences against boys	64	Against boys	86
Single offence against girls	28		
Single offence against boys	56		
Multi-offences against both	42		

Phallometry's lack of success in differentiating boy-orientated paedophiles from girl-orientated ones is confirmed by another study (Freund *et al.*, 1991). Differences in arousal to male and female stimuli were examined in men in the following categories:

(1) Paedophiles preferring boys;
(2) Paedophiles preferring girls;
(3) Offenders against adult females;
(4) Volunteers who preferred women; and
(5) Volunteers who preferred men.

Men who sexually prefer adults showed marked differences in sexual arousal to men and women, whereas paedophiles showed relatively little gender differentiation; they were aroused more equally by both sexes.

Comparisons between Extrafamilial and Incest Offenders

Conventionally, incestuous fathers are regarded as psychodynamically different from extrafamilial offenders. Thus, it would be of considerable theoretical significance if it were demonstrated that incestuous fathers either (i) show no arousal to erotic materials depicting children, or (ii) show a strong response. The latter would indicate that they are basically paedophile.

There is one piece of research highly pertinent to this issue. Previous research had been equivocal on whether paedophiles and incest offenders responded differently to depictions of children. Different studies had produced opposite results. They also differed methodologically—one used slides whereas the other used audio-taped descriptions, one used inpatient offenders whereas the other used outpatient offenders. In an attempt to clarify the situation, a further study used both audio and visual stimuli with pure groups of (i) heterosexually orientated paedophiles, (ii) homosexually orientated paedophiles, (iii) incest offenders against daughters/stepdaughters and (iv) mixed incest/paedophile cases (Murphy *et al.*, 1986). Not surprisingly, there were more single men in the paedophile groups than in the incest groups.

Penis *circumference* was measured using a metal-band strain gauge. The slide stimuli featured seven age categories—5-, 9-, 12-, 15-, 18-, 25- and 35-year-olds—each presented for two minutes. The audio tapes were in seven categories, which varied according to the level of sexual aggression and physical assault involved. The categories were: (i) child initiated, (ii) child/adult mutual, (iii) adult non-physical coercion, (iv) adult physical coercion, (v) sadism, (vi) physical assault with no sexual content and (vii) adult mutual. The audio tapes were two minutes long and described activities involving children of 8 to 10 years. The slides and tapes were chosen to reflect the sexual preferences of the offender. The findings were complex and not always consistently statistically reliable. Homosexual paedophiles had a greater response to the *tapes* involving children than those involving adults; this was also the trend for heterosexual paedophiles. The incest and mixed groups showed more response to adults than did the paedophile groups. The pattern for *slides* was somewhat different, although the two paedophile groups showed far greater response to the child slides than to those of adults. Incest offenders responded more to slides of adults. The mixed group responded to adults and children approximately equally.

The characteristics of individual offenders' sexual arousal may be clinically more important than comparisons between groups. Significantly, even with the slide stimuli (which produced generally lower levels of arousal), 40% of incest offenders actually showed an equal or greater erection to pictures of children than to those of adults. So, whatever the role of family dynamics in incest, such offenders also frequently demonstrate deviant arousal patterns to underage children.

Another study compared paedophiles (who had offended against under 12-year-olds) with a group of biological fathers and stepfathers plus social "stepfathers" (Freund, Watson and Dickey, 1991). Only men who denied interest in minors and sexual fantasies of underage children were used. A further group consisted of offenders against women. Penis *volume* changes to erotic material involving different age groups were measured. Incest offenders were three times more likely to be diagnosed as gynephiles (i.e. having their greatest sexual responses to women) than were paedophiles. The non-incest child molesters were more likely to be diagnosed as paedophile rather than gynephile, but not so convincingly. Offenders against adult women were overwhelmingly diagnosed as gynephiles. Presented in this way, the results suggest strongly that circumstances or opportunity enhance the likelihood that "normal" heterosexual men will offend against children if any are "conveniently" available at home. In other words, incestuous abusers are sexually normal; laboratory tests demonstrate their preference for adult women. This is somewhat illusory, since taking the proportions of each group identified as primarily erotically attracted to adult women by phallometry reveals the following:

- Offenders against adult women: 68% gynephile
- Incestuous offenders against single child: 49% gynephile
- Incestuous offenders against two or more children: 38% gynephile
- Non-incest offenders against single child: 45% gynephile
- Non-incest offenders against two or more children: 16% gynephile

The rest of the cases are made up of men who were faking, who were low on responsiveness to any stimulus, who were aroused to adults and children more or less equally, or who had a paedophiliac preference for children. This, in general, is not strong evidence that there are major differences between incestuous and non-incestuous child abusers. We should also be aware that Freund, Watson and Dickey (1991) classify on the basis of *relative* responses to child and adult stimuli; they provide no evidence other than this of the extent of the men's arousal to children in absolute terms. We do not know how much the men are responding to children except in comparison to their response to adults.

Clearly, phallometric laboratory assessment is far from an infallible "acid test" of a man's sexual activities in the community.

False Allegations and Phallometry

There is good reason to suspect that some allegations of sexual abuse may serve purposes other than the interests of justice and child protection. In recent years there have been well-publicized cases of public figures denying accusations of sexual impropriety with children by impugning the motives of their accusers. Allegations of sexual abuse may be made, for example, during divorce proceedings where the custody of the children is in dispute. One does not have to assume that malice or manipulation motivates these allegations; an ex-spouse may well feel genuine but misplaced concern. It would be of importance if phallometry could differentiate between false and true accusations. Are characteristic patterns to be found in men who are accused of abuse during child custody disputes?

The clinical records of men who had been referred for phallometric sexual arousal assessment either by their lawyers or by child care workers were examined in one study (McAnulty and Adams, 1990). Some were in child custody disputes, others were not. Over 70% had been formally charged with child molestation and the remainder were awaiting the results of investigations. As many as a quarter of the cases were rejected for further analysis because they showed little or no erection to any of the sexual stimuli. The *circumferences* of their erections were measured (Marshall, Barbaree and Christophe, 1986; Quinsey, Chaplin and Varney, 1981) as they listened to audio-taped descriptions of explicit sexual activity. These were narrated in the second person by a man while an appropriate colour slide of a nude person was shown at the same time. The female child stimuli included fellatio, intercourse and genital fondling; the male child stimuli described partner-initiated fellatio and the child as receptive partner during anal intercourse. These clearly showed prepubescent children. Other slides depicted women.

A statistical analysis (discriminant function) suggested that sexual arousal to the male stimuli was largely responsible for distinguishing the custody dispute cases from the rest. Eighty per cent of dispute cases could be correctly identified from this variable alone and 56% of the non-custody dispute cases. Dividing the maximum response to child stimuli by the maximum response to an adult (i.e. Abel's paedophilia index) and using a ratio of 0.6 between the two as the cut-off point resulted in nearly half of the custody dispute and two-thirds of the non-custody dispute men being classified as deviant.

It should be noted that although response to male children was the best predictor, the majority of the offences were against female children. There was no difference between the two groups in terms of their response to adult females. Half of the non-custody cases responded to male children:

> "As a final caution, the results of this study are not to be misinterpreted as criteria of 'innocence' or 'guilt' which are legal decisions. The findings do show that involvement in a custody dispute is not sufficient as a sole criterion for determining the presence or absence of pedophilic arousal in accused sex offenders. Some individuals accused of child molestation in the context of custody disputes present deviant patterns of sexual arousal while others do not. Additional criteria are necessary for determining whether the accused offender is likely to have committed the alleged sexual offense."
>
> (McAnulty and Adams, 1990, p. 554)

PHALLOMETRIC FAKING

The possibilities of the participants faking the outcome of a phallometry assessment are well recognized. The main possibilities are as follows:

(1) Faking arousal:

a. Secretly masturbating to produce an erection. Some arrangements reduce this possibility by making it physically difficult to reach the penis by using an obstruction.
b. Contracting muscles around the pelvis such as those in the abdomen or between the anus and the scrotum (perineum). These constitute attempts to simulate erection by increasing the strain on the apparatus.

highly stimulating theme which is
he stimulus material being shown or

arousing themes while the clinician
l.
cting mental task such as mental
otic material is being shown.
he content of the visual material by
eriphery.
stimulus to detract from the erotic
causing pain by clenching one's hand
vily on parts of the apparatus.

vary widely. One obvious reason for faking *disinterest* is its utility for the offender's disposal, since it may support his claims that he does not need therapy or even that he is innocent. One should not forget, either, that many people undergoing therapy are highly hopeful of its success, so faking may also serve to demonstrate that their progress in therapy has been good: if the offender is no longer aroused by pictures of naked children then surely this is progress? After all, therapy is partially designed to help offenders to suppress deviant thoughts. Similar motives may underlie faking *interest*: if the offender can show that he is aroused by adult men or women, then this is a contraindicator of his paedophilia or evidence of the success of the treatment he has received. In other words, a faking pattern may emphasize apparent interest in adults and minimize apparent interest in children. Furthermore, an offender who is keen to demonstrate that he is helpful and cooperative may fake arousal in keeping with his pattern of offending. Overall, faking may take into account the reasons for the assessment, the benefits available to the offender as a result of demonstrating a particular pattern in the assessment, the beliefs of the offender about the measurement process, how it is seen by those responsible for his disposal through the system and the nature of the relationship between the offender and the staff dealing with him.

Research on faking has largely confirmed that the outcomes of assessment may be influenced by the use of particular instructions. For example, Abel, Blanchard and Barlow (1981) gave one of two alternative instructions to groups of rapists, homosexuals, exhibitionists, paedophiles and others. Each was instructed either to "let himself become sexually aroused" or to "voluntarily suppress his erection to that stimulus by mental means" (p. 27). The suppression instruction worked well enough, although not completely successfully. Similarly, Quinsey and Carrigan (1978) studied a community sample of (presumably non-deviant) men. They were asked, for a reward, to fake a sexual preference for slides of 5–11-year-old girls in various stages of undress although they had previously demonstrated a socially acceptable preference for young female adults. Four out of five of these men managed to fake the paedophile pattern. Quinsey and Carrigan suggest that paedophiles may not have this level of control over their arousal. Using a procedure in which lights signalled an erection, it was found that only 30% could achieve control over their arousal. Supplementing this procedure with a mild electric shock as well as the signal light only increased the percentage who had control to 50%. Perhaps more important is the study by Hall, Proctor and Nelson (1988), which demonstrated that overwhelmingly men were able to suppress their arousal to previously arousing material when given instruction in this. Four out of five completely eliminated signs of arousal; less than 4% were unable to reduce their levels of arousal to the previously arousing material.

Preventing Faking

While it is possible to reduce faking, most research using phallometry has not controlled for faking. Some clinicians and researchers scrutinize their pen records for what they consider to be tell-tale signs of crude faking, but this may only deal with faking's tip-of-the-iceberg. Studies of faking prevention have largely tried to ensure that the participant engages with the erotic material presented and does not use masking fantasy or simply ignore the materials. For example,

Laws and Rubin (1969) used an irregularly flashing light during a 10-minute erotic film; participants had to signal when they detected it. In this way, hopefully, concentration on the film in question would be enhanced. Nevertheless, participants were still able to inhibit erections to the film. Some of them created competing mental tasks such as doing sums to help them. Interestingly, participants found it much more difficult to maintain an erection in the absence of filmed erotica than to inhibit erections to erotica. Henson and Rubin (1971) upped the difficulty of the task by requiring participants to describe the contents of the film. Even in these circumstances, when instructed to do so, some of the men were able to inhibit their erections. Possibly, describing a film's contents is so distracting that it is relatively easy not to become aroused.

In an attempt to overcome the faking problem, Quinsey and Chaplin (1988) recruited a sample of men from the local community through newspaper advertising. The recruits admitted to no sexual offences. A mixture of stories were used, involving non-sexual interactions between male and female, consenting sex, rape stories involving brutal, physically violent forced sex and violent stories including mugging but with no sexual content. Participants received (at different times) (i) normal instructions about what to do in the study, (ii) instructions to fake sexual arousal to sexual violence and non-sexual violence, and (iii) instructions to fake sexual arousal to these same materials but they also had to monitor the films and press either a sex button or a violence button each time these occurred. Three-quarters of the participants in the research demonstrated a "perfect" pattern. In other words, they behaved in exactly the same way under the instructions to fake if they had the button pressing task to do as they did without instructions to fake. When just asked to fake without the additional task, faking was successful. In other words, the button pressing activity largely prevented faking. All of the participants said that it was difficult to create their own fantasies when required to monitor for violent and sexual content. Nevertheless, a few of them succeeded: one claimed that he jammed his finger into a protruding nail in the apparatus in order to turn himself off, another was a pilot who claimed that he was trained to do two things at once.

Thus, a high percentage of men are capable of faking the outcomes of a phallometric test, although this is most clearly and decisively shown for the suppression of sexual arousal. Furthermore, it is possible to complicate the task sufficiently to prevent the commonest forms of faking in most men. Nevertheless, practitioners cannot eliminate the small minority of men who can fake irrespective of the procedures employed. The fact that when encouraged to do so many men are capable of faking does not mean that the majority of men actually do fake during assessment; some may, but we do not know how many:

> "... while nobody believes that penile tumescence *is* male sexual arousal or that relative penile responsiveness to sexual cues constitutes sexual preference, the discriminative power and face validity of phallometric technology make it easy to forget these distinctions, particularly inasmuch as paraphiliacs' reports of their sexual preferences are much more likely to be at variance with their actual histories of sexual behavior than are the results of phallometric assessments. The distinction between the phallometric measure of sexual preference and the psychological construct of sexual preference itself is of paramount importance in interpreting changes in sexual preference, reflected by penile measurements, that are occasioned by behavioral treatments."
>
> (Quinsey and Chaplin, 1988b, pp. 56–57)

Quinsey and Chaplin (1988) describe how some of the offenders at their institution had been instructed by their peers on how to fake on the phallometric test! Because of this, research on phallometry there is largely limited to new clients at the institution who might not have been so influenced. Clearly, phallometry is not a simple, infallible measuring procedure but something involving complex social contingencies about which only limited knowledge and speculation are available. The question is the degree of faith one can have in available findings about phallometric differences between offender types.

Phallometry is not a "sexual lie detector" (Farrall and Card, 1988) because it is not sufficiently precise to divulge whether a man has offended or is likely to do so. It would be virtually useless as a community screening device to search for likely offenders. There would be too many false identifications to make it worthwhile and too great a possibility of faking. Nevertheless, it does have uses: it gives strong pointers as to the ages and sexes that are arousing in men who may have difficulties in admitting their socially unacceptable sexual feelings. In such cases, where the phallometric data is at variance with what is disclosed, the additional information can be helpful in taking the therapy forward if used sensitively.

COMPARING PHYSIOLOGICAL AND SELF-REPORT MEASURES

Much research on physical arousal to deviant sexual stimuli fails to address the question of its power versus that of other approaches. The degree to which the phallometric and other approaches tally is taken as evidence of the validity of phallometry. Some studies compare groups of men with different offending characteristics (e.g. offenders against boys with rapists of adult women) to assess whether the known offender groups differed in their physical response to different types of deviant material. We have seen many examples of this already. Others compare the amount of erection to the deviant stimuli as measured by the machine with the offenders' self-reported arousal to the material.

Although these provide a degree of confidence about the worth of phallometry, they do not in themselves demonstrate the superiority of physiological methods over, say, questionnaires for identifying the man's deviant sexual characteristics. In practice, the questionnaire might be more effective at discriminating between the types of offender. Research needs to address the relative power of the different methods of assessment—a sort of shoot-out between the two.

Day *et al.* (1989) took rapists and sexual offenders against children. One objective was to examine whether the physiological methods could distinguish between violent and non-violent offenders. To this end, police and probation reports prepared at the time of sentencing were used to assess whether the offender was violent—a third were by the criteria of injury, verbal abuse or the use of a weapon. Penile *circumference* was measured using a mercury-in-rubber strain gauge in response to slides of adults and children of both sexes, audio tapes and video tapes. Indexes were developed based on arousal to the following types of content:

(1) Rape
(2) Male child consenting
(3) Male child non-consenting
(4) Female child consenting
(5) Female child non-consenting
(6) Homosexual arousal to adults
(7) Heterosexual arousal to adults

Self-reported sexual behaviour was assessed using the Multiphasic Sex Inventory (Nichols and Molinder, 1984), which consists of 300 true/false questions dealing with many aspects of sexual activity. Subscales from this deal with child molestation, male child orientation and female child orientation, rape behaviour, homosexual orientation and heterosexual orientation as well as other aspects of the offender's sexual behaviours. Using complex statistics, it was found that the different aspects of sexual arousal as measured by phallometry correlated fairly well with self-reports of similar behaviours. However, the amount of variation shared between the two types of measures was only 25% of the maximum possible, implying that phallometry and the questionnaire were largely measuring different things. It appears that a dimension from homosexual/non-coercive sexual preference to heterosexual/coercive sexual preference mainly accounts for the association. That is, coercion and heterosexuality were correlated.

A number of analyses were carried out in order to maximize the discrimination between offenders on the basis of type of victim. For the child molesters, the *physiological measures* could distinguish offenders against boys from those against girls. The men who were aroused by material including male sex partners were more likely to have offended against boys, and arousal to rape themes identified those who had offended against girls. *Self-reports* subjected to a similar analysis also discriminated. The child molestation measures were associated with known child molesting, as were the rape measures with known rape offenders. The sex of the victim of child molestation was fairly well predicted by sexual orientation (homosexuality versus heterosexuality) and preference for male children. However, having girl victims was associated with rated preference for female children and rape.

While the general impression is of the superiority of the self-report measures, especially in terms of consistency, the best evidence comes from the relative abilities of self-report and physiological measures to predict offending history. Day *et al.* found, using discriminant function analysis, that self-reports correctly classified 95% of the sample by known type of offence—rape or child molestation. Eighty-six per cent of the child molesters were correctly classified on their victim's sex, and 85% were correctly classified on the use of violence in offending. In every comparison, "hit" rates for self-report data were better than those for the corresponding physiological measure. Thus, only 74% were correctly identified as rapists or child molesters; 82% of molesters were correctly identified according to their victim's sex and 74% on the use of violence.

According to Day *et al.* (1989), self-reports may measure history of offending and the physiological reports tap "aspects of the potential to offend" (p. 122). The authors fail to address the question, "why bother with either the physiological data or the self-report data?" The key data of offending is seen as the criterion by which these other aspects are judged. Why not just leave things at that? There are a number of possibilities, of course. One is that, clinically, the additional information may reveal problem areas that the offending history in itself is unable to show—offending is more extensive than arrest. Furthermore, while a good proportion of offenders may decide to be truthful, many may choose not to reveal accurate information about themselves or, indeed, may be unable to do so due to lack of self-insight. As Pithers and Laws (1989) suggest:

> "Often, the offender views his disorder as problematic solely because it led to his arrest, conviction, and imprisonment. For such individuals, leaving prison and treatment as soon as possible, rather than achieving attitudinal and behavioral change, represent the goals of therapy."
>
> (Pithers and Laws, 1989, p. 83)

Unfortunately, appealing as this is to common sense, it remains an open question as to what aspects of a penile plethysmograph can be interpreted diagnostically in the absence of secondary confirmation by the offender through interview or other forms of self-report.

Faced with the complexities of abusers' cognitions about their offending (and the possibility of lying and denial), it is not surprising that some clinicians have sought to use apparently objective measures such as penile plethysmography. That it is probably as problematic and uncertain as any other approach to the assessment of paedophiles means that we should be wary of relying on it as a major criterion of the success of any treatment or therapy (e.g. Jenkins-Hall *et al.*, 1989) in the absence of evidence from recidivism data.

PSYCHOLOGICAL TECHNIQUES

Most of the evidence of the worth of psychological questionnaires in the assessment of offenders is subjective. Questionnaires are used because of their pragmatic value rather than anything else. Salter

(1988) states that the only crucial psychological test in the assessment and treatment of sex offenders is the penile plethysmograph, which she describes as "objective". She implies that, with the exception of the Minnesota Multiphasic Personality Inventory (MMPI), most tests lack research support for sexual offenders. Salter presents a list of possibly useful tests (as do Pithers, Martin and Cumming, 1989) and Barnard *et al.* (1989) describe an interactive computer system which assesses offenders on several psychological and sexological dimensions to produce an offender profile. But it needs to be recognized that psychological measures are used for relatively broad purposes during therapy rather than simply sex offending alone. Thus, among the battery of tests that have been used in the assessment of offenders are a number of general measures of psychological functioning that may bear on his offending only obliquely:

Minnesota Multiphasic Personality Inventory. This is unusual in that there is some evidence that it discriminates among offender types. Particular profiles on this have been found to be characteristic of child rapists but not incest offenders, for example (Armentrout and Hauer, 1978; Panton, 1979), although others have found no differences between sex offenders and other types of offender (Quinsey, Arnold and Pruesse, 1980).

Beck Depression Inventory (Beck, 1967).

Buss–Durkee Hostility Inventory (Buss and Durkee, 1957). "Once in a while I cannot control my urge to harm others."

Fear of Negative Evaluations Scale (Watson and Friend, 1969). "I become tense and jittery if I know someone is sizing me up."

Interpersonal Reactivity Index (Davis, 1980). "I sometimes feel helpless when I am in the middle of a very emotional situation."

Rotter Locus of Control Scale (Rotter, 1966).

Situational Competency Test (Chaney, O'Leary and Marlatt, 1978).

Social Avoidance and Distress Scale (Watson and Friend, 1969). "I feel relaxed even in unfamiliar social situations."

Social-Trait Anxiety Scale (Spielberger, Gorsuch and Lushene, 1970).

Wechsler Adult Intelligence Scale (Wechsler, 1981).

Michigan Alcoholism Screening Test (Seltzer, 1971). "Have you ever awakened the morning after some drinking the night before and found that you could not remember a part of the evening?"

Internal/External Scale (Nowicki and Strickland, 1973). "Do you feel that if things start out well in the morning it is going to be a good day no matter what you do?"

The following are psychologically based measures that have been held to be particularly pertinent for use in the psychosexual assessment of offenders. Many of these are reproduced in full in Salter (1988):

Alert List (Silver, undated). This is a list of behaviours that might signal offence linked behaviours if present in significant numbers: "Any invasion of child's privacy, e.g., entering their bedroom or bathroom unchaperoned without being asked to."

Attitudes Toward Women (Spence and Helmreich, 1978). "It is ridiculous for a woman to run a locomotive and for a man to darn socks."

Clarke Sexual History Questionnaire (Langevin, 1983).

Cognitions Scale (Abel *et al.*, 1984). This is a measure of distorted cognitions about sexual offending: "An adult can tell if having sex with a young child will emotionally damage the child in the future."

Multiphasic Sex Inventory (Nichols and Molinder, 1984).

Rape Myth Acceptance Scale (Burt, 1980). Another measure of distorted beliefs about sexual offending, although not primarily directed to child sexual abusers. "Many women have an unconscious wish to be raped, and may then unconsciously set up a situation in which they are likely to be attacked."

Relapse Fantasies (Marlatt and Gordon, 1985).

Sex Fantasy Questionnaire (Wilson, 1978). This is a measure of frequency of fantasizing about themes like: "Whipping or spanking someone."

Sexual Interest Card Sort (Abel and Becker, 1985). This evaluates sexual interest in a number of types of deviant and unusual sexual thoughts. A typical item from the measure is: "I'm lying back naked on the bed with my daughter sitting on top of me. I'm stroking her naked body with my hands and pushing my fingers into her cunt."

Although it is not appropriate to debate the detail of the use of such psychological tests and measures in the assessment of sex offenders here, it is important to stress that such tests can often have a spurious air of objectivity which they may not deserve. Campbell (1992) presents a case study of the use of psychological measures in forensic work in which a psychologist failed to meet professional standards in the interpretation and administration of the tests. He concludes that, "standardized tests can confer such an appearance of expertise upon psychologists that their potential for leading judges and juries astray should not be underestimated" (p. 46). Too little is known about the worth of many of these tests. Although they may be used in clinical settings largely to aid with planning and progressing therapy, this does not mean that shortcomings in their use are of little consequence. The overlap between a psychologist's role of therapist with that of a professional contributing to decisions about the disposal of offenders inevitably means that the right of the client to a fair evaluation risks being jeopardized by the requirements of the psychologist's institutional responsibilities.

THE VALUE OF THE TECHNOLOGIES

In this chapter I have presented some unvarnished facts about the physiological and psychological technologies that have been applied to paedophiles (and other sex offenders). It may appear a little negative to do so given the lack of a strong database for theory and clinical practice. Despite their drawbacks, these measures, especially the physiological ones, have been highly influential in the development of theory about the nature of paedophilia as well as other forms of sex offending. So, when we find that they may be relatively easily faked, or that they do not reveal particular trends consistently or strongly, or that they may not do the job so well as less technological approaches, we should be less willing to assume that theories and assertions based solely on them are firmly established. Understanding paedophilia is an important task, but it needs to be based on realism rather than hope.

CHAPTER 5

Theories of Paedophilia

> "The image of child sexual abuse of 1885 was that of the helpless victim sold as a 'five pound virgin' to satisfy the jaded lusts of a perverted aristocrat. It was a mercenary, loveless, heterosexual event across a wide chasm of age, power and social class."
>
> (McIntosh, 1988, p. 9)

It is wrong to regard theories of paedophilia as being solely about why some people offend against children. Numerous issues bear critically on our understanding of the paedophile, which reflect structural and ideological matters in society as much as the individual's psyche. Questions about paedophilia engage broader debates than of hormones, cycles of abuse, pornography and perversion. Explanations have ranged across the historical, sociological, cultural, psychological and biological. Some theories arise out of empirical research, others out of clinical observation, and others still out of vested interests. Not surprisingly, such disparate approaches share relatively few assumptions and are built on radically different foundations:

(1) One theory sees the origins of paedophilia in the psychological development of the child, another in terms of social conceptions of childhood.

(2) One theory argues that paedophilia is a social construction in which beneficial relationships between adults and children are criminalized, another that paedophilia is motivated by destructive forces.

(3) One theory blames masculinity for paedophilia, another mothers of paedophiles, and another adolescent sexuality.

(4) One theory sees paedophilia as a perversion, another will see it as central to human development.
(5) One theory argues that distorted thinking is used to excuse paedophilia, another that irrational thinking within society criminalizes the paedophile.
(6) One theory sees the paedophile as a skilled manipulator, another as an incompetent adult unable to relate to others.
(7) One theory sees paedophilia as the result of deep psychological conflict, another as the product of incidental learning.
(8) One theory sees the paedophile as psychologically sick, another as a typical man.
(9) One theory sees the paedophile as the victim of time and culture, another as a victim of childhood experiences.
(10) One theory holds that paedophilia is caused by a single factor, another by a multiplicity of interrelating factors.
(11) One theory sees paedophilia as a sequenced process, another as a characteristic of the individual.
(12) One theory will have implications for therapy, another will not.

Although some theories appear to be relatively sophisticated, nevertheless one can see elements of wider social attitudes in some of them. So, for example, moral stances are central to several of the theories. It is secondary, if not misleading, to raise the issue of the best theory. They explore such diverse domains that they often complement each other rather than compete to explain the same things. While some seem not to extend our understanding overly, knowledge of their limitations may prevent us falling into oversimplistic viewpoints. Even the most complex of the theories fails to deal with many aspects of offending.

The following are the major perspectives to be considered in this chapter:

(1) Paedophilia as sexual learning
(2) Paedophilia as preconditions
(3) Paedophilia as cognitive process
(4) Paedophilia as psychodynamically determined
(5) Paedophilia as gender politics
(6) Paedophilia as biological anomaly

Each of these may involve several different theories.

1. SEXUAL LEARNING THEORY

Despite many therapies assuming that relearning or unlearning needs to take place, the ways in which paedophilia is learnt are rarely discussed. More usually, its origins in childhood's complex psychological dynamics are alluded to. An exception to this trend is discussed by Howells (1981). Children are known to engage in various forms of sexual activity quite frequently during childhood. Granted these high rates of sexual experiences with peers in normal childhood, the association of sexual arousal with the immature body characteristics of other children might condition a long-term sexual response to immature bodies, the strength of the sexual drive during puberty possibly enhancing the likelihood of such a learning process. Given that puberty begins at various ages, there is a possibility that a child experiencing his or her first sexual arousal at puberty might be responding to a similarly aged, but pre-pubescent, peer.

Howells' thesis could be extended to take into account the reward and punishment contingencies associated with these early sexual experiences. Not all early sexual experiences are likely to encourage paedophilia. Haugaard and Tilly (1988) surveyed students at a mid-Atlantic state university about their sexual experiences before *13* years of age. Sexual partners below the age of 16 years were considered by the researchers to be peers. Forty per cent of the students claimed such sexual episodes; hugging and kissing, exhibitionism and fondling were most characteristic. Intercourse, oral sex and attempted intercourse were rather infrequent. Typically, the children were of very similar ages and the average age discrepancy was just a few months. Friends of the opposite sex were the most common "partners". Girls were considerably less likely to initiate sexual activity (9%) than boys (49%). Coercion and same-sex experiences generated the most negative feelings. Interestingly, the sexual activities were largely unrelated to how the child felt about the episode. Coercion influenced how negatively sexual activity with other children was experienced but was not so important with adult partners. Adult–child experiences were more likely to be seen negatively even when coercion was not involved.

While Howells' theory easily explains how sexual attraction towards children begins, it does not explain why so many people pass through adolescence having had adolescent sexual experiences without becoming adult paedophiles. Howells suggests that peer rejection and parental hostility may act as punishments which create an aversion to adult-orientated sexuality. The maturing individual may thus feel anxious about the prospect of approaches to sexually mature people. Furthermore, sexual fantasies about other children during masturbation may reinforce the paedophile imagery; there is some evidence that sexual offenders start masturbating younger than men in general (Condron and Nutter, 1988). Sometimes, adult paedophiles may act as models for this lifestyle. Problems in relating to adults may result in the now sexual youngster failing to "grow out of" his paedophilia. A similar learning model can be applied to adult offenders:

> "It is at least possible, for example, that child stimuli acquire the capacity to induce sexual arousal as a *consequence* of repeated sexual behaviour with children (a process of classical conditioning."
>
> (Howells, 1991, p. 6)

Like most theories of paedophilia, this leaves many important questions unanswered—such as why such men offend in the first place.

2. PRECONDITION MODEL

One of the most widely acknowledged explanations of paedophilia is the precondition model (Araji and Finkelhor, 1985, 1986). Essentially, this categorizes factors that characterize offenders and the circumstances leading to offending. Research findings are used, wherever available, to confirm possible explanations of paedophilia. The model is based on the assumption that offenders are *diverted* from adult relationships. Remarkably, despite the apparent research basis of the theory, much of the evidence used is technically poor, weak or lacking. In a curious way, the theory's strength stems from this weakness since it stresses multiple causes of paedophilia—aetiologically disparate patterns for different offenders. This encourages clinicians to explore widely for the idiosyncratic determining factors involved with each offender.

In developing the approach, Araji and Finkelhor (1985, 1986) reviewed empirical research on explanations of paedophilia categorized into four basic types. (An asterisk indicates that they believe that the relationship is reasonably well supported by research, although others may dispute this.):

1. Emotional congruence. This is the paedophile's emotional need to relate to children. It is usually expressed in terms of paedophiles having difficulties relating to adults. Sometimes children meet the paedophile's emotional needs, which adults cannot. Evidence for this factor includes:

(1) That paedophiles are attracted to children because they lack dominance, so the offender can fulfil his need for dominance by expressing it against children;
(2) Paedophiles are psychologically and socially immature;
(3) Paedophiles lack self-esteem;
(4) Paedophiles have been sexually abused in childhood and cope with the experience by the repetition of the offence or by identification with the aggressor*;
(5) Paedophiles are narcissistic, extremely emotionally centred upon themselves; and
(6) Men are socialized to be dominant and, due to social inadequacy, paedophiles are forced to exercise this over children.

2. Sexual arousal. This concerns why children are sexually arousing to offenders. Of course, it is not proven that they all are. Nevertheless the evidence for this includes:

(1) Laboratory tests which show that at least some paedophiles get erections to deviant images of children*;
(2) Sexual abuse in childhood conditions sexual arousal to children*;
(3) The experience of abusers in childhood provides a model for deviant sexual behaviour patterns*;
(4) Hormone abnormalities;
(5) Paedophiles mistakenly interpret physiological arousal as sexual arousal; and
(6) Paedophiles are socialized by child pornography or advertising to regard children as sexual objects.

3. Blockage. This consists of things that make adult sexual and emotional gratification unavailable. Aspects of paedophilia held to be relevant to this are:

(1) Difficulty in relating to adult females*;
(2) Deficient social skills: some support from uncontrolled studies*;
(3) Anxiety over sexual matters: some support from uncontrolled studies*;
(4) Unresolved oedipal dynamics;
(5) Disturbances in adult sexual romantic/sexual relationships; and
(6) Repressive norms about sexual behaviour*.

4. Disinhibition. Why are some adults not deterred by normal prohibitions against sex with children?:

(1) Impulse disorder: true of a small proportion of offenders*;
(2) Senility;
(3) Mental retardation;
(4) Alcohol*;
(5) Failure of incest avoidance mechanisms, e.g. higher rates of abuse in stepfather families*;
(6) Situation stress; and
(7) Tolerance of incest within the culture or subculture.

Araji and Finkelhor were well aware of a major problem with this model: the bulk of the relevant evidence comes from highly selected samples, almost invariably from prisoner or offender populations. Consequently, the characteristics of the system may bias our understanding. Thus, paedophiles may appear shy and ineffectual because these are the sort of people who get arrested; their apparently low self-esteem may be the result of the arrest process and the disdain with which they are treated by other prisoners; and offenders may learn the "language" that will help them to get early release. Finally, control groups, if used, may consist of students, who differ from offenders in many ways unrelated to the offence.

Newer research bearing on the model provides only partial support (Howells, 1991). Particularly important is the failure to replicate previous research (Howells, 1978) concerning paedophiles' preoccupation with dominance (Horley, 1988). Without evidence of broader motivations for paedophiles' attraction to children, the notion of emotional congruence becomes little other than a self-evident truism. Howells (1991) supports Finkelhor's ideas about deviant sexual arousal on the basis that they are consistent with recent evidence. Finkelhor regarded sexual arousal to children merely as a possible factor in offending, not a necessary one. One argument related to this suggests that changes in offending should follow from therapeutic reductions in deviant sexual arousal—if deviant sexual arousal facilitates sexual offending against children. Although Quinsey's (1983) data showed that pre-treatment arousal to nude children predicted post-treatment arousal and post-treatment recidivism, nevertheless reductions in deviant arousal *over the course of treatment* were not correlated with decreased recidivism. Thus the notion that *laboratory measured* deviant sexual arousal to children contributes to offending is in doubt. Similarly, Marshall and Barbaree (1988) also found that deviant sexual arousal could be modified by treatment but that these changes were unrelated to recidivism.

A number of comments need to be made. Laboratory-based arousal measures may be invalid, for example, due to "cheating" by the offender. Furthermore, the assumption that nudity is the sexually arousing feature of the child slides may be unwarranted, despite seeming reasonable. Howitt and Cumberbatch (in press) found, for example, that paedophiles' sexually arousing stimuli are often quite legal materials. So, for example, a television programme for children featuring children at play might be a sexual "turn on" whereas "kiddyporn" is of no interest. In other words, crucial aspects of sexual arousal may be ignored in standard laboratory "erection" measures. There is another difficulty. In the simple behavioural model it is assumed that the offending serves to directly relieve sexual tension, the putative causal sequence being that the offender becomes aroused sexually and the offence satisfies these sexual needs. This may be mistaken in a proportion of cases. Some offences against children do not result in orgasm. For example, fondling a child through his or her clothing may not be directly associated with sexual climax. Such offences might help in the creation of fantasies for use during masturbation to achieve orgasm. If correct, such an explanation would cast further doubt on the use of phallometric assessment to test hypotheses about the role of sexual arousal to children in offending.

Howells (1991) suggests that Finkelhor's preconditions imply different forms of treatment. So, for example, if relationships with adults are blocked, techniques such as assertiveness and social skills training which improve relationships with adults may be useful.

3. COGNITIVE DISTORTION THEORY

Some theories of paedophilia have a moral-cum-ideological basis. Wyre's views (in Tate, 1990) illustrate this. Such approaches often have little basis in systematic research and theory; nevertheless their capacity to attract publicity makes them influential. They may be advocated during training courses for professionals and thus gain currency away from the public record (Jenkins, 1992). Wyre argues that paedophiles use whatever means they can to validate their activities—thus, pornography is a source of reassurance. In pornography, for example, offenders see other adults doing much the same things that they do or want to do. This creates an aura of normality about offending which may disengage their inhibitions against offending as part of an "escalation" process:

> "They may start off with mutual masturbation, but even that disturbing level of behaviour appears to escalate under the influence of child pornography so that they will follow the images through oral and vaginal sex to full anal penetration."
>
> (Wyre, in Tate, 1990, p. 24)

He rejects the suggestion that pornography serves as a "safety valve" which diverts sexual energy away from offending. Paedophilia is an addiction, not cured by providing fuel to that addiction.

Among the characteristic cognitive style of paedophiles is minimalization of their offending. Due to this, offenders' criminal records are usually incomplete or inaccurate:

> "I would make an assumption that ... there may be a whole range of undisclosed offending that we do not know anything about. Again in practice it may not be true but this is an assumption I would make."
>
> (Wyre, 1989, p. 17)

Furthermore, the offender's choice of language may redefine the abuse as something consensual and desired by the child:

> "If he says that he had 'oral sex' I would immediately confront that and say 'no, you put your penis in his mouth'. I know he is using the term 'oral sex' in order to imply there was mutual consent."
>
> (Wyre, 1989, p. 19)

Child abusers often excuse their offending on the basis of family break-up or unemployment. Blame is also attributed to wives who refuse sex or to pressures at work. These are nothing but excuses:

> "When they eventually become honest about it—if they do—they admit they are sexually attracted to children and that their masturbation fantasies, far from being those of normally adjusted men, are those of fixated paedophiles who have had and will continue to have sex with children."
>
> (Wyre, in Tate, 1990, p. 56)

Partly for this reason, incest and paedophilia should not be regarded as separate and different phenomena; they are "inextricably linked". All types of offender are "just ordinary men" who are adroit at hiding their sexual feelings.

The excuses also extend to blaming the child. Claims that the abuse was an accident are common:

> "One offender told me that the abuse of his daughter happened when he turned round and his penis 'just went in her mouth.'"
>
> (Wyre, in Tate, 1990, p. 106)

This propensity to shift the blame has to be confronted in order to begin to control abusers. Professionals (police, psychologists, social workers) may inadvertently reinforce this other-blame due to ignorance:

> "... if you don't treat the behavioural side first you are colluding with them and they will grasp that—they will grab any excuse they can to shed the responsibility for what they have done. And you must remember that paedophiles are very manipulative people—they are generally of above average intelligence and they are very good at manipulating concerned professional workers."
>
> (Wyre, in Tate, 1990, p. 264)

It is counterproductive to treat the man primarily as part of the family system since this merely allows him more freedom to lay the blame on the dysfunctional family or another family member.

4. PSYCHODYNAMIC APPROACHES

Psychodynamically based theories of paedophilia are also rarely based on research. Clinical experience is usually their only empirical foundation. Much stems from Freud's (1905/1977) suggestion that homosexuals in general may have sound personality structures. This did not extend to child molesters—those who offend against children were seen as aberrations:

> "It is only exceptionally that children are the exclusive sexual objects in such a case. They usually come to play that part when someone who is cowardly or has become impotent adopts them as a substitute, or when an urgent instinct (one which will not allow of postponement) cannot at the moment get possession of any more appropriate object ... One would be glad on aesthetic grounds to be able to ascribe these and other severe aberrations of the sexual instinct to insanity; but that cannot be done. Experience shows that disturbances of the sexual instinct among the insane do not differ from those that occur among the healthy."
>
> (Freud, 1905/1977, p. 60)

This theme was reiterated many years later when Storr (1964) suggested that the paedophile "has been unable to find sexual satisfaction in an adult relationship" (Storr, 1964, p. 102).

Freud's account of paedophilia is woefully inadequate; it explains virtually nothing that is known about such offenders. For example, the thesis accounts for few, if any, of the factors discussed by Araji and Finkelhor (1985, 1986). Freud's ideas would explain why *any adult* in sexual privation would turn to children. Since only some adults are sexual with children, the theory is little more than a statement of what paedophiles do.

In a modern psychoanalytic account of paedophilia, Socarides (1991) distinguishes between what he calls *paedophiliac behaviour or fantasy* and the true *obligatory paedophile pervert* who must have sexual activity with a child or suffer "intolerable anxiety" (p. 185). The situational offender is by far the more common, according to Socarides, whereas the obligatory offender is relatively rare. The seductive and affectionate child causes some men to offend against their sexual natures, as do intoxication and privation of sex with other adults. He even goes so far as to suggest an epidemic of paedophile behaviour, similar to epidemics of homosexuality, which occurs when society fails to prohibit sexual license (Socarides, 1988)! According to him, there are two types of paedophile, differing in terms of the developmental stage at which their deep seated psychological conflicts were fixated. The evidence for this is based entirely on clinical experience, and there is very little to suggest why paedophilia is the chosen psychological defence rather than any other of the possible mechanisms. Socarides concludes his position as being:

> "... the major mechanism in homosexual pedophilia was incorporation of male children in order to reinforce the sense of masculinity, overcome death anxiety and remain young forever, as well as return to the maternal breast."
>
> (Socarides, 1991, p. 189)

It is difficult to know where this leaves us in terms of insight into paedophilia, especially as it holds most child molestation to be the consequence of the child's seductive behaviour, the offender's inebriety and the lack of an alternative means of sexual relief.

Paedophilia as a Perversion

Common sense may suggest that paedophilia is a perversion. Caution is appropriate. Without a clear concept of the meaning of the term "perversion" there is a danger of attributing too much to what may simply be somewhat unusual. Scruton (1986) regards perversions as the sexual interest in a less than fully regarded partner. Sexual interest in dead people (necrophilia) is the essence of a perversion since in this the very existence of another person is a threat to sexuality:

> "In other perversions, the other is wanted, not in absent, but in diminished form. The paradigm case is paedophilia, in which the other is wanted, not in spite of the fact that he is a child, but *because* he is a child. There is a natural instinct to cherish what is young, and to vent our desires upon what is fresh and beautiful. The paedophile, however, directs his attentions not to a 'young human being', but to a 'child'. The difference here parallels that between sex and gender. The idea of the childlike belongs not to material, but to intentional, understanding ... The child is the prelude to the person, and with a child full reciprocity is neither possible nor desirable ... When the childhood of the other plays a constitutive role in desire, desire is deflected from its interpersonal aim."
>
> (Scruton, 1986, pp. 284–285)

Scruton's thesis works best as an identifying thread between activities such as sex with animals, dead bodies and children (Johnson, 1990). None of these can be regarded as complete or full persons. Johnson describes the theory as matching "a mass of ordinary intuitions" (p. 210) despite remaining a little vague:

> "Perversion is what happens when I seek sexual congress with some body without giving due recognition to the person who *is* that body."
>
> (Johnson, 1990, p. 209)

It should be noted that masturbation may also be seen as a perversion since it ignores the pleasures and pains of adult interpersonal desire. Not only that, sexual fantasy seems also to possess the major defining feature of a perversion—not dealing with the other as a complete human being. Much as it would be useful to know what is quintessentially a sexual perversion, Scruton, in fact, provides little other than a moral position on what proper sexual relationships should be—that is, with the full person as a full person. In general, notions of deviance have not easily withstood psychological or sociological review. Sexual matters, since the Kinsey reports (Kinsey, Pomeroy and Martin, 1948; Kinsey *et al.*, 1953) have been difficult to define as deviant since it emerged that many socially condemned sexual activities are very common.

The Jungian View

Depth psychology has not contributed extensively to the theoretical treatment of paedophilia, with the exception of one group of Jungian analysts (Kraemer, 1976). Gordon (1976) suggests that in order to understand paedophilia it is essential to appreciate its healthy basis—*normal paedophilia*. By this she means the sort of interaction between adult and child that is mediated and altered by the characteristics of childhood. For example, a large forehead in relation to the length of the face is a stimulus that releases fond and pleasurable feelings towards the child. In humankind, there is an added dimension to the protection of the young—the need to preserve the "inner child" in ourselves (qualities such as innocence of perception and curiosity). The loss of the "inner child" creates an inability to readjust to the environment or engage in aesthetic activities such as religious experience and artistic creativity.

Initiation ceremonies and other rituals help to maintain a rigid distinction between adulthood and childhood, and provide the opportunity to emphasize the differences in the ways in which adults and children are regarded. In Western society this has included the definition of childhood as non-sexual.

It is an aspect of perversions that one part of the structure of the personality predominates at the cost of disregarding the rest. Thus, another person may be related to only in part rather than totally—for their age, their figure or some other partial characteristics:

> "This characteristic of deviation—the sacrifice of wholeness and totality to a part—often goes with marked obsessive–compulsive charac-

> teristics. Hence the pervert is often ruthless, single-minded and driven in his need to satisfy his desire."
>
> (Gordon, 1976, pp. 41–42)

Perversions come from preoccupations and anxieties related to different aspects of development. In relation to the paedophile, these preoccupations may be with the size of the penis or fears of ridicule by potential adult sexual partners. In the paedophile, there may be a tendency to hold an idealized longing for the purity and innocence of childhood.

Gordon suggests that female paedophilia can be seen in those women who relate effectively only with younger children. One of the signs of this is the replacement of a child with a new baby at regular intervals: "the compulsive need to have more and more babies, always new, fresh babies" (p. 43). The reason why society has tended to ignore the perversion of such women is that their means of expressing it is socially acceptable. She argues that paedophilia is most easily recognized when it is directed to an external object such as a child; it is less easily seen when it is internally directed towards youthfulness (as in Dorian Gray).

One feature to emerge out of the analyses of paedophiles is the great sense of vulnerability stemming from being the object of an unconscious sexual seduction by one or other or both of the parents. The means of dealing with this is to adopt a persona or façade of toughness and adulthood; situations which disturb this can produce great feelings of panic. Furthermore, in later reliving the experience, the paedophile may reverse the roles in a sadomasochistic way—repeating the threatening nature of the childhood experience. In one case study Gordon writes:

> "He remembers that he used to sleep in his mother's bed even when he was seven or eight, though he cannot remember when this stopped. He thinks that she wanted it and his conscious memory is of his wanting it too. Yet he also remembers that he used to put on all the available clothes before going to bed, because bed was thought of as a sort of polar region."
>
> (Gordon, 1976, p. 54)

One of the difficulties with this explanation is that it does not explain the overt sexual acts that are the focus of the usual concerns about paedophilia. On this, Williams (1976) claims that the horror of ageing is set against the renewing properties of sexuality:

> "Such morbid preoccupations could only be banished by erotic activities. The erect penis symbolized vigorous life which was constantly renewed and was indeed eternal. Alas! this renewal could be only transitory: hence its compulsive nature. Compulsive behaviour is always aimed at a once-and-for-all experience which inevitably fails to reassure."
>
> (Williams, 1976, p. 145)

Lambert (1976) takes a similar perspective in recognizing an essential component of development in paedophilia:

> "The age-old phenomenon of paedophilia may be understood as an environmental ingredient that is fundamental to the growth processes of children, even, to some extent, in its less benign seeming forms. However, if imperfections in the 'primal scene' become too great, then critical and cynical aspects of it in the child's mind begin to develop as a substitute: fantasies of sexually perverse, sadistic deviations. Perverse paedophiliac adults may lead the young thus prepared into premature sexual experiences of this sort in an over-enthusiastic attack upon the 'primal scene' and family life which have been experienced as 'not good enough'."
>
> (Lambert, 1976, p. 127)

The primal scene involves the two parents, the boy, the girl and the unborn baby. This provides the context for a powerful mix of emotions such as love and hate, creativity, violence and jealousy. When the dynamics of the family become stultifying or even destructive then this can dominate the whole personality.

The Jungian perspective contrasts markedly with some other explanations in so far as paedophilia is used for something that can be positive, pathological only when the process is diverted from its relatively healthy course. It is also another perspective which holds the mother to be fundamentally responsible, since Kraemer (1976) believes that the origins of paedophile tendencies lie in early mother–child interactions. The self-loving qualities of the mother may be transmitted to the child in excessive proportions. Because of the need of the mother to be idealized in return by the child, the process by which the child and the mother become separate individuals is substantially delayed. A crucial feature of this Jungian approach is the use of some case studies involving adult females as paedophiles.

A Psychiatric View

The degree of psychological disturbance in the offender may be related to the age of his victim (Glasser, 1989). The younger the victim, the greater the psychological disturbance. He also has negative feelings towards adult sexuality. These are feelings of fear or condemnation or a mixture of both. There is a *secondary paedophilia* which is the consequence of other pathologies such as schizophrenia, physical disorders of the brain and conditions in which the personality disintegrates, leading to a range of perverse behaviours. *Primary paedophilia* provides a certain amount of integration of the paedophile's ego and a consequent stability of his personality. Glasser suggests that there are two broad classes of primary paedophiles, the *invariant* and *pseudo-neurotics*. The two types may be characterized as follows:

(1) The invariant paedophile:

a. Long-term and exclusive involvement with children or adolescents;
b. Most often involved with boys;
c. No interest sexually (and often socially) with adults;
d. "Rigid, meagre personality";
e. Very limited interests and activities;
f. Solitary;
g. Little or no shame or guilt about offences;
h. There is a characteristic "dullness", causing in others "mental paralysis", which Glasser sees as the consequence of the paedophile's disinterest in making contact with others driven by anxiety.

(2) The pseudo-neurotic paedophile:

a. Appears usually heterosexually orientated towards adults;
b. Shows neurotic symptoms such as intermittent impotence, sexual apathy and tension and distress with his partners;
c. Sometimes, apparently due to stress or some chance factor, offends against a child or adolescent;
d. Claims great feelings of guilt or shame;
e. In reality, below the surface veneer he is deeply and consistently paedophile;

f. Paedophiliac fantasy may be used to enable seemingly normal intercourse with his adult partner.

This boils down to the pseudo-neurotic paedophile being fully perverted sexually towards children. Surface impressions have to be set aside, otherwise one would see these men as fairly normal adults pushed to paedophilia by circumstance. Quite clearly there are profound differences here from the fixated and regressed typology frequently mentioned, and discussed earlier. The pseudo-neurotic paedophile is truly eroticized towards children and not suffering from a regression in any meaningful sense.

For Glasser, paedophilia is one of a group of perversions that share a "core complex" of two major components:

(1) Aggression: this should not be confused with sadism, which has as its aim the imposition of suffering. This aggression is essentially to neutralize threats to the individual's mental or physical survival.

(2) Annihilation: while people demonstrate a wish for close, intimate unions with other people, such relationships are seen as dangerous or destructive by the pervert since he will be taken over completely by that other person.

He illustrates this with the case of a young Spanish man whose paedophiliac activities involved 7- to 11-year-old boys:

> "When a divorcee with whom he was on friendly terms expressed her desire to go to bed with him, the prospect of physical and emotional intimacy led him immediately to experience a mixture of terror and revulsion. He said he just couldn't stand her touching him and then said he had an image of steel arms clasping him to its belly and then of a Venus fly-trap closing round an insect."
>
> (Glasser, 1989, p. 4)

Or, elsewhere, Glasser (1988) refers to Karpman's (1950) case description of a paedophile's early experience of a woman neighbour's paedophiliac approach to him. When he was seven years old, she told him to undress while she did also, revealing what he describes as the hairiest vagina he had ever seen. She lay with him on top of her, when he felt that he "was going to be swallowed up within this mass of hideous hair".

Such strong feelings of danger in terms of relationships with other adults can be dealt with either by *narcissistic withdrawal* into himself bringing about "profound isolation" and feelings of worthlessness or by destroying this threatening, dangerous individual. The problem in the latter case is that the threatening person in his early life is his mother—the very person from whom the child seeks gratification. The outcome of all of this is that the pervert either converts this aggression sexually into sadism or into masochism where narcissistic withdrawal had taken place. The emotional focus of a paedophile's relationships with others is essentially on himself. In the case of the invariant paedophile, apart from family and one or two others, people are present as shadowy figures. They become significant only if they meet his needs. The pseudo-neurotic type accounts for the individuality of others rather better but in an exploitative manner:

> "His love is primarily self-gratifying and does not really concern itself with the autonomy and personal needs of the child itself. This is demonstrated indisputably in the paedophile's sexual activity with the child in its discounting of the child's own developmental relationship to sexuality, the stereotyped nature of the activities pursued and the inevitable sadomasochism involved. These considerations help us to understand why it is that the age of the children to whom he is attracted is generally the age at which he was himself sexually molested."
>
> (Glasser, 1989, p. 7)

There is an important question—how a paedophile can offend against children when the whole of society, including criminals, condemns such activities. Glasser's explanation is that societal standards (the superego) do not become integrated into the individual's personality because of the strong rejection he felt for parents and other authority figures who treated him badly in childhood. In paedophiliac activities, the protest against this is pursued. Nevertheless, there is inevitably a struggle between the individual's internal psychological needs and societal pressures (the superego) which results in the self-deception characteristic of the paedophile. A directive or proscriptive therapist readily produces a sadomasochistic relationship during treatment as a consequence.

5. FEMINISM: PAEDOPHILIA AS GENDER POLITICS

> "... don't tell us we like it, we want it, we need it or we agree to it. Don't tell us you're freeing us from sexual repression, educating us for a more fulfilling adult life. Don't tell us you do this because you love us, don't tell us you do this because nobody loves you. Don't tell us we are dirty. Don't tell us we are worthless. And don't tell us we can't recover. You may have fucked our bodies, but you're not going to fuck our minds."
>
> (MacLeod and Saraga, 1988, p. 39)

Feminism has a special claim to authority in that the identification of sexual abuse as a major social problem lay in the women's movement. Women attending crisis centres began to reveal a pattern of sexual abuse in their childhoods which had largely gone unrecognized by professionals. The feminist understanding of sexual abuse of children developed out of and secondarily to earlier concerns about family violence and sexual violence against adult women. Consequently, the major themes of this earlier stage colour feminist approaches to child sexual abusers. Ideas in the classic feminist texts on rape contain powerful clues about the nature of sexual offenders:

> "Man's discovery that his genitalia could serve as a weapon to generate fear must rank as one of the most important discoveries of prehistoric times, along with the use of fire and the first crude stone axe. From prehistoric times to the present, I believe, rape has played a critical function. It is nothing more or less than a conscious process of intimidation by which *all men* keep *all women* in a state of fear."
>
> (Brownmiller, 1975, pp. 14–15)

Brownmiller's insistence that *all* men are implicated and that male social power is exercised through sexualized violence has been a common theme. More empirically based publications by feminist and other writers confirmed that it is difficult to understand rape simply as a sexual crime aimed at sexual relief (Brownmiller, 1975; Burgess and Holmstrom, 1979; Sanders, 1980). Sexual crimes, like rape, can involve violence, brutality and terrorization way beyond what "sexual relief" would demand. This, together with evidence that men rape even immediately after having sex with a partner, greatly reduces the viability of any theory of rape based on notions of an out-of-control libido.

Feminist sexual politics have a number of important consequences. Firstly, explanations of paedophilia that relate it to the activities of *all* men are encouraged. Secondly, feminist writers dwell on the family as the context of abuse, thus extending the family violence tradition. This is achieved partly through a redefinition of concepts to meet the requirements of feminist theory. Howitt (1992) discusses how terms like "incest" become redefined to include, for example, acts perpetrated by "social uncles" with no legal or biological ties to the child. By extending the boundaries of the "family" in this way, offences come to have extra connotations of power and overtones of danger which the word "neighbour", say, singularly lacks. Incest is:

> "...'all unwanted sexual advances that occur between individuals who are involved in relationships of trust and in which one individual is subordinate to and possibly dependent upon the other'. This definition highlights the feminist principle that personal relationships involve power relationships which make the private realm a political one, thus making sexual politics an integral part of male–female and adult–child interactions..."
>
> (Dominelli, 1989, p. 297)

Of course, this should not be regarded as a deception, merely as a perspective on the issue which makes use of an opportunity to elevate the notion of male power to centre stage. As such, it is political in precisely the same way as are attempts by paedophile organizations to normalize paedophiliac activity. Another major characteristic of feminist discourse on sexual offending against children is its attempt to widen awareness of what might be considered abusive, especially by the children. Thus, while paedophile activists seek to present "flashing" as a relatively harmless nuisance crime, some feminists define it not only as sexual abuse (Kelly, 1988) but also as very dangerous.

> "Generally boys and men learn to experience their sexuality as an overwhelming and uncontrollable force; they learn to focus their sexual feelings on submissive objects, and they learn the assertion of their sexual desires, the expectation of having them serviced. Obviously this is a crude account of a complex phenomenon; male sexuality is not one-dimensional, and within a culture oppositional ideologies exist (for example, men as caretakers of their families, gentle lovers and protectors of their daughters), and have their impact on self-definition and cultural practices. Thus all men do not abuse, and sexual violence against women and children will have a different meaning, and different prevalences, within different societies at different times."
>
> (MacLeod and Saraga, 1988, p. 41)

Nevertheless, the problem is masculinity.

Feminist theory probably has more to say about the needs and treatment of the victims of sexual abuse than it has about the perpetrator. There is little pressure from within feminist theory to explain the difference between perpetrators and non-perpetrators. Given that children are commonly abused by adults with no particular demonic qualities, the potential to be an abuser can be seen as a male characteristic. After all, the rape of adult women is pervasive in all classes of males (Ellis, 1989). The high frequency of rape during dating is a strong pointer towards seeking what most men have in common rather than seeing what is different about those men convicted of rape (Russell, 1988).

Some aspects of feminist theory of sexual aggression have been absorbed into or are shared by other theoretical perspectives. In particular, the issue of distorted thinking in offenders is one given considerable attention. This partially relates to the myths about the offence and the victim that are held to support the offending (Burt, 1980). But it extends more widely to arguments against any attempt to transfer the blame to others—such as the wife of the offender. Why only some men offend has to be explained as a consequence of a sort of "hypermasculinity" in which some men have more offence-prone cognitions.

Frosh (1993), while taking on board much of the feminist viewpoint, adds his own emphasis:

> "The painful mixture of impulse and over-control, of separation and intimacy, of fear and desire—this mixture so common in men is also something that infiltrates men's relationships with children, sometimes leading to abuse. As sex is the only form of intimacy allowable to many men, all intimacy tends to turn to sex; as emotion is so linked with mastery and power, so threatening to it, then power is used where emotion would be more appropriate; as nurture is so feared, it is renounced, denied, brutalised. This is not true of all men, of course not. But this is what all men struggle with, at least now, at least here, at least while our experience is so pervasively, so damningly gendered."
>
> (Frosh, 1993, p. 54)

Whether this does more than move the explanation back to sex is a moot point. It does not explain why sex with adults does not provide intimacy for some men. Furthermore, as Frosh produces no evidence from offenders for his thesis, it may be regarded as suspect given the lack of reliable evidence for paedophiles' concern with power (Horley,

1988). It also clashes with the view that some wish to promote of the paedophile—as someone engaging in an unproblematic and affectionate relationship in which reciprocity rather than exploitation dominates (Sandfort, Brongersma and van Naerssen, 1991).

6. PAEDOPHILIA AS A BIOLOGICAL QUIRK

The simplistic hope that such complex sexual and social issues as homosexuality can be accounted for by a genetic or constitutional characteristic is attractive to many people. While paedophilia is often considered solvable by physical castration, research has not been extensive on possible biological abnormalities in paedophiles. One obvious possibility is that the sex hormones of paedophiles are in some way peculiar—they have too many, too few, too much or too much at the wrong stage in their lifecycle. Lang, Flor-Henry and Frenzel (1990) reviewed research on the sex hormone profiles of paedophiles and incestuous men. Summarizing previous findings, they concluded:

> "Overall, the findings indicate that a proportion—perhaps 5 to 15 percent—of sexually anomalous men appear to have some type of hormonal abnormality which may be linked to their sexual potency, testicular size, hypogonadism, end-organ resistance, and Leydig cell dysfunction. However ... there is no clear unusual hormonal profile in sexually aggressive or, for that matter, paraphilic men in general who engage in a nonviolent pattern of deviant sexual activity (incest or pedophilia)."
>
> (Lang, Flor-Henry and Frenzel, 1990, p. 63)

To gain better understanding, Lang, Flor-Henry and Frenzel took substantial samples of incest offenders, paedophiles and community controls. Details of the men's arousal to various slides using the penis volume measure were used to validate aspects of their sexuality. The hormones in blood samples taken early in the morning following fasting were analysed; there were differences in the mean amounts of the hormones prolactin, cortisol and androstenedione. Between 20 and 44% of *incest offenders* and between 9 and 20% of *paedophiles* showed clinically abnormal levels of these hormones; the order was always (from lowest to highest) controls, paedophiles, incest offenders. The researchers were somewhat reserved in their conclusions. For example, differences in levels of the hormones prolactin and cortisol may simply be due to the effects of different levels of stress present prior to the stressing life experiences of arrest and prosecution. Furthermore, psychological events and hormonal patterns do not exist in isolation from each other; they mutually interact and influence each other.

This theme of hormonal problems in paedophilia was dealt with more practically by Harrison *et al.* (1989) in a case study. Hyperprolactinaemia is a sex hormone abnormality involving prolactin which results in difficulties in sexual libido, arousal and ejaculation. Their patient, a 29-year-old storeman, had admitted indecent assault of a six-year-old, offences that continued for a further four years. The crimes:

> "took the form of kissing and fondling, after which he would masturbate, although with impaired potency and ejaculation. Sexual interest was only partly directed towards this girl, in that he also reported sexual fantasies involving adult women."
>
> (Harrison *et al.*, 1989, p. 847)

He was a poorly educated, shy and solitary person whose adult sexual experience involved just one woman, a relationship which ended two years before the offending began. Sexual problems contributed to the failure of the relationship. Low sex drive and difficulties in erection and ejaculation had disrupted sexual intercourse.

The drug bromocriptine was given and his prolactin levels achieved normal levels within six weeks. Simultaneously, there was a renewal of his libido, his erections and his ability to ejaculate. He claimed that his sexual fantasies were now solely about women and he was not interested in children, but his release from custody coincided with this so his claim seems particularly convenient. No relationships had been formed with adult women and it is an open question quite what his sexual proclivities actually were. The authors theorize how sexual dysfunction forced him towards children. On the other hand, this man was apparently capable of masturbating to thoughts of women but chose to masturbate over a young girl. Put in another way, what really drove him to offend against the child?

Other researchers have looked at the neuropsychological characteristics of paedophiles. Scott *et al.* (1984) compared sexual assaulters with paedophiles in a secure ward of a Nebraskan state psychiatric facility. All had been ordered to undergo evaluation for possible categorization of "mentally disordered sex offender". Men with signs of neurological impairment (e.g. a history of seizures, mental retardation or head trauma) were excluded. The control group consisted largely of non-hospitalized people:

> "... 55% of the subjects who had forcibly assaulted an adult male or female performed in the brain damaged range. The performance of another 32% could best be described as borderline. Eighteen percent of the subjects in this group performed within normal limits. In the pedophiles group, 36% met the criteria for diagnosing brain dysfunction, 29% performed in the borderline range, and 36% were neuropsychologically normal."
>
> (Scott *et al.*, 1984, p. 1117)

Neuropsychological information correctly classified 68% of normals, 50% of forcible sexual assaulters and 64% of paedophiles. While seemingly impressive, the misclassification of individuals is actually quite large; a third of normal men would be misclassified as either sexual assaulters or paedophiles. The authors claim that "for a large proportion of the rapists and paedophiles, cerebral dysfunction may be a contributing or dominant factor" (p. 1118). This particular sample of offenders had been referred to the hospital for assessment for mental disorder, thus they may have been pre-selected by the system in a way that ensured more neurological abnormalities than is generally the case.

A similar approach measures brainwave activity using the electroencephalograph (EEG). Flor-Henry *et al.* (1991) compared a large sample of court-referred paedophiles at forensic services at an Alberta Hospital, Canada, with a community sample recruited by newspaper advertisements. Phallometry and interviews were used to categorize men as paedophiles, hebephiles and incest offenders. Although the offenders were much the same as the controls in general, paedophiles differed in terms of the power and coherence of their EEG traces:

> "The general pattern of increased delta, theta and alpha power with reduced interhemispheric but increased intrahemispheric–interhemispheric coherence, with normal EEG state during spatial processing, suggests in this sexual deviation a neurophysiological instability of the dominant hemisphere, with dysregulation of interhemispheric relationships."
>
> (Flor-Henry *et al.*, 1991, p. 257)

The authors hold that sexual deviation may be the result of abnormal ideas that are the consequence of changes in the functions of the dominant cerebral hemisphere. Pathology of the dominant hemisphere encourages abnormal sexual ideas and is involved in problems in the communication between the two halves of the brain (the non-dominant hemisphere being involved in the orgasmic response):

> "Thus it would appear that the male pattern of brain organization—more lateralized for both verbal and visuospatial cognitive modes—and also more vulnerable in its verbal–linguistic dominant axis, carries with it an increased susceptibility to aberrant sexual programming."
>
> (Flor-Henry *et al.*, 1991, pp. 256–257)

Considerable reservations ought to be expressed about this theory. It suggests that offenders have problems with the organization of thoughts within and between the different halves of the brain. For some reason this results in deviant sexual thoughts. Since the cerebral organization of men is more susceptible to problems, this might explain paedophilia's relative absence in women. But there are difficulties with this. First of all, it is not a finding that has received independent confirmation. Secondly, why are not all of the thought patterns of the offender deviant if cerebral malfunctioning is responsible for sexually deviant thought? There is little evidence that deviant thinking is characteristic of all aspects of paedophile thought. Indeed, paedophiles tend to be psychologically similar to men in general.

Pontius (1988) illustrates the brain dysfunction implicated in sex offences with a case study of a child molester with a temporal lobe dysfunction in the left-hand side of the brain. Mr M. was a single man of average intelligence who graduated from high school; a heterosexual, he was the father of a six-year-old son. Nevertheless, when he was babysitting his son's playmate, another six-year-old boy, he fellated him:

> "Mr M. had no previous history of pedophilia, nor of any homosexual contact; he claimed he never masturbated and felt he needed only sporadic heterosexual contact since age 15. He had not been sexually abused as a child; the beginning of such a potential attempt by an adult male was aborted at the stage of exhibition when Mr M. was about 8 years old. Around the time of the incident of 'rape of a child,' as the charge was called, Mr M. did not feel sexually aroused. He had had some beer and some drugs ('pot' and possibly some cocaine and/or 'speed'), but was not drunk and recalled the incident quite well."
>
> (Pontius, 1988, p. 150)

The man was horrified by his actions and was intensely remorseful. For two years he had nightmares of the death of the child during the offence. Other bad dreams included wolves "tearing people apart" with heads and arms being bloodily ripped off. He was born with defects to his chest, foot and hand on the left side of his body and had received head injuries at the ages of 9 and 13; the resulting seizures were controlled by drugs.

The lack of systematic data of the association between this type of neurological problem and paedophilia makes such a single case study difficult to interpret.

Brain symmetry has been studied by some, including Wright *et al.* (1990), who examined the brain scans of a variety of sex offenders and non-violent non-sex offender controls. It is notable that the left brain hemispheres of offenders tend to be smaller than those of normal controls, although paedophiles were more like controls than sexual aggressors against adult women or incest offenders. Paedophiles differed from controls and the incest offenders and sexual aggressors against adult women—a far greater proportion of them had smaller left brain hemispheres than right hemispheres. This possibly suggests that structural abnormalities are commoner in the brains of sexual offenders.

Castration and Other Biological Remedies

> "...I know from experience that if we cut the balls off an offender as punishment, the first thing he would be likely to do when we release him is to castrate or mutilate another child. It's simply a question of anger. Equally, it is my experience that chemical castration is not reliable, and I have worked with a number of men who have offended whilst they were taking treatment."
>
> (Wyre, in Tate, 1990, pp. 272–273)

Castration as a treatment for paedophiles has an emotive appeal for some. One cannot escape the odium that sterilization engenders and the considerable ethical and moral imperatives associated with it. Nevertheless, it is generally held to be a successful treatment for sex offenders by reviewers. For example, Crawford (1981) suggested:

> "Castration, if it is to be used at all, would seem most appropriate for those offenders whose sexual drive is so strong that they experience overpowering sexual feelings which they are unable to control. The habitual aggressive rapist, for example, would intuitively seem to fit

> into this category. For the majority of pedophiles, however, the notion of excessively high levels of sexual drive and overpowering sexual urges motivating their offences seems inappropriate. The feelings they report towards children are more often ones of love and tenderness, emotions which are not reportedly eliminated by castration."
>
> (Crawford, 1981, p. 184)

Some argue that castration is extremely effective in reducing recidivism rates (Bradford, 1988). He mentions four studies indicating that, following surgery, the recidivism rates are under 4%. This contrasts markedly with recidivism rates of 60% or more prior to castration.

Judicial castration has a fairly distasteful pedigree (Sturup, 1972). For example, it was introduced in Kansas in 1855 to deal with black men who raped or attempted to rape white women. Similarly, Nazi Germany in 1933 allowed castration for men who murdered to satisfy their sex drives and for men who were evaluated as being dangerous sex criminals who had previously offended or had received a sentence of a year or more. Between 1899 and 1921, therapeutic castration was employed in the United States although it was finally abolished as unconstitutional. Some countries (Denmark and Germany) have legislated to help doctors to carry out therapeutic castration rather than for its judicial use.

Recidivism rates in studies in Denmark, Germany, Sweden, Norway, Holland and Switzerland for mixed groups of offenders are substantially under 10%, with a range from about 1 to 7% (Sturup, 1972). These are not out of line with his own study of 900 men castrated between 1929 and 1959. At the time of surgery 44% were at institutions for mental defectives; only 18% were not institutionalized. Forty per cent were castrated following just one offence. The follow-up period varied, but over 60% were followed up for more than six years. A small percentage retained their sexual drive for lengthy periods after the operation. When crimes followed castration, their severity tended to be less extreme. It is difficult to say precisely what the recidivism rate is; Sturup suggests less than 4% but this includes those whose sexual patterns did not really change and was based on the assumption that all of them were in the category of repeat offenders. A figure of 1% is a truer reflection of the actual data. One must qualify recidivism rates with the caution that official recidivism may only be a fraction of reoffending itself. Furthermore, the men in these studies were essentially volunteers, which might be indicative of their success in any form of therapy, and it is not clear how many men were returned permanently to the community. Nevertheless, Sturup concludes:

> "The social results of this technique can now be demonstrated on the basis of large numbers of cases followed for a long period of time. In any case, castration seems no more harmful to a man's potential for a normal life than the alternative of a very long imprisonment."
>
> (Sturup, 1972, p. 381)

Such arguments appear to make a convincing case for castrating paedophiles but this is not quite so, because the treatment was generally given to undifferentiated groups of sex offenders. Thus, little is known of any paedophiles among them. Sizeable numbers of paedophiles confine their sexual activities with children to those for which libido and erections are unnecessary (touching through clothing, for example). When one considers also the case histories of paedophiles who show very little interest in orgasmic penetrative intercourse with any sort of partner, one wonders what function castration would serve in these circumstances.

The alternative to surgical castration is medical castration through the administration of drugs. This began in the 1960s in Germany and Switzerland with cyproterone and cyproterone acetate (CPA). These drugs were not made available for research, so substitutes were found in medroxyprogesterone acetate (MPA) or Depo-Provera (Money, 1972) in the USA. This synthetic steroid, which counteracts sex hormones (Wettstein, Kelly and Cavanaugh, 1982), has been shown to reduce plasma testosterone and, perhaps as a consequence, sexual interest and activity. Injection into muscle may lower testosterone levels for between 7 and 10 days. The greater the dose, the greater the loss of libido, then erections, then orgasms. Treatment of sexual deviations with the drug diminish sexual fantasy and yearnings while maintaining or increasing acceptable sexual activity. Money (1972) writes of the drug's effects as:

> "Loss of the capability of erection and ejaculation is accompanied by a concomitant reduction of the feeling of sexual urge or lust ... It may be reported as loss of drive or as a lessening of tension and nervousness. It is not reported as unpleasant or anxiety-producing, although it may seem strange ... Recognition of personal deprivation is offset by knowledge that the effect is reversible and by the feeling of release from a nagging sexual compulsion ... Loss of the feeling of lust does not entail automatic loss of ability to be attentive to stimuli formerly associated with sexual arousal. It is rather that the frequency of

> attentiveness is diminished, and the carry-through to behavior is impeded or inhibited."
>
> (Money, 1972, pp. 354–355)

Wettstein, Kelly and Cavanaugh (1982) mention the case of a man in his 40s who was referred following two arrests. He had a 15-year history of convictions for sexual involvement with boys although he had never been sent to prison. Psychiatric treatment for low self-esteem and feelings of inadequacy had little tangible effect on his paedophilia:

> "He lived with his parents, had never married, and had visited female prostitutes through the years. His medical history was remarkable for obesity, hypertension, and borderline diabetes mellitus. Family history was also positive for diabetes."
>
> (Wettstein, Kelly and Cavanaugh, 1982, p. 158)

The drug was injected intramuscularly, and eventually blood testosterone levels reduced to one-tenth of their pre-treatment values. Sexual fantasies declined as well as sexual urges and inappropriate sexual behaviours. Other gains included decreases in anxiety and irritability and improved relations with his family and workmates. He was involved with psychotherapy at the same time.

Single case studies of this sort tend to be a triumph of hope over evidence. Hucker, Langevin and Bain (1988) carried out a more impressive trial of the effects of the drug on reduction of paedophile activity. They argue that earlier studies demonstrate that about a quarter of offenders drop out of medical treatments. Refusal to take part in such treatments ought to be considered also. A study of 100 consecutive cases referred to the forensic service of a Canadian institute of psychiatry illustrates these factors well. All of the men had been charged with or convicted of contact sexual offences with children. Only 48 were willing to take part in a comprehensive assessment programme. But of most importance for those who consider voluntary physical or chemical castration a solution to sexual abuse, just 18 men were prepared to participate in a three-month double blind trial of MPA versus placebo control. Homosexual paedophiles predominated among those agreeing to this treatment. To this chapter of difficulties, it should be added that one case was dropped on emerging health grounds and another was apparently not taking his tablets (hormone changes that should have happened with MPA did not). Worse still, five more dropped out on their own account.

A clear correlate of refusing or accepting treatment was that the acceptors were brighter. Those dropping out during treatment tended to have higher levels of sexual fantasies about children and adults during treatment, although they did not differ prior to treatment. Few significant changes were found on the sexual urges questionnaire. While the authors claim that the drug significantly reduced sexual thoughts and fantasies, this cannot be sustained. The data actually show that the amount of change for the placebo was 28.0 sexual thoughts down to 8.7, and for the experimental group, 11.6 down to 5.8. One could claim on the basis of this that the placebo was actually more effective than the real drug! Masturbation, intercourse and total orgasms did not change significantly—indeed, for masturbation and total orgasms the big changes were in the control group. Nevertheless the authors conclude:

> "The side effects seen in the present study were infrequent and justify the continued use of MPA for pedophiles. Most common were mild depression, fatigue, and increased salivation. In no case was a clinically noteworthy change witnessed which required major medical intervention or discontinuation of the MPA trial. Certainly MPA appears effective. The major problem facing clinicians is increasing compliance in pedophiles by educating them about the usefulness of MPA for their sexual problems."
>
> (Hucker, Langevin and Bain, 1988, pp. 240–241)

In the light of such difficulties, one should be cautious about the likely success of chemicals on paedophilia. Some claim success. Bradford (1988) reviewed seven studies of drugs and suggests, in particular, that CPA is effective. Recidivism prior to the drug treatment was commonly between 50 and 100%. Following the administration of the drugs, the recidivism was claimed to be zero in all but one study. Cooper and Cernovovsky (1992) discuss some of the evidence which suggests that the effects of CPA on phallometric assessment is variable and that responsiveness to erotic stimuli may increase in (perhaps) isolated cases. In Cooper and Cernovovsky's study laboratory arousal while awake was varied under CPA and showed nowhere near the decrease that nocturnal erections did. They suggest that the mechanism by which CPA influences the offender is to diminish cognitive processes, especially fantasy. That these are not eliminated entirely may not be important compared to the way in which a reduction enables the offender to get his acting out under control. Meyer (1992) carried out a study of Depo-Provera (MPA) on recidivism in a group of mainly paedophiles. While on the drug the men were less likely to reoffend than when this treatment stopped. For the paedophiles, recidivism was 13% while under treatment but 28% while not taking the drug. A "control" group of paedophile patients who refused the drug treatment had a reoffence rate of 50%.

Despite this data, however, physical and chemical castration have relatively few advocates among specialists in the field. Not all reviewers are as keen on castration as the authors discussed so far. Travin *et al.* (1985a) are less than advocates of castration since they argue that following castration sexual activities are common among men. So, for example, 40% of men continue with intercourse after castration and half get full erections while watching sex films.

ON THEORIES

The clearest impression left by the theories of paedophilia is that there are a good many ways of understanding it. What is uncertain is which approach is the best and for what purpose it is best. But such conclusions probably should not be drawn. For anyone working with sexual offenders some of the theories may create anger because they appear sympathetic to the offender; others may annoy because of their simplicity and failure to engage widely with the issues involved in offending. Nevertheless, it is valuable to be aware of the variety of viewpoints available in order to retain openness of mind. The risk is that offenders are understood in terms of relatively simple formulae for action which stifle judgement rather than aid it (Howitt, 1992).

CHAPTER 6

Paedophilia and Fantasy

> "'I hate to bother you with my little PERSONAL PROBLEM,' says the caption over a beautiful two-year-old on the front of a greeting card. Curiosity aroused, you look inside. She is sitting in her nappy, no other clothes. The caption reads, 'BUT I'M HORNY!!' The card, published by Mark 1 from the US, is readily available in stationery shops throughout the UK."
>
> (Elliott, 1992, p. 215)

With good reason, the relationship between sexual fantasy and sexual offending has yet to be clearly understood; little research has put fantasy centre-stage. For example, in a recent major book on sex offenders and their victims (Hollin and Howells, 1991), sexual fantasy is indexed for just a single page. The role of violent fantasy in serial murder has been researched (MacCulloch *et al.*, 1983; Ressler, Burgess and Douglas, 1988) but its role in paedophilia largely neglected. Eliciting fantasy in the usual psychiatric and penal institutions settings of research is not easy. The offender may associate fantasy with mental illness or as being something that the authorities will regard as a bad indicator of his future conduct. For such reasons, he may prefer to present his crimes as a momentary lapse rather than a lifetime erotic focus on children; he might advance "explanations" in terms of stress at work or the breakdown of his marriage rather than reveal that he harbours criminogenic fantasies about sex with blond-haired nine-year-old boys. Detailed discussion of our sexual fantasies is not everyday practice despite jokey allusions to them. But this sort of banter really only touches upon the still taboo topic of masturbatory fantasy. Given this, people are unlikely to find it easy to discuss their fantasy with strangers in the early stages of therapy, let alone during a prison assessment interview.

What do we know about sexual fantasy and offending? This may not be a simple question of cause and effect but one or more complicated matters of the interplay between the two. Do, for example, the themes of an offender's fantasy indicate likely offending patterns? In some cases there seems to be considerable divergence between the two; others show a more perfect match. An offender, for example, may fantasize that he is copulating with or buggering a child but, in a lifetime of abusing, limit his overt physical contact to fondling children through their clothing. The imperfect match is not restricted to offender groups. Seemingly normal women, for example, may report sexual fantasies largely unrelated to their sexual practices or even desires in real life:

> "Before I was married I went out with a crazy guy, not black, but very far out. I remember once lying on the beach, there was no one else around, and I was lying on my stomach. He stood up, and the first thing I knew he was peeing on my bare back. I screamed and jumped up, but I was laughing—I was mad about him—and our tussle on the beach ended up with him inside me, needless to say. I have never wanted to be peed on in reality, before or since, but this idea of the very well-endowed black man peeing for ages onto my clitoris ... it's a winner every time."
>
> (Friday, 1976, pp. 167–168)

This fantasy seems to be a complex mixture of cultural myths, personal experience and fulfilment in the imagination. In other words, the fantasy exists in a separate domain from overt actions despite being a synthesis based on experience. It does not require acting out in reality in order to be satisfactory, since it functions effectively as an accompaniment to masturbation or sexual intercourse to maximize pleasure.

Offenders who are persuaded to talk intimately about their fantasies reveal them to be varied in their extent and nature. They range from "obsessive" fantasizing which dominates waking time to the individual who denied that fantasy had a significant role in his thoughts (although this man claimed to be a "skilled" dreamer on sexual matters). Sometimes the fantasy is no more vivid than a dim image, much as a faded black-and-white "snapshot" photograph. On the other hand, the imagery of some men was much more detailed, with touch, smell, texture and other sensations. In some cases, the offender was capable of "editing" the fantasy at appropriate points, rewinding the "film", and changing faces of children for other, more preferred, ones. Nevertheless, by and large fantasies veered more towards the mundane and limited.

THE PORNOGRAPHY QUESTION

> "Pornography does predispose some men to commit sexual abuse, and I have little doubt that the predisposition for some men can actually lie solely in the area of pornography. In other words, for some men it is just pornography—and nothing else—which creates the predisposition to commit sexual abuse."
>
> (Wyre, 1992, pp. 237–238)

While no one has demonstrated decisively the relationship between fantasy and action, the lay public and some experts on sex offenders tend to regard the link as a matter of proven cause and effect. Wyre, for example, apparently never has to date presented a single detailed case study of a paedophile in print, let alone one which demonstrates his thesis. Perhaps, as a consequence, one need not spend too much time on his assertion that fantasy can be the precursor to crime, obtained from the fantasy content of pornography. Common-sense theories tend to be contradictory. For example, there is a lot to be said for the notion of fantasy as substitute for action, a largely separate stream of experience or a substitute for reality. The original psychoanalytic view of fantasy as wish fulfilment took a similar stance. Nevertheless, there has been little acknowledgement of this in the debate on the effects of pornography and the legislation that has accompanied it (although exceptions include McCormack, 1988; van Naerssen *et al.*, 1987; Vine, 1990). The feminist slogan "pornography is the theory, rape the practice" (Morgan, 1978) encapsulates the view that fantasy is the precursor to action. Some theorists see it as a cognitive process in which the offender learns false social norms and expectations from pornography. Thus, the role of pornography may be different from creating vivid sexual images which, at first, are used to accompany masturbation but later are inflicted on a victim. While some therapists see fantasy as part of an escalating offending cycle (once again, Wyre (1990) being an extreme case in point), the direct evidence for this is slight. One cannot simply take evidence that offenders use and buy pornography as sufficient to implicate pornography causally in their offending. The most reasonable assessment based on the available research literature is that the relationship between pornography, fantasy and offending is unclear.

Often issues get confused when pornography is debated. The control of pornography might well be desirable simply on the grounds of its intrinsic offensiveness to sectors of the public (e.g. Cowan, Chase and Stahly, 1989; Eysenck and Nias, 1978). Unfortunately, the offensiveness issue tends to be confounded with public concern about the harm done by pornography. Of course, harm to the user of pornography is a common legal test of obscenity—its ability "to deprave and corrupt" (Taylor, 1984)—but the modern feminist view has emphasized the additional harm condition whereby people—women and children especially—are increasingly at risk of sexual violence because of pornography's sexually violent themes (Howitt, 1991; Russell, 1988). Such arguments are commonly made by opponents of pornography; frequently they are promoted by the mass media themselves (Howitt, 1994). Controversies concerning other social issues use the same structure. Drugs, media violence, poverty, promiscuity and education yield similar harm theses. Despite being superficially different, the rhetoric remains much the same. Third parties, not oneself, are held to be at greatest risk (Innes and Zeitz, 1988).

Harm theses are usually expressed simplistically; that looking at pornography will make men commit sex crimes takes a commonsensical appearance. This can also be seen in the political response to official reports such as the US Commission on Obscenity and Pornography (1970) and the British Williams Report (1979). Latterly, Howitt and Cumberbatch (1990) failed to find strong evidence of the adverse effects of pornography which prompted one government minister to comment:

> "There can be little doubt that pornography has an insidious and dehumanising effect on attitudes to women and family relations."
>
> (The Home Secretary, Home Office press release, 20 December 1990)

Similar attitudes have spawned much research into the effects of pornography since the late 1960s, when the United States government first commissioned psychological and other research into obscenity and pornography (Commission on Obscenity and Pornography, 1970). Indeed, the origins of social scientific interest in pornography trace back to this single initiative; virtually no research had been done until then. A major theme in this earlier research was the effect of pornography on sexuality in general, including such matters as promiscuity and illegitimacy—major social and moral concerns of the time. During the 1970s, under the influence of feminist ideas (Brownmiller, 1975; Burgess and Holmstrom, 1979; Lederer, 1980; Russell, 1975), the research emphasis shifted to the question of sexual violence (Cumberbatch and Howitt, 1989).

Despite changes in emphasis, questions concerning pornography continue to be framed mostly in terms of effects. The debate has been acrimonious and controversial, not only within academia but also in the responses of politicians and pressure groups (Brannigan and Goldenberg, 1987; Cline, 1974; Wilcox, 1987). Psychology has been central to the debate, largely because of experiments (e.g. Donnerstein and Linz, 1986) that allowed causal interpretations—though at the price of ecological validity (Brannigan, 1987).

Attention ought to be directed towards sexually violent crime rather than peripheral matters such as sexual arousal or promiscuity, which are only tangentially related to the crime issue (as are most laboratory studies, which demonstrate a marked lack of even superficial validity). Statistical investigations of crime statistics have dominated the more ecologically valid studies of pornography. These studies have had a variety of foci, but especially changes in the known crime rates in response to putative changes in the availability of pornography and similar time series analyses (Court, 1977, 1984; Kutchinsky, 1973, 1991), as well as comparisons of sex crime rates in regions differing in the amounts of sex magazines in circulation (Baron and Straus, 1987, 1989). Of these authors, Court alone suggests that pornography causes sexual crime. It is well known that Kutchinsky's rejection of the "pornography causes sex crime" thesis has been controversial (e.g. Bachy, 1976). An obvious limitation of such studies is that they consist of macro level analyses which, at best, can tell us little directly about how offenders use pornography and are possibly influenced by it psychologically. To emphasize the point, in general the authors of these studies have not implicated pornography in sexual crime, although others have interpreted the data differently (e.g. Baxter, 1990).

Investigations of sex offenders themselves, rather than official crime statistics, might offer greater insight into the links between sexual crime and pornography. Whether or not using appropriate control groups, these studies tend to show fairly high levels of exposure to pornography during late childhood and adolescence among sexual offenders in general. But, set against fairly high levels of exposure to such material in the general population, the differences found between sex offenders and others are often relatively small and statistically insignificant, or tend to suggest that offenders have less experience with pornography (Carter and Prentky, 1990; Carter *et al.*, 1987; Cook and Fosen, 1970; Gebhard *et al.*, 1965; Goldstein, 1973; Goldstein and Kant, 1973). Similarly, studies of the age of first exposure to pornography show offenders to be no different from controls or to become involved with pornography later in adolescence (Condron and Nutter, 1988; Walker, 1970). Whatever else, a clear-cut adverse link between sexual crime and pornography has not been demonstrated by such statistical studies—neither for age of initial use of the material nor for the amount consumed.

Studies that treat sex offenders as a relatively homogeneous group, undifferentiated according to offence (Knight and Prentky, 1990; Knight, Rosenberg and Schneider, 1985) find no differences in offenders' potential to be aroused by or preferences for different types of pornography (Carter *et al.*, 1987; Cook and Fosen, 1970; Johnson, Kupperstein and Petters, 1970). Consideration of research examining different offender types might reform this impression. Rapists of adult women are especially aroused by images of violence against women (Abel *et al.*, 1977; Barbaree, Marshall and Lanthier, 1979; Hinton, O'Neill and Webster, 1980; Quinsey, Chaplin and Upton, 1984).

Turning to the current use of pornography at the time of their offending, it has been shown over the last 30 years or so that there is no strong and consistent trend for sexual offenders to be more avid consumers of pornography than other men. Cook and Fosen (1970), Goldstein *et al.* (1970), Johnson, Kupperstein and Petters (1970) and Walker (1970) all suggest that offenders are similar to non-offenders—what differences emerge imply that offenders are less frequent users of pornography. Langevin *et al.* (1988) interviewed over 200 offenders and 150 controls but found no evidence that pornography was a factor in the offending. Goldstein (1973), in contrast, reports that many more of his rapists claimed to have been aroused to masturbate by pornography than his control group did. The proportions of offenders blaming pornography for their offending vary. Becker and Stein (1991) found 10% making such a claim, while half of child molesters claimed incitement by pornography in Marshall's (1988) study.

Offenders' claims about pornography's influence on their lives may be self-serving; for example, by helping them to avoid self-blame for offences. Research on offenders demonstrates a paucity of interest in the development of deviant sexual fantasy. The use of self-completion questionnaires in much of the relevant research may not be conducive to complete disclosure of something as sensitive as fantasy. It would appear that the existence of deviant fantasy among some offenders is established (Carter *et al.*, 1987). Nevertheless, it might be naive to speculate that particular detailed types of fantasy accompany certain types of offence, let alone suggest what these types might be. It is a matter of conjecture how early sexual experiences might relate to fantasy (Howitt and Cumberbatch, 1990) but even mainstream research suggests that it is fairly common for offenders to have been physically and sexually abused as children (Becker and Stein, 1991; Carter *et al.*, 1987; Seghorn, Prentky and Boucher, 1987). Significantly, Rhue and Lynn (1987) found that high levels of fantasy were associated with severe physical abuse in childhood—a characteristic not uncommon in the childhoods of paedophiles, as we have seen.

Surveys and other statistical approaches have failed to provide clear information about the ways in which sexual offending relates to the use of pornography. There has typically been very little opportunity taken to investigate in detail the interplay between the offender as an individual and his experience of pornography. Virtually no extensive case studies are available on offenders, with the exception of Kutchinsky's (1976) account of the long-term sexual history of a "peeper". He was an active sexual deviant many years before first seeing pornography; his deviant impulses were channelled by pornography, not created by them.

Following an extensive review of the research on pornography and sexual violence, Howitt and Cumberbatch (1990) wrote:

> "... the general assumption of the available research is that normal men and deviants get the same sorts of things out of pornography and that it is exposure as such which is the critical factor. Of course, this is an assumption which is useful to researchers, it does not itself mean that individuals with deviant tendencies process pornography in exactly the same way as 'non-deviant' men."
>
> (Howitt and Cumberbatch, 1990, p. 44)

Case studies reveal the complexity underlying the superficially simple question of how sexual fantasy, perhaps stimulated by pornography, is involved in paedophile offending. The case studies discussed in this chapter are men with long-standing criminal paedophile records. The choice of research location is vital to enable the elicitation of fantasy material, since the institutional context may inhibit disclosure by encouraging denial or motivated distortions, for example, because offenders make assumptions about the interrelationships between researchers and management. I decided to research a group of paedophiles in a treatment setting in which this particular motivated distortion was less likely. The men were all well into their assessment or treatment programmes, in which disclosure concerning the offences, pornography and histories of being abused, *inter alia*, had been stressed. An atmosphere of disclosure seemed to be more conducive to effective research. Certainly there was little or no evidence of the denial that some see as characteristic of sex offenders in the early stages of assessment (Wyre, 1987). Spontaneous comments during the interviews indicated that sensitive information would have been withheld in penal settings. Only a smallz amount of the material gathered can be reported; topics are confined largely to the use of and experience with pornography, fantasy and sexual history, especially related to childhood sexual experiences.

Case 1: Brian

When Brian was about 10 years old, he first saw pornographic magazines which his stepfather kept in a cupboard. By 13, he was masturbating to magazines obtained from a friend; titles such as *Fiesta*, which are considered to be of the "soft-core" type. Brian's fantasies were not of women in the main—his sexual history reveals little or no involvement with them. In his adolescence he used "non-pornographic pornography":

> "things like clothing catalogues, that is you've got children in their underwear or dressing gowns, whatever or even in the toy catalogues ... they show you an outdoor swimming pool inflated and they show the children in it, but the children would not be naked and that sort of thing ... Just normal clothing catalogues from like Kay's [a mail order company] ... children that are dressed in underwear or nightdresses or swimming costumes ... Sometimes I would deface the pictures as well. By drawing penises into their mouth or vagina or draw them urinating ... things like reading ... in the paper about abuse, that would cause

> masturbation ... you'd see young children getting into bed, or young children undressed naked, there was quite a lot of that on TV, and even simple things like adverts ..."

This erotic interest notwithstanding, he claims not to have seen commercial child pornography. It is his belief that his "non-pornographic pornography" had an indirect role in his offending because it strengthened the desire to be involved with children. Similar self-made pornography is discussed in Holmes (1991). In terms of childhood sexual abuse, Brian claimed:

> "... I first became a victim when I was 10, I was getting abused ... I felt our parents sent us out to the park on a regular basis at weekends, 'cause they wanted to get rid of us, 'cause we are under their feet ... I had a brother who was eight and a brother who was five and ended up getting involved with this guy or should I say that this guy got involved with us, paying us money for sexual acts ..."

His abuse of other children began at 13 years, when he was in a children's home.

Case 2: Bernard

Bernard has had a long-term fantasy of sex (vaginal and anal) with a particular physical "type" of woman as well as an obsession concerning his beliefs about the small size of his penis. Although he said that he had been interested in "blue videos", he was deterred because of the largeness of the male genitals in such material. He admitted to enjoying magazines containing pictures of naked women which:

> "gave me ideas ... sometimes I would fantasize [about] them but basically I'd say the fantasy [of vaginal and anal sex with a particular physical type] was the overriding thing ..."

It was not until he was in the army that he saw pornographic material. He suggests that:

> "... I am weird because my fantasy stayed constant since I was young ... throughout my life since I was say 13–14 it has always been women's bottoms and girls' bottoms ... been with me all the time."

He claimed that newspapers or films in which a woman "showed" her "bum" would start him fantasizing. Bernard had extensively photographed adult women although he had not taken "self-made" pornography of his girl victims, although:

> "with the two girls involved this last time I actually brought a Polaroid camera with the intention of taking pornographic pictures, but I just couldn't bring myself to do it."

His offences were indecent assaults on females.

Case 3: Adrian

Adrian is a prolific fantasizer capable of manipulating his imagery extensively. His offending had been against boys and had started while he was still at preparatory school. He had used pornography as part of the "grooming process"—the preparation of circumstances appropriate to initiating the offence. His collection of pornography had at one stage been worth £7000 cost price and included "hard-core" material such as *Boys International*, *Golden Boys* and *Male International*. He claims to have first seen this sort of material at the age of 16 while he was still at boarding school. However, his sources of fantasy included videos and television:

> "Walt Disney is very good ... There are a lot of children's videos and some of them like *American Scout Troops* and things like that ... *Grange Hill* [a school series] type of things you know ..."

He also used other sources such as naturist beaches:

> "... or I would be watching the television and a boy who's blond would come up on the television, clothed, fully clothed ... but then I would take that picture of the boy, use my fantasy to undress him, I put the parts that I had in my memory to fantasize and to build up ... I could see a boy ... who was clothed, say, on a bicycle. I could take that boy I could put him into shorts so I could see what he looked like ... A typical example ... if I watch *Huckleberry Finn* on the television, I can get to a point that I am going to think about him, I might even change the whole situation, by fantasizing and masturbating over him ... [A] poster with three boys or three girls, or a boy and two girls, sticking their tongues out on a big poster by the side of the road; and I fantasized of how the boy would look ... so that he was naked."

Case 4: Garry

Garry admitted that he had looked at pornography in prison but that it did not interest him really:

> "I think it's a right rip-off the price they charge for it. I have watched a few blue movies but neither here or there ... I think I might have gone into some photographic stuff 'cause I was up on top of the tower block and I was in a very privileged position in the summer especially when I could look down onto lots of back gardens and there was quite a few back gardens which had kids ... The only ... magazine that I got ... the odd one that was brought to work, and that was the spanking magazine ... and that was normally schoolgirls about 13, 14 that type of age ... I think a lot of them turned me on because I was so horribly treated when I was 13 or 14 myself and I think it's me getting back at them ... revenge."

This refers to incidents with female peers during adolescence. He had seen videos of a soft-porn sort but tends to regard them as humorous:

> "I get turned on more by what they're wearing ... suggestive ... if they were completely bare with a bare backside it wouldn't really turn me on ... if they were wearing certain clothes it would turn me on more ..."

He denied using pornography in pre-offence preparation. Although spanking was part of his later offending, it was he who was spanked—a reversal of his fantasy. His initial offending was indecent exposure to children but later on there was contact abuse. Garry had been sexually abused by a stranger at the age of about 10 or 11, which involved masturbation and oral sex to the man. He also claims to have witnessed men indecently exposing themselves before this age.

Case 5: George

George's offending involved touching girls in the 8- to 15-year-old age group under their clothing. He had not seen any pornography until his late 40s. *Esquire* type magazines he found interesting but repetitive. A couple of years before the interview he had a collection of soft-porn videos. None of this material had been used in relation to his victims. George had neither seen any pornography involving children nor taken photographs of his victims. Describing his sexual fantasies, he said:

> "I would suddenly be in a dream and there would be one there but it was a loving relationship. I wouldn't dash her on the ground and jump on her or anything like that. It was kissing and hugging."

He describes his fantasies about children as being very similar to this fantasy with adults.

Case 6: Charlie

Charlie's earliest sexual experiences were with other boys during adolescence. His first heterosexual experience was with his future wife while at university following a period of time in the army. However, sexual fantasies involving boys tended to dominate over heterosexual ones even during this time. His preferred age group with boys was the 9- to 13-year-olds, particularly blond haired, blue eyed, athletic types. For a period his paedophiliac contact was largely "horseplay", which created sexual arousal but did not reach the stage of illegality. He would cut pictures from scout magazines, which provided erotic arousal. Nudity did not feature and the material was personally selected "non-pornographic pornography". Early on, his fantasies did not involve nakedness but this changed in his 40s after he moved in for a while with a family, when he saw his victim in various stages of undress every day—in the shower and so forth.

Case 7: Michael

Michael sees the origins of his fantasy in childhood visits to Saturday morning children's movie matinées. He identified strongly with the heroes:

> "I remember at 10 or 11 years of age being sexually aroused by the … heroine tied to a chair or a railway track or wherever, and when I was 11 or 12 … we often used to have large family get togethers and my cousin who was almost my age (a girl) and we used to be left to our own devices, the family would talk 'adult' talk, we would go away and play with my train set. But very often through that 11, 12, 13 we would play kidnap games where I would tie her up and I got great arousal from that, and of course I used it as fantasy and masturbation and got sexual pleasure/enjoyment out of it … It seemed fun, we both looked on it as fun and I never saw anything sinister about it, and it was the first moment of sexual arousal and it sowed the seeds for what has become a pattern of offending throughout the years."

This pattern of tying up an adolescent/pre-adolescent girl and going elsewhere to masturbate in private reflects the man's adulthood offending very precisely:

"... I would tie her up, talk through a story (I would invent a story) and then I would leave her to go and masturbate and then come back and untie her. In fact most of the girls weren't even properly tied because one of the devices when I had finished I would say 'just untie yourself' which they could."

His use of pornography in the conventional sense seems to have been nil, but he did report that:

"There was a period when I discovered a bookshop ... where they had bondage magazines and occasionally I would smuggle a magazine like that, I think I worried myself sick for the duration and ended up putting it in the bin somewhere far away. I was scared of discovery ... these were photograph magazines, sometimes in the form of a weekly story which was really just a vehicle for the bondage."

This was during his late teenage years to early 20s. In his 30s, living away from home for the first time:

"... if I saw bits and pieces of cartoons where someone was tied up I would cut them out and make a collage. And when I was feeling isolated or needed a bit of stimulates [sic] I would fantasize to these pictures."

During his offending period in his middle age, he began to use Polaroid cameras to take picture of his "target" child but nudity as such was of little or no interest to him in his fantasy:

"In fact I have seen a couple of the heavy bondage magazines and they completely turn me off. I can't understand them at all ... If I was watching television which showed some girls or even grown ups (because I fantasized about grown ups through television as well), I would video the film and then watch it when I was alone finding the particular point in the film that I could masturbate to."

Case 8: Terry

Terry abused his three stepdaughters, including having full sexual intercourse with one of them from 10 to 18 years. A feature of his early life was sexual assault at the age of 4 to 6 years by his elder brother, including oral sex, and a sister from about 7 to 10 years. Although he knows his father sexually abused his sisters, he did not abuse Terry. More dominant is his first sexual intercourse with an underage girl two years older than his 12 or 13 years and another girl slightly later while he was at boarding school. His fantasies largely centre around these girls, who seem to correspond to his preferred physical type:

> "... the same length hair, and same body proportions, and very similar in each case ... as the girls which were at school ... the fantasy would always revolve around what actually happened at school, where I would be in the bedroom having sex with either girl ... just sort of going on old experiences ... I started noticing the stepchildren as being of the same proportions and then the fantasies would be going on with the schoolgirls which I had actually had sex with and the stepdaughters would come and take the place ... in the situation at school ... eventually it became then in the home setting, and then the fantasy led to abuse."

His experience with pornography went back to his early childhood, perhaps as young as five years, when he saw pornography that his brothers had hidden away:

> "I remember one particular, it was only a small book, it wasn't one of the big ones, and there are pictures—ladies bums—and I used to sit on the toilet looking at them."

His experience of pornography involving females of his fantasy age group was minimal:

> "The only things I have seen anything remotely to do with that is a couple of books on ... *Health and Efficiency* [a naturist magazine] and there have been a couple of immature looking girls in there. But it has never been enough to sexually arouse me more than ... a fully formed woman ... like 20, 22, 23 and upwards which have been more stimulating than the actual young child's form ... I saw one ... which one of my neighbours had once, ... she had half a fish up her anus and another half ... coming out of her vagina. And another one where there was a pig and [someone] screwing it, but that sort of repulsed me more than anything ... I never sort of seeked it out any more than that, because they were pretty illegal I think ... I suppose you can get hold of them but I never sought it out."

Case 9: Graham

The background of Graham has already been described in detail in Chapter 1.

Case 10: Mike

He has a 22-year history of abusing extrafamilially, which included indecent assaults on both sexes and masturbation on boys, although he had not engaged in penetrative sex with them. He would afterwards masturbate to the fantasy of the offences. His offending had started at the age of 17:

> "I was abused by a relative of mine, my father's brother, at the age of 14. I was also raped at the age of 17 by four lads who actually held me down whilst this other bloke raped me."

Only since entering treatment had he started to have sexual fantasies about adult women. Pornography was used by his uncle as part of the abuse perpetrated on Mike—this was generally available heterosexually orientated men's magazines such as *Playboy*. Pornography, he claims:

> "wasn't involved in my offending. But I can use a man's magazine today, say like something like the *Knave*, and read the stories out of there which will make me excited. And I would masturbate to the thoughts of that story of the man and the woman having sexual intercourse or the woman masturbating the man, or the man caressing the woman. I could masturbate to them thoughts ... Not the pictures they turn me off ... I cannot stand the sight of a woman being plastered all over a magazine like they do, that downgrades a woman."

He had never seen child pornography but mentioned some television commercials that contained scantily dressed women which he was able to masturbate to.

Case 11: Paul

Paul's offending history was a long one, going, as he put it:

> "as far as finger rape, there were girls and there was boys and my finger was against the boys in their anuses, and some of the girls who were older, fully developed or who I felt to be fully developed, then I would use my finger to masturbate them".

His fantasy might start:

> "... with walking out in a field or something like that, because with a fantasy you can do all sorts of things with it. You can do what you like with a fantasy. But to go into a fantasy it could be if I'm making love to

my wife. I could be in a fantasy, not of my wife but of this child ... I used to change the picture, that I'm not making love to my wife but I am loving the child ... you cannot make love to a child. They cannot give consent for a start, it's illegal rape that's what it boils down to. So I'm treating that child as an adult, now that's in the fantasy ..."

He has seen pornography:

"... but not child. That has never appealed to me. I have never been into that. I have seen it and I have read the stories but they were not all that fantastic. It turns me dead. I am not interested. But yet I could put a *Parade* picture up and that to me was art but also helped with my fantasies. I could use it—relieve my frustrations and I like it that way."

He wanted to, but never did, take photographs of the children he abused because of fear that they might be discovered:

"I did use club books [mail order catalogues] with children in their panties. They turned me on."

He videoed children's television programmes: "I actually tried to freeze the pictures so I could masturbate".

Such comments present a number of dilemmas for the literature on the effects of pornography on offending. These stem from the fuller picture provided by the case studies, in which additional factors in offending can be considered besides pornography. Nevertheless, the research also provides confirmation of some previous findings from research. One can seriously doubt whether reliance solely on questionnaires given to offender populations or experimental studies of offenders can fully illuminate precisely the role of pornography in the offending process. There are a number of reasons for this. In particular, our experience in collecting the case study material is that certain information, such as times and sequencing, is very difficult for participants to recall quickly and accurately. Also, in the case study approach, information is revealed that might not fall within the frame of reference of the survey questionnaire. The compressed case studies presented here omit material that does not bear directly on pornography. For example, it spontaneously emerged early in the research that the paedophiliac offenders' sexual fantasies frequently involved themselves at a far younger age (especially adolescence).

Another unpredicted aspect of paedophiles' fantasy emerged

regularly in these case studies. It seems clear that commercial pornography is only of limited interest to many offenders. Very little interest in child pornography was expressed by most of the paedophiles—if by child pornography we mean nude children explicitly posed or involved in sexual activity (see also Marshall, 1988). Some of the offenders expressed strong distaste for that sort of thing although few had actually seen it. Nevertheless, some of the offenders had an affinity for imagery that they found to be sexually stimulating. This was to be found in licit newspapers and magazines, television programmes and videos that did not normally involve nudity (although occasionally television advertisements with bare babies or toddlers were mentioned). The range of such materials was quite extensive, varying from pictures of children in their underwear found in mail order catalogues through to Walt Disney videos. It is unlikely that normal adults process this material erotically.

Not quite so surprising is the choice of "pornographic" materials, which was largely limited to general heterosexual pornography of the so-called "soft-porn" type. It has to be stressed that some of the offenders expressed a distaste for this sort of material as well. A sizeable proportion of the paedophiles seemed to use heterosexual pornography more as an entertainment rather than to promote paedophiliac fantasy. Previous studies have not found very strong evidence for specific arousal factors in different types of pornography, with only tentative exceptions (Howitt, 1991). There may be several reasons why this should be the case. Firstly, a proportion of paedophiles show a pronounced erotic fixation on a particular age group and physical type which may not be well catered for by the pornography trade. Secondly, conventionally defined child pornography may well fail to include powerfully erotic stimuli. For example, if an offender finds glimpses of children's underwear particularly sexually arousing, child pornography featuring nudity or adult–child sexual involvement quite simply fails to meet his sexual needs. Thirdly, many paedophiles also seek to engage in heterosexual relationships with adult women. The apparent lack of interest in child pornography may be due to concern about being "caught" with certain illicit materials in their possession. Finally, since offenders tend not to construe their involvement with children as primarily sexual, interest in child pornography might put this "distorted" thinking under strain.

But, of course, these men have chosen to exercise their paedophiliac feelings directly through assaults on children. As a consequence, they may be less likely to need paedophiliac pornography for use in masturbation since they generate fantasy through their offences. Only a few of the paedophiles actually reported orgasm as part of their offending; many would masturbate to fantasy arising out of their offending at a later time. In this context it is interesting that some paedophiles take photographs of their victims or would like to have taken such photographs. Given these factors, perhaps it is not surprising that the men did not put effort into obtaining illegal materials when they had ready sources of fantasy in their offending, in licit materials and in children they observed in the street or elsewhere.

In the literature on pornography (especially Burgess and Hartman, 1987; Tate, 1990), suggestions are made concerning the function of pornography in the "grooming process" (Wyre, 1987). Grooming, as we have seen, is the steps taken by paedophiles to "entrap" their victims and is in some ways analogous to adult courtship. One suggestion is that offenders show children pornography (especially adult–child sexual depictions) as part of this—possibly in order to make adult–child sex appear "normal". Only one of the men actually did this. This is not to deny that this sort of use of pornography occurs but merely to suggest its limited extent. Another of the men who had been abused by an adult as a child reported that this involved pornography.

One difficulty relates to sequencing. As we have seen, research has tried to ascertain whether sex offenders were exposed to pornography earlier in their childhoods than non-sexual offenders. The implicit theory underlying this is the notion of the depravation of childhood innocence. If anything, the research actually suggests that sex offenders are likely to see pornography for the first time marginally later in childhood than non-offenders (Howitt and Cumberbatch, 1990), although this is, at its strongest, only a slight trend. While at first appearing paradoxical, it might indicate that sex offenders are relatively naive about sex, making it difficult for them to form contacts with other adults. However, paedophiles do not appear to be sexual illiterates or sexually naive. In the sexual histories of all of our offenders was evidence of significant sexual activity during childhood; for example, all but one had been the victim of direct sexual abuse by single or sequential abusers. The one exception to this had been witness to a paedophiliac assault on his friend. Not all of the abusers had been adults; in some cases, an older child was involved. There is no sense in which the paedophiles themselves were anything other than sexually aware as children. Some of them described how they believed children to be sexually knowledgeable, just as they themselves were made to be as children. The rates of sexual abuse reported by our group of offenders are far greater than any survey has suggested (e.g. Risin and Koss, 1987), especially for males and particularly when peer abuse is included. Of course, it is difficult to make precise comparisons between surveys of the general population and a selected sample of offenders. The early sexualization of offenders might go some way to explaining Condron and Nutter's (1988) finding that masturbation began younger in offenders than in controls.

All of this is of considerable importance when it comes to assessing the impact of pornography on the genesis of offending. In none of the case studies in our research can be found instances of individuals who had experience of pornography of any sort prior to their early sexualization through abuse. In those cases where there was some childhood experience of pornography, this was either contemporaneous with the abuse or occurred later. As such, there is no evidence that early exposure to pornography was a cause of later offending. Indeed, in the cases reported here, there is a continuity between abuse in childhood and adult offending. Early experience of abuse leads to peer abuse, which leads to adult abuse of children. In many of the cases, first exposure to pornography appears to occur after their paedophiliac careers had started, and in relatively few cases was child pornography involved. For example, Adrian was the only offender who reported extensive use of child pornography rather than making it. This he first saw at 16 years of age, by which time his sexual career was several years long following his initial abuse and sexual involvement with peers. Quite clearly, whatever the role of pornography in his adult life, the structure of his sexual career had already been laid down by his earliest experiences.

It is unfortunate that there exists no comparative data on the use of pornography in British general population samples (Howitt and Cumberbatch, 1990), especially that which is broken down into categories of content. Nevertheless, it seems likely that for many offenders, their experience of pornography is similar to that of adult males in general. Most of this experience is with soft-core men's magazines or sex videos. Experience of child pornography was exceptional. This is not to say that the paedophiles did not find pictures of children arousing—many of them quite evidently did—but that pornography was for most of them not a prime source of arousal of paedophiliac fantasies. (There were examples of men who claim to be able to cognitively manipulate adult heterosexual pornography to generate paedophiliac themes, but this is in the mind of the beholder rather than in the material itself.) The generation of paedophiliac fantasy from non-pornographic sources may well be a special characteristic of the paedophile. Of course, we have no comparative data on this either and it is difficult to see how such data could be reliably collected. That a proportion of paedophiles seek to stimulate their sexual fantasy about children but do not turn to child pornography for this may reflect much about the strength of their erotic attachment to children.

Another issue is whether pornography has a role in heightening sexual arousal prior to offending. This is a viewpoint that has some support in the literature on rapists (Marshall, 1988). In our sample's accounts, there were many descriptions of how the sexual interest of the offender was aroused by a particular child or type of child. Often this led to fantasy about the child and eventually to the offence. None of our sample reported using pornography in a similar sort of way. Their lack of interest in child pornography in general may explain this. The reasons for the lack of interest in child pornography may be intimately tied to the nature of paedophiliac offending by these men. The offending process was rarely, if ever, described in terms other than "grooming". Children involved in these crimes had often been targeted because they possessed characteristics that were sexually arousing to the offenders. "Grooming" is often portrayed as a discriminating process by the men. It is not as if the sexual drive is triggered by factors external to the victim, then satisfied by the abuse. In these circumstances, pornography might not contribute to offending. Furthermore, much paedophiliac sexual offending involves acts that do not require sexual arousal for their execution, and penetrative sex is not typical of the offences. Thus the offence itself may provide imagery for later masturbation. Conceived in this way, the offence does what pornography is thought to do by some—that is, provide sexual arousal.

The implications of these findings for legislation concerning pornography have to be tempered by the limited range of offenders included in the present study, and by other factors. We have noted that most paedophiles seem not to be attracted by child pornography. Given that the possession of such material is currently subject to legal penalties, there is a hefty deterrent to its distribution. Some of the offenders expressed concern about being found in possession of materials involving children. There is an implication that the illegality of child pornography may serve as a deterrent against seeking the material. Paedophiliac fantasy is unlikely to be effectively controlled by the exclusion of pornography. The legal alternative sources of fantasy seem to dominate in the lives of most of the offenders, and it is difficult to conceive of legislation that could effectively limit the visual materials that paedophiles process into paedophiliac fantasy.

None of this is to suggest that explicit child pornography is acceptable; Tate (1992) argues that the phrase "child pornography" is actually misleading:

> "It is not pornography in any real sense: simply the evidence—recorded on film or video tape—of serious sexual assaults on young children."
>
> (Tate, 1992, p. 203)

Given the illegality of child pornography throughout much of the Western world, the "commercial" aspects of the distribution of the material may be seen as a "cottage industry"—individual paedophiles make pictures and films of themselves abusing children, which are then bought or swapped by other offenders:

> "In effect, legislation aimed at eliminating child pornography has merely eliminated the middle man, requiring paedophiles to deal directly with each other."
>
> (Tate, 1992, p. 208)

Despite the shocking nature of some of the material found by the police and customs officers, in itself this is merely evidence that the material is available and of interest to at least some offenders. It does not mean that it either causes offending or even that it maintains molestation patterns. Indeed, it is not even established precisely who buys it. Nevertheless, there is clearly a proportion of offenders who spend a lot of time and money on accumulating it.

THE MEDIA'S ROLE IN FANTASY

The way in which offenders "extract" fantasy from television, videos and the printed media deserves special attention. While complaints about sexually explicit material in the mass media are familiar, little of the material used by the offenders is indecent, let alone pornographic. One of the traditional dichotomies in the mass communications literature is between the direct influence of the media on the audience and the use of the mass media by the audience in ways that "fit in" with their general personal and social values, interests, attitudes, needs and lifestyles (Howitt, 1982). A similar distinction seems appropriate about the mass media's influence on fantasy; fantasy may draw from the mass media but is not directly caused by the media. The alternative is that the media put fantasies directly into the minds of individuals. Thus there are at least three ways in which the media might be involved in paedophiliac fantasy:

(1) As a direct cause of paedophiliac fantasy;
(2) As a source of imagery to be incorporated into existing fantasies and used by the paedophile; and
(3) As a cause of sexual arousal.

The detail of the material that the offenders found stimulating is in many ways bizarre and only fully understandable if we assume that what the offender puts into his experience of the media is important, not just the media's objective content. Brian reported:

> "... you'd see young children getting into bed, or young children undressed naked, there was quite a lot of that on TV, and even simple things like adverts, There is a *Comfort* advert on at the moment where the young girl is just standing naked and then wrapped in a towel ... you don't get a full frontal shot but like it's enough to start off the imagination. [And that would lead to masturbation] sometimes not always. It depends on how I'm feeling emotionally myself ..."

Terry reported:

> "[T]here's a really pretty girl in *My Two Dads* I don't know if you have seen that on telly? It's an American programme ... and there is a 14-year-old girl in there and she is really a pretty girl, and she has got a relatively nice body and she sometimes wears very ... short skirts and sexy clothing, but it doesn't do anything for me. I have never actually had a sexual fantasy about her ... I have thought about that girl in *My Two Dads* when I have been masturbating ... she has flashed in and flashed out, and I have pushed her out ... There was one actually a little while back, she was in ... *My Girl and Me* ... she was quite stimulating, quite nice, I think ... She was a schoolgirl in that but she wasn't actually, she was about 17, 18, but she was made up to look like a schoolgirl, I had quite a good time with her."

The information gathered about the role of the media is remarkable. In particular, it illustrates that apparently innocuous material may become incorporated into the fantasy of paedophiles. Walt Disney films, situation comedies and the like were moulded around the psychosexual needs of the paedophile in ways that might be virtually exclusive to him.

THE ORIGINS OF FANTASY IN EXPERIENCE

If pornography is not the origin of the major themes of the deviant fantasy of paedophiles, then what is? Very little has been written on this matter. Indeed, in some ways, the neglect of the question is the result of the common view of fantasy as existing independently of reality. Reality–fantasy is a dichotomy that places fantasy in a separate realm of experience from real life. Freudian theory eventually chose to regard fantasy as the expression of things that were psychologically too dangerous to reveal, even to oneself. Ultimately this has meant that fantasy is construed as a stream of consciousness far removed from everyday thought. But this assumption has not been very productive in helping us to understand paedophile fantasy. There is reason to think that much sexual fantasy is grounded in early experience, just as is offending behaviour. Modern researchers have often concentrated on the role of fictional materials in creating mental representations of many different aspects of experience. A rare study of the development of fantasy in childhood is Kirkendall and McBride's (1990) retrospective study using male and female students at an American university. Fifty per cent claimed that their childhood fantasies had been influenced by childhood sexual experiences. These early sexual experiences provided food for the fantasy in many cases. Although the authors give no details, some who had unpleasant sexual experiences found that these inhibited fantasy. Most typical by far was that sexual content involved a heterosexual encounter in which the fantasizer was seduced. Although fantasy could "mature" and fantasy people were replaced by people they were involved with, in 59% of the students the earliest sexual fantasy still remained their favourite fantasy, although we are given no details as to the sexual activities and sexual partners involved. This is important, bearing in mind the following about paedophile fantasy.

There seems to be a marked tendency for paedophiliac fantasy to reflect at least broadly the childhood experiences of offenders, especially those of a sexual nature. In other words, real-life experiences were responsible for the sexual fantasies, not vice versa. This is clearer than any evidence that pornography was implicated in causing deviant sexual fantasy. The broad themes of fantasy appear to be laid down early in life, the details obtained from a variety of sources. In other words, the broad framework of sexual fantasy relates closely to early sexual experiences in childhood and adolescence. Furthermore, some non-sexual elements of early experience may make important contributions to the sexual fantasies of some offenders.

Garry, whom we first discussed in Chapter 3 to illustrate the nature of the "grooming" process, was essentially sexually aroused by indecent exposure and public masturbation. His sexual history fits in very well with this, and much the same theme dominates not only his offending but his early sexual experiences:

> "... I first started off back when I was 14 or 15 and the first memorable case I had was in the Boy Scouts when I was in the tent with 11-year-olds, I was one of the older ones. And I was masturbating in the tent and one walked in on me by mistake ... what I had done is set it up really because I had the feeling that somebody would walk in ... Before that, I don't know, exactly the first time I was shown how to masturbate was about 11 or 12 by my brother ... Well he masturbated in front of me and came and that showed me how to do it. I hadn't really bothered doing it before then ... [A]bout 8 and 9 ... I'd seen other blokes around the same time, down on the ... canal, masturbating behind bushes ... [He was also paid money to give a man oral sex.]"

"Flashing" characterizes his offending. It should be mentioned, however, that one of his attempts at contact abuse involved oral sex, which he had tried to persuade some of his victims to allow him to do. Although no amount of persuasion allowed him to get his way on this, it remained a long-term wish:

> " ... [While having sexual intercourse with adult women] I would be fantasizing about screwing a 12- or 13- or 11-year-old girl ... most of [my] early masturbation fantasies were just exposing myself in front of boys, blond boys with blue eyes, slender boys with lovely rounded bottoms ... so what I was doing in real life was actually in my fantasies or I would masturbate fantasy over an incident that happened that day ... of a boy or odd times very rare a girl ... I would go back to my inner mind and pick out an incident that stuck out in my mind or an incident that day ... [T]he fantasies did change later on, punishment did come

into it ... they used to cane me and I used to cane them in my fantasies, but in real life it was only one way—the girls used to cane me ..."

Garry attributes his caning fantasy to a bad experience with a girl in his adolescence, but it was he who wished to punish her. Despite Garry's "top" fantasies being of oral sex and caning girls, he never did these things to a child. Although there are close parallels between some of his fantasies and his offending, as he explains, fantasy was not always enacted as it was pictured—for example, the caning was done by the child to him.

Or we can take the case of Bernard, in his late 60s when interviewed. His sexual history starts very young:

"And then [when he was 63] a family moved along the same road that we lived in and there was a young schoolgirl there. She was 12 and she was very well developed, quite a big girl for her age, and she used to wear short skirts and I did try and fondle her and abuse her. But she wouldn't have any of it, but I did another girl and that was my first offence ... that was indecent assault.

"[My] earliest recollections of sex is about the age of five. I can remember then I always used to be interested in girls and exposing myself to them and always chasing girls. And about the age 7 I started masturbating quite a lot and then that's when fantasy started I should imagine around about then ... [M]y most vivid recollection I think, the one that affected me my whole life, my mum first caught me in bed masturbating and, of course, she told my father and also the brother and elder brother. And they kept on to me what'd happen to me if I kept masturbating. And to cap it all they even marched me up to school one day and the headmaster stood me out in front of the class and told everybody what I was doing, what a weakling I was and I'd be a physical wreck if I carried on. And that stayed with me. And then at that time, I would say about 12, 13, I came to realize then that, now I blamed masturbation for all of this, I was very small build. In actual fact, at the moment, I am about like a boy of 6 or 7 sexually you know, sexual organs you see. And it was pointed out to me by other children at school, that I was a lot smaller than what they were. The girls, when I used to chase them, used to also point out to me that I was a lot smaller than boys of my age group."

Bernard's belief in the smallness of his sexual organs is not unique among sex offenders. The immaturity of his sexual organs contrasts markedly with his sexual fantasies in which he is a "super-stud"—so much so that the fantasy appears to be an overcompensation for his beliefs about reality. Fantasy reversed reality in this sense. A great deal of the sexual behaviour that Bernard describes is governed by his obsession over his self-proclaimed genital inadequacies. Intimate contact with women is avoided because "his secret" would be revealed and attract comments that would disturb him:

> "[T]he fantasies basically, from when I was 12 ... 14 have stayed the same all the time ... [N]ormally it would be in my own home. I would always get a woman into my own home and we would start off by just normally kissing and cuddling and put my hand down over her breasts and basically undress them and kiss them all over their bodies and kiss their vaginas and things inside her thighs ...—I think now and again oral sex came into it but not significant—never really, now and again I would think. I would fantasize that a woman was having oral sex with me. I'd shove it in her mouth you know but never any great significant part ... I would get undressed and we would have normal sex but there again ... when she saw my penis she would say you have got a really big one ... that was still there all the time that I was bigger than any other man ... we have sex two or three times and I'd always want to turn them over and have anal sex. Even in my fantasies a lot of women wouldn't agree to it and with schoolchildren the same thing but something in my mind told me that I couldn't have it both ways ... I couldn't really be built like a stallion and then have anal sex with them ... it would be too painful ... [I]n my fantasy all the women were all very [well] built women, voluptuous women, there was the breast, the bottom, everything. [Then, speaking of his first real-life victim, he said] I was mixing with women and one of them, in particular, her daughter she was between 12 and 13 ... she fitted the fantasy perfectly. She had the figure, she had the look. [The mother] would come round to my flat quite often and the girl used to come and sit on my knee a lot and things like that although, knowing the risks, it was a long time before I actually started touching her."

So, for Bernard there is a partial match between fantasy and reality. In particular, fantasy begins over a particular type of woman or girl. The sexual acts involved are considerably different from the reality of his sexual activity but interrelated with his sexual concerns. Anal sex is a common theme in Bernard's fantasy but he had never attempted buggery with anyone irrespective of their age or sex. Fantasy went substantially further than reality but his interest in anal sex bears a significant relationship with the small size of his penis—perhaps so small that he believes that it would not hurt his partner or victim. His fantasies stopped when he got to know a particular woman or girl better.

Turning to Brian, his sexual experience covers the gamut from adult homosexuality to paedophiliac activity with children of both sexes. Some of his youthful sexual experiences parallel his adult offending to a remarkable extent. This is not quite true of his fantasy. In other words, his fantasy and childhood experiences differ. In particular, the adult fantasy tends to involve activities like penetrative sex with young females or them engaging in fellatio with him, which were not characteristic of his offending. Indeed, heterosexually he was a virgin:

> "... I ended up in a childrens' home when I was 13 ... and I had a young girl sitting on my lap and I just started touching her up ... I left there after a year and went back home ... and at this time my sister was about two and a half ... I put my hand into her nappy and I asked her to [urinate] on me ... [As a teenager] I was abused in the public toilets ... I know it included oral sex and that a guy paid me more money if he could have ... anal sex on me ... I was doing oral sex anyway ... memories of that are very vague ... [T]here was an incident when my stepfather got me to wash his penis ..."
>
> "... I still carried on abusing and I got involved with a family of five children. I knew the oldest two from a church I was going to. I'd already decided that a church was an easy place to meet people when I first came to London, having gone to church in prison and ... I realized that's the social place that's OK ... So having walked them home on a number of occasions, not having met the rest of the family, I was hoping to call round and find out ... why they hadn't been around ... So I got invited in, got to know the mum and all the rest of the family ... I found out that their dad had died and that's why they'd stopped coming to church. And from that ... I had just been larking around sexually with these two oldest girls, you know, unclipping her bra and things like that [they were 11 and 13 years old] ... I started abusing the oldest girl ... but that didn't carry on ... but it did carry on with the next girl and the boy who was about 8 at the time ... and the other girls they were about 6 and 4 at the time. [Or, concerning another family met via the church] I was left to babysit them when they were about 3 years old I suppose, and then did oral sex on the youngest girl and the boy was the twin brother. He saw what went on. And for a couple of months I still tried to touch the girl up ... through her clothing and she said don't be rude. So that stopped.
>
> "[The fantasies] vary ... young girls, sometimes young boys and sometimes blokes ... [W]ith children who I see ... in the street ... I can ... picture ... about her undressed or thinking of being sexually involved with me in relationship to all sorts of incidents from the past like my sister being in bed with me or my sister [urinating] over me or some of the involvements with different children ... with boys like the buggery with the boy and things like that ... it could be oral, it could be them [urinating over me], it could be intercourse, could be caressing, could be being in the fields and then ... the children would first start to come to me and undressing me and I undress them ..."

Brian's fantasy overlaps with his offending to a degree but the relationship is far from perfect, the most significant difference being that he claims that he did not carry out penetrative intercourse with any of the girls although penetrative sex is part of his fantasy. Although he attempted anal sex with one boy this was a marked departure from his paedophiliac activity. His fantasy "partners" are not recognizable as individuals.

Clearly, many paedophiliac contacts are substantially different from what is implied by the "SEX MONSTER" type of newspaper headlines. Based on our sample and general survey findings, much paedophiliac activity is, for the want of a better description, of a less serious nature than the headlines imply. It has to be acknowledged, though, that some commentators would consider it inappropriate to use descriptions like "less serious" (Kelly, 1988, 1989). In the context of legal definitions, such phrases are more precise than are general terms like sexual abuse.

OFFENCES AND FANTASY

So what is the relationship between fantasy and paedophilia? The possibilities range from (i) a close match between the two to (ii) no relationship at all. Of course, the facts may not be so straightforward. For example, some paedophiles report fantasies of sexual relations with women and/or men. What do these say about their paedophilia? Furthermore, what about paedophiliac sexual fantasies during sexual intercourse with an adult? The range of lifestyles of paedophiles is as varied as the ways in which fantasy is employed. Generally, a close relationship exists between the broad contents of paedophiliac fantasy and offending. In many respects this is to be expected; it is analogous to the adult who gets aroused by touching another person then may well masturbate to fantasies of this. Similar fantasies may be "created" by men who are sexually aroused by children. What about cases in which fantasy is totally spontaneously created in an individual's mind and then enacted against a child? We did not come across any such cases, and they may not exist.

There may also be substantial differences between offending and fantasy. Some men's fantasy includes sexual acts not to be found directly in their offending. A process of active negotiation may occur between fantasy and offending. For example, fantasies of buggery may be very arousing but its physical expression rejected because of the physical pain it might cause. In some cases, fantasy reverses reality. The offender who imagines himself the abused victim is a good example of this. Rather than being a script or plan for offending, fantasy engages with significant aspects of the experience and lifestyle before being expressed in action. In addition, it is often wrong to see offending as the source of sexual relief. Much sexual offending lacks immediate sexual release, and orgasm is not characteristic of all offences. In some cases sexual arousal and not sexual relief appears to be the main motive.

CHAPTER 7

The Treatment of Paedophiles

> "If the paedophiliac interest remains at the level of fantasy and therapeutic interventions do not appear to be effective in modifying them, one treatment option that remains is to help the patients to accept their fantasies—so long as they continue to be fulfilling to him and do not affect others ... A last consideration might be to recommend those whose motivation for change is minimal to move to an environment, e.g. parts of Morocco and Turkey, where legal and social constraints against non-coercive paedophiliac practices are less extreme than in our own society."
>
> (Yaffe, 1981, p. 91)

Beliefs about the value of therapy for paedophiles have changed markedly over the years. The traditional view from the classic writers on sex held paedophilia to be an intractable sexual orientation, unresponsive to treatment (e.g. Freud, 1905/1977; Krafft-Ebing, 1922). It has been suggested that this received wisdom led to the neglect of the treatment of paedophiles. During the second half of the twentieth century behavioural modification methods were developed and applied to sexual deviations. This was an era of greater optimism and new faith in the worth of therapy, justified or otherwise by facts. An important implication of these then new behaviour therapies was the de-emphasis on the past cause of the paedophilia in its treatment. Previously, psychoanalysis and related therapies assumed that the elimination of "symptoms" such as paedophilia required understanding of the individual's psychological history responsible for the problem; only by unravelling childhood experiences could a "cure" be effected. Treatment might last several years, with insight gradually unfolding about hidden childhood trauma.

Irrespective of the efficacy of such forms of treatment, they were characteristically expensive because they were carried out on a one-to-one basis with a therapist. Consequently, they were not commonly available to sex offenders. There are few reports of significant instances of such psychotherapy with paedophiles. Freud, for example, describes the psychoanalyses of several patients who had been sexually victimized as children but apparently undertook no analyses of perpetrators themselves. This is remarkable given the vilification he has received in the child abuse literature for putatively changing his mind about the role of sexual seduction in childhood by adults (and the consequent adult hysteria). Pressure from his colleagues pushed him towards the view that these seductions were merely fantasy (Froula, 1985; Masson, 1985). Such a denial of the sexual abuse of children has been construed as being partly responsible for the neglect of sexual abuse in clinical work during much of the twentieth century (Baartman, 1992; Bayer and Connors, 1988). Despite these claims, it is far from certain that Freud was actually convinced of the fantasy basis to seduction (Howitt, 1992); it has been claimed that Freud was sexually abused at the age of two (De Mause, 1976). *Family systems therapy* has some of the characteristics of the depth psychologies. Rather than seeing the issue lying in pathological childhood experiences, sexual abuse is held to be the outcome of pathogenic family relationships. Responsibility is thereby spread among family members and treatment of the abuser requires treatment of the family.

In the 1960s, the *depth therapies* were being challenged in terms of their therapeutic assumptions and effectiveness. The major characteristic of the new *behaviour therapy* school was its characterization of “symptoms” as learnt behaviour, not the sign of fermenting psychological conflict. Psychological techniques that promoted the unlearning or inhibition of the behaviour were sufficient. Psychological learning theory became a major theoretical domain in clinical psychology at this time and combined academic theory with therapeutic practicalities. This was held to be a powerful combination. Purely behavioural methods dipped somewhat in popularity as thought (cognition) was increasingly incorporated into psychological theories. The most popular of modern therapies for paedophiles are, indeed, described as *cognitive–behavioural* in nature. This largely means that beliefs, self-justifications, myths about child victims, attitudes and other aspects of paedophiliac thinking will be tackled during therapy alongside the more purely behavioural strategies aimed at stopping offence-related behaviour.

The "fly in the ointment" of behaviour therapy for the treatment of sexual deviations relates largely to ideological homophobic issues. Many of the early behaviour therapy treatments for paedophilia emerged from attempts to make homosexuals "normal" or, at least, stop "doing their thing". While this was ideologically unproblematic when it was socially acceptable and medically tenable to regard homosexuality as a "disease", time was running run out for such points of view just as behaviour therapy was gaining popularity. The increased rejection in professional circles of pathological conceptions of homosexuality created a climate inimical to behaviourist techniques. Giving a "patient" painful electric shocks if he showed signs of an erection to slides of naked men was at variance with the radical ethos of homosexuality as a psychologically healthy personal choice promoted by the Gay Movement from the late 1960s.

But Gay Liberation quickly disentangled itself from the paedophile groups with which it originally marched and protested. While attitudes to homosexuality changed, there was no corresponding change towards paedophilia among professionals. Consequently, paedophiles remained appropriate clients for behavioural modification techniques during the 1970s. The ideological basis of therapy for paedophilia, by and large, remained hostile and based on its elimination. A very small number of therapists have adopted a rather different stance much more supportive of the paedophile. Such approaches illustrate by contrast some of the moral, ethical and ideological implications of conventional treatment. They are described as *support therapies*.

As we will see, there is a degree of uncertainty about the effectiveness of even the best researched therapies for paedophiles. There are a number of reasons for this. Many of the therapies have not been subject to specific empirical evaluation of any sort; some have been tried with only a few clients. Often the criteria of therapeutic success have fallen well short of evidence of a decline in recidivism in offending, obviously one of the most important criteria. Research that includes a control or an alternatively treated group is in the minority of the evaluations. With a situation like this, claims of therapeutic success may sometimes be wishful thinking on the part of the clinician, the client or both.

The overall effectiveness of therapy, though, is only one matter to raise about therapy. Equally important is what sorts of paedophiles succeed best in which sorts of therapy. Little attention has been addressed to these issues. Similarly, questions such as the risk factors predicting recidivism following treatment have hardly entered the frame.

THERAPY FOR PAEDOPHILES

The range of therapies used with paedophiles is extensive. Some may not be generally applicable. For example, one technique involves groups of naked paedophiles standing in front of a mirror touching various parts of their body while describing how each part feels and why he likes or dislikes that part (Prendergast, 1991). Quite clearly, it is neither possible nor desirable to document or describe such apparently idiosyncratic techniques here. What is feasible is to present in some detail the main sorts of therapy.

Behavioural Treatments

In general, behavioural treatments for paedophilia are relatively clear in their implementation. Wherever possible, the details of the procedures have been given in order that the approaches can be understood much as they might have been experienced by the offender.

Classical Conditioning

A simple approach to the use of behavioural therapy in treatment can be found in the classical conditioning procedure described by Beech, Watts and Poole (1971). This was initially carried out on a young student who found young girls sexually arousing and sought opportunities to spy on them voyeuristically. During his assessment period, he was shown a set of photographs of female nudes, which ranged from sexually immature girls lacking breasts and pubic hair to heterosexually orientated soft-porn type pin-ups. The man's erection was measured while he fantasized to these pictures. Mature females were seen by him as repugnant and produced little by way of arousal. On the other hand, fantasizing about young, immature girls gave him a sizeable erection.

Classical conditioning involves the simultaneous presentation of a stimulus that produces a physiological response with one that initially on its own has no effect. Over a period of time the initially ineffective stimulus gains the power to elicit much the same physiological response as the initially effective one. In the case of this man, the conditioning procedure presented the sexually arousing pictures of immature girls with the initially ineffective stimulus of nude mature females. The offender was asked to create sexual fantasy about each picture. There were two such conditioning sessions each week for three months. Sexual arousal was successfully conditioned to all of the photographs, irrespective of their contents:

> "After three weeks of treatment the subject reported having experienced sexual arousal with mature females outside the treatment situation, and that his interest in young females was declining ... a few months after the termination of the formal parts of the treatment program he had satisfactory intercourse."
>
> (Beech, Watts and Poole, 1971, p. 402)

This would seem to be a remarkable success, although it raises numerous questions. Why, for example, should this treatment result in a *decline* in sexual interest in young females? This is akin to Pavlov's dogs ceasing to salivate to food! And if things are as easy as this, does it suggest that deviant sexual arousal is equally easy to condition in sexually normal individuals?

Operant Control of Approaches to Children

Wong, Gaydos and Fuqua (1982) describe a system of rewards and punishments, which they employed to stop an offender approaching children. Their patient was a 31-year-old, intellectually retarded man who had been sent to a state institution following allegations that he had heterosexually molested a young girl. While in the institution he initiated homosexual contacts with other inmates. Claims were also made that he was molesting local children. While he had difficulties communicating, he understood instructions given to him well enough. Nevertheless, he clearly lacked many of the prerequisites for modern treatment designed to change his sexual preference to adults; for example, he would not have been a good candidate for group therapy. Instead, a procedure was designed simply to reduce his habit of approaching children. The patient was "tailed" as he took walks in the nearby suburbs. Observers were substituted frequently in an effort to ensure that they went unnoticed by him. The circumstances were recorded whenever the patient approached either (i) females 18 years or under or (ii) males of 12 years or less. Because the patient was physically small, older boys were not considered at risk. During times when the patient was within a radius of 25 feet of a proscribed person, any approach to such a person was noted. The reliability between observers was high, with over 80% agreement about whether an approach had taken place. Staff had shown him pictures of the types of person to be avoided. If he went up to young males or females, he would immediately be confronted by the observer, who explained his misdemeanour and took him back to the hospital. There he was punished by confinement to his bedroom for the evening and the cancellation of his parents' visit the next weekend. Praise was given by staff if he avoided children.

After the third confinement session for transgressing the non-approach rules, he avoided going up to children during an eight-month follow-up period. This contrasts markedly with the pre-treatment observation that on half of the occasions when he was near girls he would approach them; the corresponding figure for boys was 75%.

Aversive Modification of Fantasy

Unpleasant or obnoxious punishments have been used in modifying paedophile fantasy. Marshall's (1973) procedures for aversion therapy are a good illustration of how this might be done. Working together, the therapist and the client generate a range of sexual fantasies. Those that were the most effective at giving the client an erection were retained for use in treatment. The offender selects a photographic slide to facilitate the imaging of each fantasy scene. Each fantasy was split into six audio-taped segments: (i) thinking about doing the deviant act, (ii) going to a situation in which the act might be expected to occur, (iii) seeking out the object of the deviance, (iv) approaching that object, (v) beginning the deviant act and (vi) finishing the deviant act and achieving orgasm. The therapist and client had previously determined an aversive level of an electric shock.

The fantasies were played back to the client. During each segment he was given the painful electric shock. Just before the shock was delivered the therapist shouted "stop" in order that the word served as a conditioned punishment to replace the electric shock itself. Initially, each segment was accompanied by a shock but eventually only 50% were on a spasmodic basis. Intermittent rewards and punishments are known to be more effective than continuous ones. For each client, deviant fantasy was paired with actual or conditioned punishment more than 300 times over a one- to two-month period.

During a postal follow-up several months later, a large proportion of the men claimed no further deviant behaviour. Marshall claims a 75% success rate.

Covert Sensitization

Cautela (1966) was the first to report the use of covert sensitization. In some of its forms, covert sensitization is quite similar to aversion therapy. The big difference is that the punishment is a psychologically unpleasant fantasy image rather than electric shock or a similar physical punishment. The client is helped to fantasize a situation similar to his offence. An unpleasant consequence such as a prison term is then incorporated into the fantasy. The fine detail varies. One group of therapists describe their procedures with paedophiles as follows:

> "... there are four categories of thoughts: neutral thoughts, child-molesting thoughts, aversive thoughts, and pleasurable thoughts associated with consensual sex with an adult partner. The offender is asked to develop detailed fantasies and scenes involving these four categories. With the child-molesting scene he breaks down the sequence in discrete steps, going from thought to cruising to approaching and on to molesting behaviour. Using a tape recorder, he tapes fantasies from the different categories of neutral, child molesting, aversive, and consensual sex thoughts. For the aversive scenes he must come up with several different types of unpleasant effects that may occur if he is caught molesting a child. These are highly individualized, but include such things as being verbally rebuked by his family, having his own children harassed by other children when they learn that their father is a child molester, the thought of imprisonment and rape by inmates when they learn that he is a child molester, or contracting the deadly disease AIDS."
>
> (Barnard *et al.*, 1989, p. 142)

In fantasy, the offender follows the child molesting sequence through but breaks into it with an aversive fantasy episode. This effectively stops him reaching the stage of abusing the child in fantasy. He dispels the aversive thoughts by moving into fantasy of pleasant consensual sex with an adult partner. When successful, the covert sensitization process will have ensured that his future abuse fantasies will be short-circuited by aversive thought intrusions. In this way the process of building up to real-life abuse through fantasy is stopped.

Orgasmic Reconditioning

Rather than interrupting a fantasy, orgasmic reconditioning employs fantasy during masturbation. This procedure, derived from studies using homosexuals as participants (e.g. Conrad and Wincze, 1976), was improved and adapted to paedophiles by Van Deventer and Laws (1978). The aim is for the client to learn new, socially acceptable, fantasies to replace deviant fantasies about children. The treatment is described as follows:

> "... the subject is first instructed to shift his masturbation fantasy from a deviant to a nondeviant theme at the moment of orgasmic inevitability: later in training he is instructed to move the introduction of the nondeviant fantasy forward in time toward the start of masturbation ... deviant and nondeviant masturbation themes were alternated on a weekly basis for a period of six weeks ... In the first week, the subject masturbated to the deviant fantasy theme of sexual relations with young boys. Each was instructed to masturbate to ejaculation as rapidly as possible or for 20 min. whichever occurred first, while speaking the masturbatory fantasy aloud ... During the second week the conditions were identical except that the theme was sexual relations with adult females. This weekly alternation continued throughout treatment."
>
> (Van Deventer and Laws, 1978, p. 750)

The two clients discussed in the report were both paedophiles predominantly or exclusively attracted to boys. Their offences included anal intercourse. Many of the desired changes in fantasy and sexual arousal were achieved. Some evidence emerged of increased sexual responsiveness to women. The authors suggest that it is the sexual confusion created by alternating deviant and non-deviant fantasy that might be responsible for the changes. Uncertainty, depression and anger were typical of their clients' feelings half way through the treatment:

> "Our subjects indicated that the switching made them aware of differences in their feelings. As one put it, 'It's not that I feel *bad* when masturbating and thinking about kids, it's just that I feel *better* when

> doing it to thoughts of women.' Both subjects denied that masturbating to fantasies about children was aversive."
>
> (Van Deventer and Laws, 1978, pp. 760–761)

Laws (1985) essentially argues that this form of therapy is especially suitable for clients who are much more aroused to deviant imagery than to non-deviant imagery. There is little point or prospect in trying to change the fantasy of offenders unaroused sexually by deviant imagery. Those highly aroused by normal imagery do not need new fantasy conditioned; they need their paedophiliac fantasy eliminated.

In Marshall's (1973) version of orgasmic reconditioning, deviant and non-deviant fantasies were not alternated. Normal fantasy was used to block deviant fantasy throughout the treatment. Heterosexually orientated pornography was used to help the men to generate fantasies. They were told to eliminate deviant material from their fantasy, otherwise their deviance would be reinforced. Fantasy around the point of ejaculation is the most important since the contents of this are most closely reinforced by orgasm:

> "He was told to use his deviant fantasies to initiate masturbation, and to continue to imagine them until immediately before ejaculation at which time he was to switch to the appropriate fantasy. The patient carried on this practice until he was able to control his fantasy content at ejaculation. At this time the therapist advised the patient to begin to extend the appropriate fantasy further back in the sequence until it would finally serve as the initiating stimulus."
>
> (Marshall, 1973, p. 560)

There are no studies comparing the relative effectiveness of these two approaches.

Orgasmic Reconditioning without Deviant Fantasy

One of the oddities about orgasmic reconditioning as described in the previous subsection is that it involves the use of masturbation to deviant fantasy. Given the lack of clear understanding about how orgasmic reconditioning works, there is an ethical uncertainty about encouraging paedophiliac fantasy as part of treatment. Kremsdorf, Holmen and Laws (1980) describe a variant of orgasmic reconditioning using only socially acceptable fantasy material.

The paedophile involved was confined at a California state hospital for the molestation of a 6-year-old girl. He was highly sexually aroused by girls between the ages of 1 and 12 years. Although in his 20s, he was hardly aroused by women of this age and his sexual experiences with adults were minimal.

> "Following a baseline measurement period, the subject began to masturbate to non-deviant fantasies on a daily basis for a period of 8 weeks. He was instructed to masturbate to ejaculation as rapidly as possible or for 20 min, whichever occurred first, while speaking the masturbatory fantasy aloud. This latter procedural variation was included to allow greater control over the fantasy the subject was actually utilizing ... The subject was further instructed that when he masturbated outside the laboratory he was to use themes solely of a non-deviant nature."
>
> (Kremsdorf, Holmen and Laws, 1980, p. 204)

Using slides, it was found that his erections prior to treatment were to girls under the age of seven years. Following treatment, women generated the biggest erections. Eventually, over the course of treatment, the time he took to ejaculate to normal fantasy decreased.

Satiation Therapy

The use of punishment to inhibit paedophiliac behaviour appears uncommon within therapy (although Rosenthal (1973) used electric shock in his behavioural treatment of a retarded offender). Shame aversion therapy, a currently recognized behavioural treatment of sex offenders, uses humiliation as a punishment. In this the client re-enacts his offence in front of a cooperative panel which disapproves of the activity. There would, in general, be no legal or ethical problems associated, say, with having an exhibitionist do his act to such a group. It is more problematic to imagine how a paedophile's offences could be portrayed in this way, unless his sexual fantasy was made the focus rather than his acts. Marshall (1979) argues that a good alternative to shame aversion therapy is to have offenders masturbate to paedophiliac fantasy to the point of physical satiation and beyond. That is, masturbation is continued well beyond the time it is pleasurable. This is *satiation therapy*.

One of Marshall's case studies involved the masturbatory satiation of a 33-year-old married man with children. The couple's sex life seemed satisfactory and intercourse took place three times or so each week. Intercourse involved deviant sexual fantasy so was actually part of the problem; furthermore, he had a fetish for female clothing. Despite having a long history of paedophilia with girls in the 4–14 year age group, he had not abused his own children. Exposure, genital fondling and reciprocal oral sex had been its extent until the most recent offence, when he had full intercourse with an adolescent neighbour. His heterosexual paedophilia was confirmed by his erections to nude photographs of girls in the 6–8 and 11–13-year-old age groups:

> "... the patient was required to seat himself in a darkened room where his only contact with the therapist was via an audio-intercommunication system. The subject was instructed to remove his trousers and commence masturbating, while at the same time verbalizing aloud every variation he could think of on the fantasies associated with the targeted category ... For the initial six 1-hour treatment sessions ... the targeted category was female children aged 6 to 8 years. The patient was told to masturbate continuously throughout the 1-hour session so that even if he ejaculated he was to continue, stopping only to wipe himself clean if he found this necessary. Monitoring through a one-way screen and the sound system revealed that the patient followed the instructions closely."
>
> (Marshall, 1979, p. 380)

Once erections to the younger girls declined, the 11- to 13-year-olds were satiated to. Finally, the underwear fetish was tackled. When these changes in responsiveness to young females had been achieved, *orgasmic reconditioning* was carried out to adult female images. This worked in that he achieved erections to pictures of nude women and ejaculated to them increasingly quickly. At a six-month follow-up meeting, his wife reported that the improvement in their sex life had lasted and laboratory assessment showed that the new pattern of erections to nude women remained.

Assertiveness Training

Detailed discussions of assertiveness training for paedophiles are surprisingly rare, given claims that paedophiles have problems with dominance or relating to other adults. Edwards (1972) treated the three major problems of a 40-year-old doctor: (i) twice monthly sexual activity with his sons following his wife's extra-marital affair; (ii) interpersonal difficulties with adults, especially his wife; and (iii) intermittent impotence. When his wife found out that he had persuaded one of their sons to bugger him the marriage "hit on the rocks". She had known of the abuse for two years but this was the final straw. The man's family history included an overbearing mother and a disciplinarian father. Experiences with prostitutes when he was 17 were bad; both episodes gave him venereal disease. A few months later, he had his first paedophiliac contact. This was with the four-year-old son of a friend. He met his wife at medical school. Intercourse took place after about six months. Sexual activity was rapacious, when they sneaked a holiday together unbeknown to her parents. They were discovered and her parents forced their marriage but from then on sex was not at all the same. His wife had little sexual interest in him and, for example, the marriage's consummation did not take place for nearly a week. They divorced for a while after her affair but remarried. After this she became sexually the aggressive partner but his interest lessened.

During treatment he was required to stop sexual activity with anyone; instead his objective was to get to know people. "Thought stopping" procedures were demonstrated, although these are nothing to do with assertiveness training as such. When a paedophiliac image was conjured up, the therapist banged a table loudly and shouted "stop". The fantasy was thereby disrupted. This startle reaction could be brought back by the patient simply saying the word "stop". According to the man, this worked well with deviant thoughts, reducing them to once or twice a week.

Assertiveness training given by the therapist was supplemented by a training book which described assertiveness techniques in more detail. In its own terms this seems to have worked quite well but the detail of his assertive behaviour seems from another era of marriage partnerships:

> "At the fourth session he reported that he had again stated clearly that he would be the decision-maker on finances, on the bringing up of the children, and 'as a matter on fact, on all things'. She was argumentative and angry at first, but he felt himself in control the entire time. She ultimately accepted his edict which he found a highly satisfying experience. He then told her that her sexual aggressiveness upset him because she had challenged him on the 'no sex' issue and become seductive. He had, however, felt like sex with her on several occasions. Since he seemed ready to approach her, I instructed him to do so but assume at least equality in control, not to allow her to domineer."
>
> (Edwards, 1972, p. 57)

It is suggested that the paedophiliac behaviour stopped, although the case for this is largely based on anecdotes. Incest offenders, as we will see, tend not to reoffend following detection. This may emphasize the need for caution about the success of the treatment, especially as two different therapies were confounded. Modern assertiveness training would normally see dominance and aggressiveness as inappropriate ways of asserting oneself.

Modelling Social Skills

An early treatment programme for paedophiles was described by Serber and Keith (1974). This is unusual in so far as it directly tied the treatment of paedophiles with homosexuality. The programme was known as the Atascadero project after the state hospital which housed it. About 15% of the men in this large hospital were "homosexual", meaning mainly paedophiles. For the most part, the homosexual patients had either severe difficulties in relationships with other homosexuals or absolutely no experience at all with adult homosexuals. They were seen as lacking the interactive skills required for adult friendships and relationships. Feelings of inferiority in relation to other adults, according to the authors, encouraged the men into relationships with children. The homosexual patients, typically, either had never been in contact with other adult homosexuals or had experienced difficulties in relating to them. In general, the men were fairly ignorant of community groups and the support they could give.

The programme aimed simply to orientate the patients to adult partners rather than convert them to adult heterosexuality. Successfully functioning homosexual models were introduced to the hospital:

> "The group depended upon gay student volunteers from a local college campus who are successfully integrated into straight society and who functioned as instructors and behavioral models ... Role playing situations were first used with the models ... The scene used was that of a gay bar where social contacts are frequently made. After observing many behavioral samples by the gay models we isolated specific verbal and nonverbal components of gay social interactions which served as a 'behavioral base' upon which further social skills could be built."
>
> (Serber and Keith, 1974, p. 95)

A lesbian led consciousness raising groups dealing with matters such as problems involved in being gay in a heterosexually orientated world, as well as ways of dealing with family members in relation to homosexuality. The authors report no increase in sexual acting out as a result of this. Since this apparently means homosexual acts it is difficult to know how successful the programme had been.

Cognitive Programmes

It is not known what proportion of therapists rely exclusively on behavioural approaches. Most modern practitioners appear to use behavioural treatments such as orgasmic reconditioning and satiation just as components of their work. The reasons for this shift are not documented, although they may include a general disenchantment with purely behavioural methods, the higher profile given to sex abuse treatment, the need to provide corporately run treatment programmes and greater awareness of alternatives to traditional individual psychotherapy (such as group work). The failure of research to effectively identify a single cause of paedophilia may also encourage "broad-front" therapy. Research has highlighted numerous factors that may contribute to sexual involvement with children, and no single factor is generally held to be essential or sufficient in itself. Thus, a wide a range of factors are addressed in therapy. Since the social and psychological difficulties of paedophiles are often similar to those of people in general, ignoring the wider social, personal and emotional difficulties of offenders might be counterproductive.

A three-phase programme for the treatment of paedophilia is described by Rowan (1988a) and provides a useful illustration of this sort of approach. The three aspects involved are:

(1) Social skills: modelling, role playing and performance feedback, assertiveness training and anger management; sex education, legal education, correction of cognitive distortions about sex roles and sex objects challenged by peer group discussion; confrontation with an adult victims' survival group.
(2) Stress management and communication skills: individual therapy (targeting how to reduce deviant sexual arousal). A fantasy diary is kept for future use in covert sensitization as a source of negative conditioners. Ammonia is used as an aversive conditioner if this fails. Drug treatment is available to those unable to control fantasy any other way.
(3) Patients may lead self-help groups; individual treatment programmes continue; conjoint therapy is available if partner and offender agree; social skills including life skills practice if near release.

Progress in therapy is assessed on the basis of the discrepancy between a patient's own ratings of his personal progress and a pooled assessment by the staff of the institution; the smaller the discrepancy, the greater the improvement. One case study describes a man who had undergone the therapy:

> "Subject A is a 42-year-old man who reported that his alcoholic father had abused his sister but not him. As an adult, Subject A was also an alcoholic and never married. Twice, when intoxicated, he made sexual contact with his niece. In treatment he was an active participant in ward government and therapy groups and Alcoholics Anonymous ... Victim identification exercises led to great remorse and he reestablished contact with his sister, the victim's mother, to begin family reconciliation. Subject A rates his progress as high, and the staff agreed because of his openness, insight, increased self-esteem, and sincere effort to control his alcoholism. He returned to prison with a recommendation for parole."
>
> (Rowan, 1988b, p. 208)

In another publication, Rowan (1988a) adds to the list of treatments the correction of cognitive distortions. Education and insight-orientated therapy are described as the means of doing this:

> "First the perpetrator has to admit and accept responsibility for his own behavior. It is not generally true that sex-starved seven-year-olds jump out of the bushes and attack innocent, passing men. The 'why me?' question can be addressed using the four-factor model [Araji and Finkelhor, 1985] and determining how the individual meets the criteria of each factor and how these combine to explain behavior. The role of the victim must be clarified as behavior may be rationalized by observations such as 'she kept coming back' and the adult fails to take appropriate responsibility for his own actions."
>
> (Rowan, 1988a, p. 94)

Clearly, much of the above relies on changes quite distinct from those of erotic orientation.

Lanyon (1986) suggests that a systematic treatment for paedophiles should include the following steps:

(1) Immediate crisis and life problem management. Psychological problems such as depression and anxiety that are pervasive need to be alleviated. The therapist may also need to provide help and information pertinent to family and legal matters.
(2) Deficiencies in sex education should be remedied.
(3) Attention to existing and continuing adult relationships. Difficulties in the relationship may be helped by counselling with the couple. Similarly, sex therapy should be provided as

required to further the emotional quality of that relationship. In the case of incest, each member of the family will normally need to be involved in the therapy at some stage.

(4) Where there is no adult relationship the client should be helped to work towards achieving one. Skills in relationships should be developed if they are lacking and anxieties about adult relationships tackled as a prelude to initiating contacts.

(5) Behaviour therapy procedures should be employed to stop deviant behaviour and the associated fantasy. Periodic follow-up interviews will be used in addition.

While they differ in fine detail, Lanyan's and Rowan's treatment programmes overlap in significant ways. A more extensive but overlapping programme was that developed at the North Florida Evaluation and Treatment Center (Barnard *et al.*, 1989). Several hundred offenders have been treated there using the basic philosophy that:

> "... sex offenders develop their deviant behavior through multiple and diverse ways and consequently require a variety of treatment approaches to alter this aberrant behavior."
>
> (Barnard *et al.*, 1989, p. 126)

Again, treatment overlaps with that of the smaller scale programmes already discussed. Nevertheless, the programme contains features that may be of interest where resources are available. The programme aims to change the men in four ways—sexual behaviour, character, behaviour in general and physical and psychological wellness:

1. Sexual behaviour. The techniques used are masturbatory satiation and covert sensitization, much as described earlier in this chapter.

2. Characterological. Self-insight into the offender's own character with the intention of reducing maladaptive behaviour. The training modules involved include:

a. Interpersonally orientated groups. This provides the offender with an opportunity to recall his own traumatic experiences of abuse and act out the experiences within the group. Gradually with the support he is given he begins to master the trauma. He is made to understand how this trauma led to his offending.

b. Peer-facilitated groups. A group of three offenders (one of whom is in the advanced stages of treatment) is formed with the objectives of (i) mutual support, (ii) acting as an initial sounding board for ideas or matters to be taken to the larger treatment groups and (iii) mutual confrontation on distorted thinking or unhealthy behaviour patterns.
c. Role-playing. This employs video-taped role-playing of abusive experiences with the offender in both the victim and perpetrator roles. Other offenders watch and make notes and comments on the role-plays. It can be a very traumatic and emotionally draining experience for all of those participating.
d. Sensitivity training module. This attempts to integrate the body and mind—the experience of offending is often isolated by offenders through processes of denial—such that they become unresponsive to how they feel. These sessions include yoga, stretching and movement exercises, art therapy, and other activities planned primarily as "enriching" experiences. In addition interpersonal relations groups, role-playing, sensitivity training, peer facilitated groups and help with traumatic events are also available.

3. General behaviour. This aims to improve skills at dealing with the ordinary problems of life. The training methods include the following:

a. Cognitive restructuring. This confronts the offender's irrational ideas and rationalizations which served to justify offending, then attempts to increase the belief that the offender can control his deviancy. He is encouraged to confront these irrational ideas and replace them with socially more acceptable ones. Rational–emotive therapy (Ellis and Grieger, 1977) forms the theoretical foundation of this approach with its emphasis on changing thoughts and beliefs as a means of changing how events are experienced. Jenkins-Hall (1989) provides some quite straightforward cognitive restructuring methods, including (i) the provision of alternative interpretations, (ii) asking the client to consider whether his thoughts help or hinder his goal attainment, (iii) the examination of the logic underlying the client's thoughts and (iv) the disputing and challenging of the client's beliefs during therapy in the manner of rational–emotive therapy (Ellis and Grieger, 1977).

b. Communication skills. This is designed to improve relationships with adults. Self-disclosure, assertiveness training and communicating genuineness/warmth are among the sections of this module.
c. Social skills. This includes better care of their appearance, and use of non-verbal communication in conversation and listening skills.
d. Relapse prevention. By developing understanding of how offending is part of a process or cycle, the offender is better prepared to recognize how a particular action is in fact a "lapse" in a healthy, offending-free lifestyle.
e. Substance abuse. Although abuse may be linked to offending, these modules are further challenges to distorted thinking processes that will reinforce the need to change thinking styles for the offenders.
f. Stress inoculation for anger and impulse control. This includes learning to express emotions in a socially constructive manner. Thus, anger must be expressed appropriately, not destructively. The offenders keep diaries as part of this, so that factors that lead them to anger can be identified.

4. Mental/physical well-being. Better self-esteem and physical well-being are the main purposes of development in this area. Modules include:

a. Personal health project. This is a health schedule developed in conjunction with professionals. Yoga and running would be useful aspects of this. The programme excludes competitive sports as part of this though they can be played for general recreation.
b. Sex education. The client takes an assessment test and if he does well in terms of sex information he need not take the rest of the module. Otherwise there are lectures, printed materials, video tapes and so forth to provide information.
c. General learning. This can include art and music therapy, woodworking, ceramics and so forth.

All of this is far removed from the "cheap and cheerful" behaviour modification techniques. Justification for the use of extensive programmes seems to be based almost entirely on clinical experience rather than research.

Other essentially cognitive approaches include enhancing offender empathy (Hildebran and Pithers, 1989). Usually this is carried out in mixed offender groups (child abusers and rapists of adult women) in order that these alternative viewpoints (and antipathies) can work towards change. Materials on the experiences of the victims of offending are used to stimulate responses concerning victims of sex crimes. The offender is encouraged to write an account of his own offending from the point of view of his own victim. The distancing styles adopted by offenders towards their own offending need attention—these can include speaking in the past tense rather than in the present tense, extensive abuse may be reduced to a couple of phrases and the experience may be turned into a highly theatrical or dramatic scenario distanced from reality. Resisting offenders may be asked to role play the abuse as the victim with another member of the group acting as the victimizer.

Contingency Management

Inevitably, the process of doing therapy takes place in a far broader context than the time spent in the therapist's office. A wide range of external factors impinge on the likely therapeutic outcomes. Thus, there is a need to ensure commitment to therapy rather than the alternatives. Perkins (1991) suggests several means of helping offenders to move along the therapeutic path:

(1) The treatment options should be described, together with the likely outcomes of not going through therapy.
(2) Detailing to the client the rewards and punishments that are possible outside of therapy. These include the possibilities of further and longer terms of imprisonment, losing contact with his own children and the loss of his wife or other partner.
(3) The client is encouraged to view the therapy as being of his own choosing rather than the consequence of external pressures from within the institution or elsewhere. Perkins suggests that this is likely to maximize the genuine attitude changes following from therapy.
(4) Short-term benefits of therapy such as time out from tedious prison routine can be emphasized.

An illustrative case study involves a prisoner with a history of indecent assaults against girls, given a life sentence for girl rape. The man maintained that realizing the gravity of this offence had shocked him out of offending in future. He did not believe that he could be helped by therapy and saw himself, essentially, as posing no future risk. In comparison to other sex offenders, he felt himself harshly and unfairly dealt with:

> "Work with this offender began from the position of taking matters from his perspective, that is wanting to get out of prison. He accepted that the authorities would need to be convinced of his safety to the public and that this would require assembling a good deal of information about his past offending and his current propensity for offending ... He proved to be amenable to discussion about his past life and gained some insight into the reasons for his offending ... Discussion about his past sexually deviant interests and masturbation fantasies involving both young females and a degree of sadism led to the issue of how any changes in these features of his makeup might be demonstrated to the authorities. After much weighing of the pros and cons, the offender took part in an auditory [penile plethysmograph] assessment, which clearly indicated the presence of very strong sexual responses both to young females and to certain sadistic acts."
>
> (Perkins, 1991, p. 172)

The evidence provided by this directly led him to reveal how distressed he was about still having deviant fantasies. For the first time in the therapy, useful discussion was possible about his sexual deviance and what could be done about it.

Relapse Prevention

Some recent approaches to the treatment of sex offenders use techniques that help the client who has largely graduated out of therapy but has not altogether proven himself as a non-offender (Pithers *et al.*, 1988; Marshall, Hudson and Ward, 1992). The techniques are applied throughout the range of addictions (Wilson, 1992). Relapse into old ways is a clear possibility on release from an institution, and there is evidence that relapse tends to occur in the period immediately after cessation of treatment in the case of physical addictions. For sexual offences this period of maximum vulnerability is claimed to be the first nine months following discharge (Frisbie, 1969). It is important to supply the offender with the appropriate tools and techniques to recognize the danger signs of circumstances likely to enhance the risk of reoffending against children.

Empirical research on paedophiles has identified some of the precursors to offending (Pithers *et al.*, 1988, 1989). These immediate signs include planning of sexual offences (73%), anxiety (46%), depression (38%), alcohol abuse (23%), deviant sexual fantasies (51%) and many others. There is a sort of pattern that many pass through:

(1) Affective/mood changes: uncommunicative, brooding, moodiness;
(2) Fantasies of performing aberrant sexual acts;
(3) These fantasies were converted to thoughts such as the child needing to be educated into sex;
(4) Passive planning of the abuse, possibly during masturbatory fantasies.

In other words, the offence is not the result of "impulse". The offender can be taught to understand the signs of imminent further offending. It is important to make realistic claims about therapy's benefits. "Cure" is unlikely and many offenders will have deviant thoughts and sexual arousal patterns after treatment. Education into the likelihood of lapses is one way of making the client more fully insightful into his situation.

A few concepts from relapse prevention work can be mentioned for the purposes of illustration. One of these concepts is the Apparently Irrelevant Decision (AID; Jenkins-Hall and Marlatt, 1989). These are things that the offender decides to do which superficially may have little to do with offending in the mind of the offender but lead to risk situations. These are not accidents, but part of the engineering of a relapse. He needs to learn to recognize that hiring a Walt Disney film from a video store is unhealthy if he intends to use it to stimulate sexual imagery about young children. Similarly, making casual offers to babysit neighbours' children is not as casual as the offender may pretend to himself:

> "A paedophile in outpatient treatment described how he had a hectic day at work and was asked at the last minute to run an errand for his boss. This made him increasingly anxious about being late for dinner at his mother's, so anxious that he decided to take an alternate route because it would be faster. This route took him near an area of town where he had offended in the past. However, he would save about 10 minutes. As he drove through the area, he saw a child he knew from his neighborhood who looked exhausted and was carrying a heavy load. He was unaware of any sexual interest in the child, only that the child needed his assistance. The client took the time to stop and ask if the child needed a lift ... The child spontaneously gave the client a hug upon exiting the car."
>
> (Jenkins-Hall and Marlatt, 1989, p. 49)

Later he had urges which resulted in him masturbating to fantasies of a boy similar in appearance to the boy he had helped. The offender could not see the connections, but the sequence of events described demonstrates the ways in which behaviour that facilitates offending is subject to rationalization, its intention denied and the offender's feelings projected onto a child. One exercise to help prevent lapses is for the offender to fantasize a future scenario of a lapse involving a sequence of these apparently irrelevant decisions in order to see how they come together in the fantasized offence.

The Abstinence Violation Effect (AVE) is largely the consequence of the mismatch between the offender's new view of himself as a reformed person and knowing that he had lapsed in some way, thus putting himself at risk of reoffending. Such circumstances can lead the individual to revert to self-perceptions of being an offender:

> "The probability of relapse is a function of the following factors: (1) The extent to which the individual feels controlled by (or helpless relative to) the influence of another individual or group (e.g., criticism from others, anger at others) or by external events 'beyond the control' of the individual (e.g., financial hardship, boredom, depression); (2) The immediate availability of a coping response as an alternative to the dysfunctional behavior in a high-risk situation; (3) An individual's expectations about the consequences of the behavioral alternatives in the risk situation; and (4) The availability of victims (i.e., opportunity)."
>
> (Russell *et al.*, 1989, pp. 147–148)

Relapse prevention requires a highly individualized programme designed to help a particular offender to cope with his special pattern of precursors to offending, to develop his own coping mechanisms and to develop his own contract with the therapist. Pithers *et al.* (1988) argue that relapse prevention is highly cost effective. For example, it needed only $61 000 to provide relapse prevention for 15 outpatient therapy groups. The relapse rate for paedophiles following treatment was only 3% reconvictions.

Addiction Control Programmes

Superficially at least, most forms of psychological treatment have the individual as their focus. In many ways, they seek to provide a degree of autonomy for the participants in the programme. But this is not universal; there are treatments with an ethical foundation in an attitude more hostile to the offender and more geared to protecting what are believed to be broader social interests. These seek to psychologically control and contain paedophilia as their first objective. They assume that paedophilia is an addiction, to be tackled much as any other addiction would be. Salter (1988) makes the point strongly that general psychotherapy and that for sexual offenders differ fundamentally. She suggests, among other things:

(1) That voluntary treatment is *not* to be preferred. Too often the client will use the opportunity to avoid the consequences of his crimes. Treatment mandated by a court of law has the back-up threat of further judicial punishment required to keep the offender in line.
(2) It is for the therapist to set the goals of the treatment rather than the client and to forcibly reject inappropriate and exculpatory goals.
(3) The therapist must set a clear value stance against abuse and the harm done by it.
(4) The therapist must set limits on the behaviour of the offender and react strongly if the limits are exceeded. The incestuous father who engages in "tickling" sessions with his child may well be exceeding what is allowable during a course of therapy.
(5) The offender is not to be trusted as a reliable source of information. He is regarded as a liar.
(6) Confrontation is the typical style, and comments by the therapist such as "I wouldn't believe that if my grandmother swore it on her death bed" are regarded as appropriate.

It is not seen as right to regard the addict as a trustworthy person, someone who is determined to "kick" the habit. This comes across very clearly in the viewpoint of Wyre (1989) when describing the treatment programme employed by his co-workers and himself:

> "I feel the most important thing to do is to shift the power and the knowledge base from the offender to the worker. I want [him] to feel that I know what he is up to, what he thinks about and what he does."
>
> (Wyre, 1989, p. 19)

The strategy, especially early on in treatment with incest cases, may involve the use of offenders' distorted justifications for their offences. The approach is one of "appearing to collude" with the offender; skilful use of enabling comments can prompt disclosure concerning patterns of offending. These take the form of the usual cognitive distortions common among offenders:

> "I expect you found her very promiscuous when you joined the family?"
> "I suppose she saw you make love to your wife?"
> "I expect you usually told her to go away?"
> "Sometimes when you were cuddling she touched your penis and asked questions."
>
> (Wyre, 1987, pp. 32–33)

Such leading questions are geared mainly to obtaining evidence of guilt. Apart from their role in treatment, they also provide the means of preventing further abuse by having a profile of the offender for future forensic or preventative purposes. Wyre regards it as a crucial part of dealing with the offender to investigate the characteristics of the man's offending. Just how does he form the social relationships that become the basis for the sexual abuse of children? Is there a particular sort of child that typically becomes targeted by the offender? Are they characteristically a certain age or physical type? This information is then available as a profile to match with future offences for forensic purposes or to use to prevent possible offending:

> "We are meant to disclose any information we have about a known child molester ..."
>
> (Wyre, 1989, p. 19)

There is something of a culture shock for those with a foundation in traditional psychotherapy when confronted with Wyre's views. Further insight into the approach's ideology is revealed by the following:

> "If you use the psychotherapeutic model ... you're almost certain to run into trouble. It starts on the premise that you are treating the offender more as a victim than as a perpetrator—you're colluding with him to see what made him carry out these offences ... I have to make them confront the reality of the abuse, make them see the damage and understand that they had a choice as an adult which their victim as a child didn't have."
>
> (Wyre, reported in Tate, 1990, p. 264)

Although the addiction control programmes share a great deal with other forms of psychotherapy, it is important to remember the nature of their special assumptions because this highlights the distinctive ideology involved. Theory in this area is not yet systematic enough to make any great claims about major schools of thought; it may be that many of the programmes not proclaiming their basis in addiction control are *de facto* similar. After all, the approach is as much to do with the distinctive attitude of the therapist as substantially different therapeutic techniques. McConaghy (1989), writing of similar techniques mixing confrontation with support, suggested:

> "Such techniques are disturbingly reminiscent of those used to provide data for political and religious show-trials. Their underlying acceptance of a guilty until proven innocent attitude suggests the accused sex offender has become the contemporary witch, victim of the projected unacceptable sexual fantasies of the good citizen."
>
> (McConaghy, 1989, pp. 618–619)

Perhaps this is a major debate just waiting to happen.

Religious Therapies

While the addiction model dominates in his work also, Valcour (1990) describes therapy that is steeped in the Alcoholics Anonymous philosophy but integrated with religious attitudes. Twelve steps are involved in the treatment employed by the Catholic Church in the USA, apparently very successfully. At one treatment centre, 55 child molesters who completed therapy reported no recidivism or new allegations at follow-up. Over 30 of the men had returned to work in some form of ministry. Valcour insists that what he calls "Sexaholics Anonymous" does not require that the addiction concept be satisfactory in research or theoretical terms for the treatment based on it to be effective. The twelve steps are parts of a three-part treatment model: (i) accepting that there is a problem that essentially is beyond our individual power to affect though not beyond our responsibility, (ii) the desire for help beyond oneself as an individual and (iii) the "handing over of self to that healing higher power, be it God, a fellowship or therapy group, a treatment center or some combination thereof" (Valcour, 1990, p. 55). Some of the twelve steps are:

(1) Admission that life had become unmanageable because they were powerless over their lusts.
(2) Coming to believe that a greater power could restore sanity.
(3) Placing their life in the care of God.
(4) Making a moral inventory of themselves.
(5) Allowing God to take away their character defects.
(6) Naming everyone harmed and becoming willing to make amends.

(7) Praying and meditating for strength to carry out God's will for them.
(8) Evangelizing the "sexaholic" message.

Among the areas that are seen as important to deal with are:

1. Idealization. Abusers may need to be helped to see the reality of their early family life which suffers from idealization. One offender whose family moved 20 times in his childhood claimed that this was not a problem because they always had a comfortable home.

2. Self-loathing and guilt. This can interfere with therapy since what is needed, according to Valcour, is for the individual to despise what they have done but regard themselves as a "fully franchised human being loved by God and others" (p. 57).

3. Authority conflicts. Valcour suggests that offenders lack a mature understanding of authority as essential in any social system. They may have problems with the authority hierarchy of the church and in therapy may disparage the therapists as authority figures. The problem is dealt with through honest communication.

While it is obvious that such an approach has only limited secular applicability, it is intriguing because of the ideological slant it imposes. Overt hostility as implicit in some other addiction models is replaced by concerns about the whole person.

The Role of Group Work

The use of therapeutic groups for offenders against children is characteristic of recent therapeutic programmes. Much of this is similar to what takes place in general psychotherapy for non-offenders. Careful accounts of its use in relation to paedophiles are not common. The reasons for this are probably to do with its common usage in general psychotherapy, as part of the stock-in-trade of the professional therapist. Nevertheless, Breer (1987) goes into considerable detail but his interest is primarily in the treatment of adolescents who molest other, younger children. Since sexual offences are often committed by teenage offenders who then grow up to become middle-aged paedophiles, his discussion is very salient.

The group, according to Breer, is especially useful in providing sustained and confrontational pressure on a member determined to avoid the crux of the issue—his offending. Groups may achieve more than the therapist could in individual sessions. For non-residential offenders there should be no more than one group a week, lasting a minimum of two hours. Breer uses the term "family energy" to indicate that the parents of a young offender have only finite resources to devote to his problems; taxing the family's ability to devote time, money and emotional resources is counterproductive and over-frequent therapy sessions can result in family or offender resistance. Furthermore, people and families can only change at a given pace determined by their emotional strength. To push the rate of change too greatly is fruitless. A weekly group session is a compromise between all factors but is generally within the capacities of most offenders and their families. Meetings need to be lengthy because time is invariably wasted in excuses and the like before the nitty-gritty of the group work is achieved, often in the dying minutes of the meeting. Breer motivates clients using a five rung "ladder of achievement". Youngsters can ask to be considered for higher levels. The lowest rung is that of denial and minimalization of the offence; the highest involves achieving sophisticated understanding of the victim and the victim's experience.

Again, the methods are unlike traditional psychotherapy in a number of ways:

> "A degree of coerciveness and lack of confidentiality are modifications of traditional therapy essential to the successful treatment of the adolescent molester. They must, however, be balanced by a climate of warmth, acceptance, and support in the group itself. Everything should be done to create a climate of free expression in the group. For example, there should be no rules on the nature of the language used in discussion."
>
> (Breer, 1987, p. 113)

Support Therapies

One rare discussion of support therapies for the counselling of paedophiles is to be found in van Zessen (1991), who raises a number of problems with conventional treatment programmes for paedophiles. These include that they are almost exclusively designed for prisoner or psychiatric hospital populations; deal with paedophiles alongside all other sex offenders; regard paedophilia as a homogeneous issue in which the sexual rapist of a toddler is dealt with in the same way as a man having a "paedophiliac affair" with a

15-year-old boy; and risk confusing a genuine desire to change sexual orientation with a wish to get out of prison or hospital. Treatment is aimed at getting rid of paedophiliac arousal and at increasing arousal to adults, usually women, fails to distinguish between clear abuse and consensual acts, and never explores the meaning of the paedophiliac attraction in the psychology of the man.

At the Clinical Psychology Department at the University of Utrecht, for a while non-residential clients in the 25- to 50-year-old range with a preference for 9- to 16-year-old boys were put through a therapy programme. Only men having non-violent contacts and no signs of severe psychopathology were eligible. The therapy was not designed to convert men from paedophilia and so did not attempt to create heterosexual arousal or to provide heterosexual courtship skills. The men, it was felt, were too old and lacking in signs of heterosexuality to make conversion a realistic possibility. Rarely had the men sought conversion.

During assessment, it became clear that the major problems for the paedophile either concerned his erotic/sexual attraction to boys or difficulties created when trying to express his sexuality in relation to other people. Identity and realization therapies formed the nucleus of individual therapy as a consequence. The focus was upon the provision of cognitive frameworks that helped to structure understanding of sexual/erotic desires. Guilt and insecurity were characteristic of many of the men:

> "In this phase of therapy, the meaning of the desires is explored and discussed. The therapist helps to focus on the desires and to positively change the self-image."
>
> (van Zessen, 1991, p. 192)

The second phase of therapy centred on the realization of desires:

> "No one is brought up to be a pedophile and there are no visible models to follow in coping with problems. The social framework for intergenerational relationships is lacking ... Social support can be found among other pedophiles in organized settings (self-help or emancipation groups, often with a strong ideological background) or in informal situations (circles or networks of 'colleagues')."
>
> (van Zessen, 1991, p. 192)

Having made satisfactory progress in the individual therapy, some of the men would move on to work in small groups in order to improve their ability to communicate with others about the problems created by the paedophile lifestyle. Matters like paedophile "coming out"; interactions with the boys, their parents and the police; and growing old as a paedophile could be discussed. Basic conversational skills, such as listening attentively and dealing with feedback, were also developed. A pilot study suggested that the listening and contributing skills of members of the group improved.

The law in the Netherlands was conducive to such therapy as there was no mandatory reporting of suspected child abuse and a therapist could not be regarded as an accessory to a crime through accepting the sexual activities of the clients. The therapy had to be modified as Dutch society became less accepting of therapeutic support for paedophilia. The newer therapy emphasized understanding the emotional functions of their paedophilia in the lives of the men.

> "These men strive for enduring, affectionate and erotical friendships with boys; they have no interest in forced or violent sexual contacts. When a boy is very young (12 years old and under) or emotionally unstable, the counselor can suggest that the man reconsiders the relationship thoroughly, especially its sexual aspect. A non-sexual relationship with a boy, regardless of his age, is not illegal."
>
> (van Zessen, 1991, p. 196)

Again, at the University of Utrecht, van Naerssen (1991) utilized a related approach, apparently supported by the Dutch police. He agreed to take referrals from the police of men who had been involved sexually with boys or girls over 11 years of age. There were a number of provisos, such as the man had to have requested referral, had to be a non-violent offender and had to have no severe psychiatric symptoms such as delusions or depression. It was possible to break down this sample of clients into two broad categories—*self-identified* paedophiles and *identity confused* paedophiles.

Category 1: Self-Identified Paedophiles

Some saw themselves as paedophile and were very clear about this. They wished to discuss their relationships with boys and felt the lack of social support to be a problem. A sizeable group of these dealt with their relationships solely in terms of "fun and games"; attachment to the boys was difficult and long-term relationships were consequently regarded as impossible. Therapy dealt with this by explaining how relationships concentrating solely on sexual matters prevent emotional closeness. Examples of adult–child conflicts in these relationships were worked upon in order to find ways of coping with difficulties. Only a small number of these men gained confidence in their ability to develop emotional commitment even after many treatment sessions. Mostly they continued to relate only in casual sexual encounters. Another sizeable group of these self-defined paedophiles had developed emotional commitment to the children. This had its problems, since they found that the boys could not handle this emotional aspect. The therapist explained how boys develop psychosexually and pointed out that man–boy relationships are difficult for boys given social pressures towards heterosexuality. The therapy also included scenarios of conflicts that can arise in man–boy involvements. This type of client seemed to learn effectively in therapy since mostly they reported increased satisfaction with their relationships with underage boys, although this will seem an undesirable outcome of therapy to many people.

Category 2: Identity Confused Paedophiles

These did not define themselves as paedophiles with any certainty; they were confused over their sexual identity. Some wanted to undergo therapy to become "normal" in their sexual desires. They expressed great concern about their sexual feelings and worried about being found out. Sexual dysfunction was common, involving problems associated with desire, arousal and orgasm. Some were fearful of adulthood, having a sort of "Peter Pan" complex and an idealized view of childhood, and others believed that they ought to be punished for their sexual activities with boys. The therapist provided biographies in which adult–child sexual contacts were treated in a very positive way. Some of the men were capable of defining themselves as paedophiles after about 10 such therapy sessions, but a roughly equal number could not. Van Naerssen suggests that their histories involved very negative family attitudes towards sexuality, in which sex was separated from love and regarded as filthy but love was extremely romanticized. For these men, treatment goals concentrated on their ideas about sexuality rather than on their paedophilia as such. Mostly these men discontinued treatment.

Quite clearly this sort of therapy contrasts markedly with other sorts. The relatively liberal Dutch attitude towards paedophilia no doubt contributes to this. It should be noted that in 1950 over a third of all recorded sex crimes in Holland involved a minor; this had reduced to a little over a quarter by 1982.

The "Systematic" of Therapy

It is common for reports of research findings published in academic journals to portray a somewhat rosy version of the truth. This is not deliberate deception as such; it is more a case of describing events as being tidy and systematic when, in fact, the process was relatively haphazard and fraught. So, for example, whereas the researcher leapt into the research without reading previous research and without bothering to theorize overly, the final report may well describe the research in very orderly terms, in which the theoretical and conceptual reasons for doing the research are carefully melded with the empirical research. The term *systematic* has been used by sociologists of science to describe these "polished-up" accounts of research (Howitt, 1991). Descriptions of therapy are quite similar, in avoiding the somewhat embarrassing hitches and difficulties encountered. This may be partly a consequence of reporting new types of therapy after only limited trials with a few highly motivated clients. Saphira (1989) is different, in focusing on difficulties encountered using commonly employed therapies. He describes his tribulations when dealing with sexual offender prisoners in New Zealand. Attempts were made to treat over four-fifths of them. The programme of therapy was similar to those described earlier and involved such things as assertiveness training, anger and stress control, covert sensitization and risk management. About a quarter of the original sample either withdrew after the initial sessions or sabotaged their programmes. Only about 5% of the men actually completed treatment. The offenders superficially appeared to be cooperating with treatment but many scrupulously avoided changing their attitudes or behaviour.

Among means of sabotaging the programme, Saphira mentions the following:

(1) Evasion: taking up the treatment session with matters relating to the prison rather than to their offending.
(2) Denying access/information: the therapist might be forbidden to contact older children of the offender or the offender may deny earlier abuse of now grown up children. This interferes with attempts to relate earlier stress to the start of offending.
(3) Printed materials provided for use during treatment and for "homework" may be "lost" or forgotten.
(4) Offenders may place themselves in high risk situations, thus undermining whatever therapeutic progress had been achieved

by this time. For example, finding accommodation next to a school clearly may enhance the potential for offending.

(5) Making excuses as to why they cannot follow their therapy programme after leaving prison. They avoid joining support or therapy groups, finding time-consuming leisure time activities or making friends.

If it is any consolation to psychotherapists, medical treatments may be similarly fraught. Hucker, Langevin and Bain (1988) intended to investigate the effectiveness of a sex drive reducing drug. Not only have drop-outs to be taken into account but also men who refuse to take the medication in the first place. They took consecutive referrals to a Canadian psychiatric forensic service. Each had been charged with contact abuse of children or had already been convicted. Of these men, less than half were willing to undertake a comprehensive assessment programme. Even these figures declined markedly when the men were asked to take part in a controlled clinical trial of the libido reducing drug—only 18% of the original sample agreed! But this was not the end of the matter. Two others had to be dropped for either health reasons or for not taking their medication, and another five left treatment of their own volition. Homosexual paedophiles, it emerged, were relatively more likely to take the therapy than heterosexuals. Despite the authors feeling that the drug was valuable for treatment where it was taken, all in all their experience puts a question mark beside the potential use of such treatments generally in therapy.

Attempts have been made to predict the likely "careers" of offenders during treatment in order to identify the best contenders. Abel *et al.* (1988) took a sample of fairly well-educated non-prisoner paedophiles entering a treatment programme. This involved social and assertiveness skills training, sex education, cognitive restructuring, covert sensitization and masturbatory satiation. About a third had dropped out before the end of the 30 weeks of treatment. Mostly they simply refused to continue treatment and did not specify the reasons. A small percentage had been imprisoned and others had been thrown out of treatment because they were too disruptive. Others moved or became extremely psychologically disturbed. Most demographic characteristics did not differentiate between those who finished treatment and the drop-outs. Rates of paedophilia and duration of paedophile careers also made no effect. Nevertheless, three characteristics did identify likely drop-outs:

(1) Self-assessed heavy pressure to be in the treatment programme;
(2) Being diagnosed as having an antisocial personality—such individuals can be socially manipulative and leave therapy as soon as they have achieved their aims of, say, avoiding greater punishment; and
(3) Being involved with boys and girls and having a range of paedophiliac acts (e.g. both exhibitionism and fondling). Abel *et al.* (1988) suggest that these may have developed too great a range of psychological defences justifying involvement with children for therapy to penetrate.

Such attempts to make systematic knowledge about the characteristics of bad risks for therapy are clearly valuable, especially in circumstances in which therapy is a scarce resource. Nevertheless, programmes in different settings vary widely in their drop-out rates. Unfortunately, the reasons for these between-programme disparities have not been researched.

Evaluation of Treatment

> "Any therapy creates for the patient a demand situation. This applies especially to procedures designed to change feelings and attitudes primarily. Even a patient who, at the start freely admitted to his anomaly, may easily succumb to this demand situation and try to influence the test result in the direction of a favourable outcome."
>
> (Freund, 1981, p. 167)

As with therapy in general, there is a gap between practitioners' confidence in their techniques and substantiated research evidence from controlled evaluations of therapeutic success:

> "We have seen many treatment failures but we have never seen a treatment which made a sex offender more deviant. In the absence of knowledge of a treatment which is totally effective across the board for all sex offenders, it is safe to say that *any* treatment which promises or produces success in the individual case is always better than no treatment at all."
>
> (Laws, 1985, p. 43)

Such pragmatic comments will appear rather cavalier to those who believe it is incumbent upon therapy to prove its worth. Theoretically, evaluation research is relatively simple—treat some, don't treat others and measure any differences. But few things are ever that straightforward. A major problem is money, and most of the treatment of sex offenders is carried out in places traditionally uninvolved in research. Often funds are very limited for the provision of therapy itself, and whatever research is done is on a shoestring.

Another major difficulty is that the best criteria of the true worth of the therapy are only measurable in contexts away from the treatment setting. Recidivism, for example, is not only intrinsically difficult to measure because of underreporting by victims and other factors, but involves a time scale that is a deterrent given the pressing, day-to-day demands of work in a therapy unit. While it is perfectly feasible to ask offenders whether their treatment is doing them any good, if they answer "yes" the inclination is to suggest "well, they would say that wouldn't they?" Offenders have a vested interest in convincing the authorities that they are responding to therapy and that they are unlikely to reoffend. Asking similar questions using formal psychological tests and measures is fraught with much the same difficulties of motivated and strategic replies.

Most of the available evaluation work is relatively short term. Simple questionnaire measures or physiological measurements of arousal to deviant pictures are usually as far as it goes. Physiological measures have a superficial scientific "objectivity", which may to some extent account for their popularity. Where evaluations are done, it is usually easier to compare treatment with no treatment than to decide which of several treatments work and are the most effective and efficient. It is important to differentiate between studies that have investigated therapy for groups of sex offenders in general and those that have concentrated on paedophiles. One should not presume that what works with a rapist will also work with a paedophile; the state of evaluation research is such that we cannot say with certainty whether this assumption of therapeutic comparability is sustainable.

In a thorough review of the evaluation studies applied to sexual paraphilias in general (fetishes, cross-dressing, etc. as well as paedophilia), Kilmann *et al.* (1982) concluded:

> "The paraphiliac treatment literature reflected severe methodological shortcomings: e.g., the failure to assess subjects' pretreatment functioning and the strong reliance upon subjects' self-reports, often obtained verbally, in the assessment of treatment outcome. Since most studies did not specify the characteristics of the therapists, the relative importance of the therapist variable could not be distinguished from other aspects of treatment. Very few of the studies included a control

> condition. The control subjects in the studies which included them rarely were matched to their experimental counterparts on treatment-related variables. Much of the literature consisted of single-case studies. Most of the small number of group studies found in the literature also were uncontrolled. The tendency in most of the group studies was to consider all variant subjects as similar, and to consider all variations as similar in terms of their origin and maintenance. This resulted in global, non-specific attempts at treatment."
>
> (Kilmann *et al.*, 1982, p. 239)

Most evaluations of behavioural treatments are in terms of success with a small number of clients, sometimes just one. Evaluations of treatment programmes in a systematic manner using outcomes related to offending are even more difficult to find. Some practitioners have been highly critical of the lack of evidence available about quite significant treatment programmes.

All of this assumes that the prime reason for treating sex offenders against children is to directly reduce the likelihood of any further such offending. This point of view is probably most endemic in the behaviourist fantasy/orgasm modification techniques. Therapy broadly directed towards the social and psychological difficulties that offenders might have nevertheless can be important. These difficulties may have contributed to the offending only indirectly, but if ignored they may interfere with therapy directly related to offending. Ultimately, it is difficult to see the justification for not helping offenders with their problems simply because this help is not geared to stopping offending.

Just as therapy usually involves compromises between what is ideal and what is practicable, so too does evaluative research. It is, as a consequence, not possible to identify research studies that get close to meeting high standards. For example, the pressures on the therapy unit to treat referrals from court may make it impossible to create an acceptable control group. The operation of the therapeutic unit as a social system may also interfere. What, for example, of problems of spill-over from treatment? Untreated offenders may well learn from offenders in treatment in the same unit; this would reduce apparent differences between treated and untreated offenders.

There is, of course, some evaluative research on sex offender treatment programmes (e.g. Groth, 1979a). A good illustration of the nature of the problems can be seen in the study of Dwyer and Myers (1990). They sent a questionnaire to men who had been treated for sexual offences—the vast majority of these were paedophiles or incest offenders (74% of the cases). The rest were obscene telephone callers, frotteurs, peeping toms and exhibitionists. Over two-thirds of those taking part were sent for treatment by a court of law. "Multi-modal" outpatient treatment was used, including interactive therapeutic work with victims and other family members, sex education, diary keeping, reading homework, behavioural tasks to develop new skills such as assertiveness and communication skills with adults, family therapy techniques to deal with psychological damage from childhood, and marital and sexual therapy. Libido reducing drugs were also employed where appropriate. All of this is important in assessing the outcome of the study. The follow-up period varied from a few months to about 10 years. Computer data-bank checks on offenders yielded information about new arrests and was combined with self-reported reoffending. Recidivism was under 4% although over two-thirds of the respondents reported urges to reoffend. The men indicated broad satisfaction with *all* techniques used in the therapy.

The study, though, involved relatively short follow-up periods in which reoffending could take place, and the men were selected as good candidates for therapy, so hard and persistent cases were excluded. These factors could explain the relatively low recidivism. Without a proper non-treated control group it is impossible to tell. Abel *et al.* (1988), using a similar programme to this one, found recidivism after a year of follow-up to be 12%, although this relied solely on reports by their paedophile clients. As this rate is several times that found by Dwyer and Myers, this variability ought to be explained. One possibility is that paedophiles are less successfully treated than the mixed population used by Dwyer and Myers. Another is that Abel *et al.* studied men who had *not* been referred by a court of law. Thus, it may well be that the greater fear of the penal system acts as a deterrent among court-referred offenders. It is notable that short-term follow-ups continue to be described. Marques *et al.* (1989) report data from a follow-up in which the offenders had only been at risk in the community for six months. While none of them had been rearrested for sex crimes, they did not differ from a non-treated volunteer control group (at risk for an average of four months) or a non-volunteer control group (at risk for seven months). They seemed to be a little better than controls in terms of violations of parole.

It can be difficult to understand the paucity of studies of recidivism in sex offenders. Although only partially dealing with paedophiles,

Furby, Weinrott and Blackshaw's (1989) extensive review of recidivism studies contains a number of salutary lessons for those inclined to assume that the pertinent data on recidivism is readily available and simple to interpret. They included 42 studies of a range of different types of sex offending. Firstly, on the matter of treatment effectiveness:

> "Two patterns are evident with respect to treated and untreated sex offender comparisons. First, eight of the nine studies of untreated offenders (with follow-up periods ranging from 6 months to 10 years) have relatively low recidivism rates, all below 12%. In contrast, two thirds of treated offender studies have rates higher than 12%."
>
> (Furby, Weinrott and Blackshaw, 1989, p. 24)

Of course, there are all sorts of artefacts that might be responsible for this curious state of affairs—for example, the studies where treatment was given might have been more rigorous in following up the offenders. The authors are somewhat critical of the studies that involve treated and untreated cases:

> "In six of these seven studies, the sex offense recidivism rate for the treated offenders is higher than that for the untreated offenders (though in one of the six studies, that difference is minuscule). However, in all but one of these studies, the treated and control groups differed at the outset in ways other than whether they received treatment."
>
> (Furby, Weinrott and Blackshaw, 1989, p. 25)

These are not definitive statements about the ineffectiveness of treatment, embarrassing as they might appear. Many of the treatments might no longer be considered "state of the art". Rather, the data can be seen as a warning shot against complacency about therapy. It is easy to sympathize with Furby, Weinrott and Blackshaw's view, "It is time that we give this issue the resources and attention it deserves" (p. 28).

As the prominent therapist Wyre has said, "It may be that I'm just creating very clever offenders" (FitzHerbert, 1993).

THE COSTS OF NOT TREATING

While this discussion might encourage a degree of scepticism over the state of our knowledge about the effects of treatment on recidivism rates, it is nevertheless important to develop approaches to evaluating the benefits that might accrue from therapy. Given that any sort of therapy costs money, time and other resources, it is possible to subject treatment to a cost–benefit analysis. The level-playing-field approach requires that whatever comparisons are made, all measurable economic costs are included. So, for example, although it is impossible to put a price on grief and suffering, it is feasible to calculate the monetary cost of treating the victim. Usually, the cost of an offence has to include those of processing the offender through the legal system and imprisonment. These are alarmingly expensive.

A cost–benefit analysis of the rehabilitation of child molesters was carried out at the Massachusetts Treatment Center (Prentky and Burgess, 1990). Using a group of inpatient child molesters for whom recidivism data were available, it was possible to compare the recidivism of this group with that of untreated offenders. The sample was generally of long-term offenders, since a third had a juvenile record and 90% a previous adult record. Over a five-year follow-up period, 25% of the treated group offended again. This recidivism rate was based entirely on the number of criminal charges made. A small number of so-called nuisance sex charges involving non-contact offences such as voyeurism and obscenity were all excluded. Finding an appropriate non-treated group causes difficulty. A randomly selected, non-treated sample from the same offender population would be ideal but this is not easily done for court-referred offenders required to take treatment by court. Instead, by using the findings of another study (Marshall and Barbaree, 1988), it was decided that the appropriate recidivism rate for a similar group of non-treated offenders was 40%. The authors regard this figure as conservative. It goes without saying that the non-treated recidivism rate is a crucial element in the calculation of the benefits of therapy. Seven years of incarceration before review for probation was taken as the likely minimum average. Imprisonment formed the bulk of the cost, with victim-related costs a fraction of this. At the time, the monetary cost of each new offence by an untreated offender was close to a quarter of a million dollars. The figure for members of the treated control group was 71% of this:

> "It appears that we resist treating child molesters because treatment is too 'humane' a response to such egregious behavior. If the overriding goal is the reduction of victimization rates, as well as of the costs incurred by victimization, and if rehabilitation of offenders can be shown to reduce the likelihood of repeated offenses, then it is

> imperative that we overcome our resistance to treating child molesters—not for the sake of the offenders, but for the sake of the victims."
>
> (Prentky and Burgess, 1990, p. 116)

Notwithstanding the limitations of the data, this reflects a rational approach to therapy. The better the results achieved in therapy in terms of recidivism, the greater the savings. Unfortunately, most therapies have not been evaluated in this way. As things stand, the available data applies at best to certain therapies in a criminal justice system giving substantial prison sentences to paedophiles. It is possible that Prentky and Burgess were being generous in their estimates of non-treated recidivism. Finkelhor (1986) reviewed the available recidivism studies of paedophiles, and appears somewhat scornful of their worth, especially their relatively short follow-up periods. The 10 studies reviewed gave figures of between 6 and 35% for sex offence recidivism. While these studies involved various mixtures of treated and untreated offenders, quite obviously the range is sufficient to imply that treatment may not be so cost effective as Prentky and Burgess imply.

It is not very meaningful to draw conclusions about therapy for paedophiles. The reasons for this are as much to do with the lack of in-depth research into therapy as they are to do with the varied ideological bases of therapy. Modern treatment for paedophilia is multifaceted. No modern therapist is on record as recommending a single psychological treatment technique even for an individual offender, although this was done in the case of the early behaviour therapies. Programmes that cover virtually every conceivable deficit in the knowledge, skills and thinking of offenders are the current recommendation. The question of why programmes have come to dominate therapy has not been answered, especially at the level of demonstrated effectiveness. No doubt the failure of research to reach consensus over a single explanation of offending has had considerable impact. Research on paedophilia itself has done little to focus therapy away from the multi-modal programme. Instead, as we have seen, causal explanations of offending stress multi-determination. It would be harsh to describe modern therapy as "shotgun", but the lack of research specifying which parts of the programmes work best invites such suggestions.

It is possible that the attraction of the treatment programme can be explained by professional and institutional requirements as much as by proven therapeutic success. A programme can facilitate the cooperation of therapists coming from a variety of ideological-cum-theoretical positions on approaches to therapy. This applies both within and between professions. Psychologists, psychiatrists, medical staff, social workers, probation officers and prison officers are among the range of professions that might be represented in a team involved with therapy. Each of these differ in terms of their skills as well as their broad professional ideologies. The programme provides a variety of niches in which different individuals may operate as part of the team. This smooths the path of interdisciplinary cooperation.

Prendergast (1991) provides a true/false self-assessment quiz which includes the following items:

(1) Supportive and non-confrontational treatment techniques work better with sex offenders than other treatment modalities.
(2) Psychotherapy itself will produce positive results with sex offenders.

FALSE is the correct answer in both cases, according to Prendergast. Some might be more inclined to wonder how confident one can be in this. What do "work better" and "positive results" mean in this context? It would appear that there is a long road to travel before we see all of the implications of the questions, let alone provide definitive answers.

CHAPTER 8

The Future of Paedophilia

> "Ann knows from personal experience. Her children were molested not once, but twice. Both times by men [patient 1 and patient 2] who were treated ... [at the clinic]. There were others like them. While a patient ... [patient 3] sexually abused three boys. While an outpatient ... [patient 4] allegedly molests a 9-year-old girl. Former ... [patient 5] is convicted for having sexual relations with boys, ages 7 to 13. While in treatment ... [patients 6 and 7] sexually abused three boys ... [patient 8] accosts and molests seven women in what the papers called bizarre sex spree. A convicted child abuser ... [patient 9] takes two preteenaged boys with him to the ... [clinic]. While he is in therapy, they drive his car into the wall of the hospital ... [patient 9] was later charged with molesting two boys."
>
> (from a television series, quoted in Berlin and Malin, 1991, p. 1573)

Berlin and Malin did not like this sort of media coverage of their clients at the Johns Hopkins Sexual Disorders Clinic. Television took an interest at a time when a well-known public figure had referred himself there for treatment. Of the nine apparently recidivist offenders that were described in the programme, the "truth" of their "reoffending" did not always match what was claimed by the series:

- Two were reconvictions while under treatment
- Three had avoided or resisted therapy
- One was mentally incompetent to stand trial
- One had sprayed women with paint but with no sexual assault
- One was not accused of having genital contact by the boys involved

- One took the boys to the clinic for evaluation at the clinic's request, although his rearrest was not unexpected

The "misrepresentation" can be illustrated by the case of a patient who was a homosexual paedophile. According to Berlin and Malin, the programme failed to reveal that his "recidivism" occurred when one of the three boys put debris into the offender's trousers when he refused to give them motor scooter rides; he put debris down their trousers in retaliation. None of the boys alleged any genital contact despite the man's history of fondling boys sitting on his scooter. At a parent–teacher association meeting, a parent had announced that there was a convicted molester living locally, which led to a police investigation. Taking his lawyer's advice into account, the patient pleaded guilty to a minor offence against the boys.

Despite Berlin and Malin's defence of the crime, some might be inclined to regard the man as being at an early stage of his reoffending cycle—exhibiting the pattern that had previously led to abuse. Similarly, the paint-throwing incident involving another of the patients may not be quite the non-sexual assault that Berlin and Malin claim it to be. They neglect that some clinicians argue that there may be serious sexual underpinnings to apparently non-sexual offences—including physical assaults on women (Revitch and Schlesinger, 1988).

The clinic's overall criminal recidivism rates for exhibitionists, paedophiles and sexual attackers of women treated at the clinic was actually quite good (less that 10%) and only 3% for paedophiles who cooperated fully in treatment:

> "Biased media presentations that focus only on treatment failures, sometimes in a less than fully informed fashion, do a disservice to patients, mental health workers, and society at large."
>
> (Berlin and Malin, 1991, p. 1576)

But who is to blame? It is easy to suggest the media but this ignores important aspects of how paedophilia was created as part of a major social issue. Did the media invent the slogans of the child abuse debate; the idea that sex offenders are never cured; the idea that sex offenders are difficult to treat; that paedophiles lie, deceive and cheat; the ideas of the paedophile ring and satanic abuse; the idea that children never lie; ritual abuse; and the idea that paedophiles are violent? Most of these are drawn directly from the public claims of child protection workers. Imagine, for now, what impression is created by the following, which combines a simplistic critique of the role of the media with a sloganistic view of child abuse:

> "Our national preoccupation with sex, particularly as reflected in the print and electronic media, cannot be overlooked as contributing to an 'ecology of deviance' that heightens the vulnerability of children to sexual assault and increases the prevalence of adolescent child bearing and child rearing. Parenthetically, I consider any sexual overtures made to children by adults, whether violent or flatteringly persuasive, as human sexual aggression. For me to think otherwise would be to accept the premise that children are the aggressors in their own victimization."
>
> (Green, 1988, p. 402)

Rhetorically, Green blames the media for everything from sexual assault to teenage pregnancies. Such a diffuse target is little other than a vehicle for a moral outcry inappropriate to a serious academic publication. After all, just a few years earlier, it was possible for another serious academic review of child victims to conclude:

> "Without doubt, the child victim's own behaviour often plays a considerable part in initiating and maintaining a pedophiliac crime. However, when we speak about victimological aspects in pedophiliac acts of children who are 'precipitating' or 'participating', it is important to bear in mind that they do not necessarily always view the pedophiliac acts in the same sexual way as the adults ... These acts can often seem to them something exciting, an expression of their stimulus-seeking behaviour, or a way to establish relationships with adults."
>
> (Virkunnen, 1981, pp. 130–131)

PAEDOPHILIA ACROSS CULTURES AND TIME?

Imagine the parents who send their adolescent son to stay with his godfather, where he is made very welcome and becomes part of the new family for a while. During this time his godfather becomes physically involved with him, culminating with the boy being deliberately ejaculated upon. The parents are so delighted about this that they insist on giving the man joints of meat. Surely a more appropriate strategy would be to call in the police and child protection workers, or beat the living daylights out of the man? This social arrangement was to be found in various parts of Papua New Guinea and Melanesia in strikingly similar ways (Bleibtreu-Ehrenberg, 1991). It was strongly believed that a young man who does not undergo such an initiation process will remain a child, incapable of marriage and fatherhood, never to become a warrior. Prior to this initiation, a boy is regarded as belonging to his mother. He is a "woman" in that he can take part in their rituals and tasks without embarrassment. He is capable of pregnancy and, if illness caused stomach swelling, attempts were made to induce a miscarriage. Contact with sperm nourishes and changes this "social woman" into an adult warrior. Changes in social relationships accompany this initiation period: from when he begins living with his godfather he becomes a "son" of the family and marriage with a daughter of the household is regarded as incestuous and taboo.

In older times, paederasty (buggery between a man and a boy) was not considered a problem or as something apart from other forms of sexuality (Bleibtreu-Ehrenberg, 1991). So, in ancient Greece and elsewhere it was not held to be different from adult homosexuality or transvestism:

> "The child in antiquity lived his earliest years in an atmosphere of sexual abuse. Growing up in Greece and Rome often included being used sexually by older men. The exact form and frequency of the abuse varied by area and date. In Crete and Boeotia, pederastic marriages and honeymoons were common. Abuse was less frequent among aristocratic boys in Rome, but sexual use of children was everywhere evident in some form. Boy brothels flourished in every city, and one could even contract for the use of a rent-a-boy service in Athens. Even where homosexuality with free boys was discouraged by law, men keep slave boys to abuse, so that free-born children saw their fathers sleeping with boys."
>
> (De Mause, 1976, p. 43)

The way in which paedophilia was conceived appears to warrant viewing it as normative rather than unusual or deviant:

> "Paedophilia was to the Greeks at first the most important way of bringing up the male youth. As the good mother and housewife was to them the ideal of the girl, so ... the symmetrically harmonic development of body and soul, was that of the boy. For the Greeks the most excellent way of approaching this ideal was the love of boys; and while ... the State expected that every man should choose a youth as his favourite, and, further, while a boy was blamed if he failed to find an older friend and lover—a lapse that appeared to be intelligible only if he had some moral taint—both man and boy exerted themselves as far as possible to develop many virtues. As the older was responsible for

> the behaviour of the younger, the love of boys was not persecuted, but fostered, to become the power that maintained the State and upheld the foundation of Greek ethics."
>
> (Licht, 1953, p. 441)

But we should be very careful not to confuse the ideal with reality. After all, Boswell (1980) suggests that one should not necessarily assume that every man's ideal of female sexuality in modern Western culture is the late-teenage girl promoted by the mass media, pornography and literature. For this reason, deciphering the scanty historical record can be a fraught exercise. Furthermore, much of this involved sexually mature males. It is something of an open question whether the sexual use of children was confined to the post-pubescent groups. De Mause (1976) suggests that this was not the case and presents evidence of it being common with younger boys and possibly with girls. Aristotle saw homosexuality as frequently the outcome of the sexual use of boys in childhood. In imperial Rome, infants were castrated by having their testicles squeezed; the boys were later employed in brothels. Ancient Jewish culture sought to stamp out homosexuality. Death by stoning was held to be an appropriate punishment for buggery with children over nine years of age; sex with children younger than this was punished by the whip because it was not considered to be a sexual act!

Condemnation by European scholars and travellers resulted in their accounts of adult–child sex in other cultures being full of moral reproval, and lacking informative detail. Some see this as leading to a situation in which:

> "... pederasty, like every other form of sexual behavior at variance with our standards, was nowhere tolerated during the period of colonialism, i.e., for no less than 500 years. It was intentionally persecuted and, where possible, eliminated ... the custom had been already exterminated before real scientific ethnological research (then called 'anthropology') began in about 1880."
>
> (Bleibtreu-Ehrenberg, 1991, p. 15)

The question of brother–sister incest and the "incest taboo" is of considerable importance in Western sexual mythology. The claims that incest was sanctioned in some cultures allows a cultural relativistic view to predominate. The evidence that sibling incest was permissible in the *royal families* of such cultures as Egypt, Peru and Hawaii is seen as support for the view that incest taboos are culturally based rather than deeper seated in biology. A belief that inbreeding results in a weakening of the genetic stock is central to this latter view, because it indicates that incest prevention is essential within the nuclear family to prevent inbreeding (Bixler, 1982). If it could be shown that incest between siblings were at all common in vigorous societies then some accounts of the "incest taboo" would be seriously challenged. There are numerous difficulties with the historical record. In particular, there is no clear distinction made between marital relations and sexual desire. Historians have recorded marriages between siblings but failed to document whether there was sexual desire and intercourse between the partners. So, in most respects, the evidence of marriage is no embarrassment to theories that postulate the primary importance of incest avoidance. Marriage between full brothers and sisters were rare in many of the cases of so-called sibling incest. Furthermore, in documented cases, the evidence about sexual desire suggests that it is far from strong. Bixler points out that at least one culture seems to buck these trends:

> "Roman Egypt is quite another matter because evidence that commoner siblings frequently married during the first two centuries A.D. is overwhelming ... Both Egyptians and Romans announced weddings that appear to have been between full-siblings ... and the incidence of sibling marriages until 212 A.D. is sufficient to seek an explanation. Because they were commoners, little is recorded beyond wedding invitations, marriage contracts and a few letters which reveal almost nothing regarding sexual attraction."
>
> (Bixler, 1982, p. 273)

In the history of sexuality, the notion that age determines suitability for marriage is relatively modern; penal statutes restraining sexual activity in young persons are a relatively recent phenomenon. There are a few rare exceptions to this. In ancient Rome boys could not marry before 14 years and girls 12 years of age. Throughout the Middle Ages, Europeans had *no* minimum marriage age, according to Killias (1991). Suitability for marriage was largely judged on the basis of reaching physical maturity. (Care needs to be taken over Killias' claims since Simpson (1987) describes how in England from 1285 it was illegal to have carnal relationships with a maiden under 12 years of age. Furthermore, this particular age was based on existing church law and in this sense was not arbitrary.) The close ties between the law, the church and morality meant that conduct unacceptable in Christian morality was in principle punishable by either the church or state. Adultery, bigamy, incest, sodomy, rape and abduction were all crimes. Sexual activity with children as such was not unlawful other than to the extent that it was illegal under any of the prohibited categories:

> "If a child was willingly involved in the commitment of a sexual crime, such as sodomy, the child was not seen as the victim of the adult partner but as a participant and therefore equally punishable ... The adult ... was not punished just because his partner was a minor. The child was protected exactly as an adult was protected—against being the unwilling victim of rape or indecent assault. This system persisted long after the Middle Ages."
>
> (Killias, 1991, p. 42)

The activities of a German priest, Johann Arbogast Gauch, are a case in point. During the 10-year period from 1735, Gauch was sexually involved with boys and a small number of girls in the village where he acted as parson. All of this was public knowledge in the village for several years until political changes in the area finally led to Gauch's prosecution and death sentence. In contrast to modern attitudes, the children were jailed for several months and the boys whipped and beaten because of their complicity. Apparently the oldest boy only just escaped a death sentence. The girls were treated rather more leniently because their "unchastity" was heterosexual and not homosexual.

Killias claims that under common law prior to 1800, in England, France, Italy and Germany, there were no legal prohibitions on the basis of age alone against sexual activities involving children past puberty. Although sexual behaviour was rigorously controlled, this was not primarily aimed at protecting young people from moral corruption (an exception being the protection of immature girls). Things changed considerably in the late nineteenth century when the division of labour altered. Widespread and lengthening education resulted in a non-adult group with a distinct role outside of the main labour market. Killias argues that the age of sexual consent gradually increased since schoolchildren with family responsibilities were a considerable problem for the system. Some evidence for Killias' thesis is provided by the 25 small states in the federation which formed Switzerland. In the late nineteenth century, these different cantons had radically different educational systems and criminal justice laws controlling young people's sexual activities. A strong correlation was found between both the age of consent *and* the criminality of sexual behaviour involving adolescents, as well as the extent and quality of the educational system. A well-developed educational system can be seen as a good indicator of the degree of separation of the roles of adult and child.

But this should not be taken as a sign that the role division caused by increasingly universal education was responsible for attempts to control childhood sexuality, which is not the same as the age for consent to marriage. From the eighteenth century onwards there had been growing attempts to limit sexuality in children, but these were often collusions between parents and the medical profession rather than a matter of state intervention. During this phase, which lasted into the early twentieth century, physical removal of the foreskin and clitoris were among the medical treatments for masturbation, along with any number of restraining devices intended to make masturbation impossible or even excruciatingly painful (De Mause, 1976; Haller and Haller, 1974; Howitt, 1992; Wasserman and Rosenfeld, 1992). In London in the eighteenth century, there is evidence that although the courts of law treated women victims of sexual violence appallingly and their attackers leniently, men who raped children, possibly because it was a putative cure for venereal disease, were severely punished (Clark, 1987).

Jackson (1990) has a somewhat different view when she suggests that "[t]he Victorians did not ... repress sexuality but on the contrary constructed it; they made it possible to talk about it, to conceptualize it. They also, in so doing, prescribed particular ways of thinking about it which continue to exert a powerful influence today" (p. 42):

> "The Victorians also established sexuality as an area of public concern in such a way that regulation of it could no longer be accomplished merely by punishing wrong-doers. More active intervention and surveillance were necessary, since what was now at issue was not merely moral rectitude but the health and stability of society. Once sexuality had been defined as of central importance to mental and physical health the sexual habits of the population at large became socially significant. With childhood defined as critical to the development of healthy sexuality anything which threatened children's purity was a threat to the future of society."
>
> (Jackson, 1990, p. 45)

The ethnographic record on adult–child sexual contacts is best characterized as sparse. Davenport (1992) raises the important question of what would be unacceptable adult–child sexual contact in those cultures that allow intimacies that Western cultures find distasteful, but he provides no answer. He prefers to dismiss the very point of comparative perspectives:

> "While this relativistic cultural point of view provides a broader perspective in which to understand panhuman variability in sexuality, it is not an appropriate perspective with which to view and confront such heinous deviances as the sexual abuse of children within individual societies and cultures."
>
> (Davenport, 1992, p. 79)

Such is cultural universalism.

PAEDOPHILIA AS A SOCIAL CONSTRUCTION

Paedophile Activist Viewpoint

One theory of paedophilia portrays the paedophile as a victim of society (Brongersma, 1984), although similar ideas have been put forward by others. Some consider such points of view as merely paedophile propaganda, but for our purposes this does not mean that they are of no interest. Paedophile lobbying is part of what we need to understand, not what we have to accept. Because Brongersma refers to how social institutions generate self-serving conceptions of adult–child sex, it can be regarded as a social constructionist account (Gergen, 1985), albeit somewhat crudely expressed. Brongersma often alludes to psychological and other social scientific ideas, and proposes explanations of anti-paedophile anger which treat it as a social construction. He is a very public figure in the micro-politics of paedophilia or the boy–love movement. One account describes Brongersma as:

> "... one of its most articulate spokespersons. He has been a member of the Dutch Parliament on and off since 1946, but his career was interrupted by an arrest in the 1950s for sexual contact with a boy of 16. He went to prison. Subsequently ... establishing the Brongersma Foundation, which houses a significant collection of paedophile literature ..."
>
> (Plummer, 1991, p. 321)

One major international conference at the University of Swansea in 1978 was subject to considerable media and public furore when he was scheduled to speak there as part of a discussion on paedophilia (Cook and Wilson, 1979; Plummer, 1981b) but was eventually denied the opportunity.

Brongersma paints a picture of history until the nineteenth century sympathetic to the notion of childhood sexuality. Up to this point children were not seen as distinct from adults and lacking in sexuality. Indeed, he suggests, the genitals of children were commonly and openly touched by adults such as their parents and friends. Children of the age of 11 could be married and sexual intercourse take place:

> "No one took offense at Dante's love for nine-year-old Beatrice. The City Fathers of Ulm, in Germany, had to make regulations to stem the flow of 12–14 year old boys to the brothels ... And in England ... 13-year-old Elisabeth Ramsbotham complained officially about the fact that her 11-year-old husband John Bridge had not yet deflowered her."
>
> (Brongersma, 1984, p. 80)

But during the nineteenth century a form of aggression against those who "love" children and "want to express their feelings for them with bodily tenderness" (p. 79) emerged. Sex between children and adults was not seen as inevitably causing damage to the child. There were no legal penalties for intergenerational sex since children and adults had identical rights; like adults, children were protected by statute from rape, violence and similar crimes. The law was not involved in preventing them from having consenting sex with adults (although see the caveats above about similar claims by Killias, 1991).

Changes in the law, which occurred fairly simultaneously throughout nineteenth century Europe and elsewhere, had nothing to do with the harm caused to individual children by sex with adults. Increasing needs for educational and technical sophistication following the industrial revolution were responsible through extended (and universal) schooling and apprenticeships. The new industrial bourgeoisie valued the amassing of money and property through the twin virtues of industriousness and thrift. In contrast, sexual reproduction was a sheer waste of human energy and was consequently deplored:

> "These two rather prosaic factors together engendered a fairy tale. Society had ... no use for a child's sexuality; so it simply declared that a child didn't have any. And so emerged the fairy tale, depicting the child as asexual, pure, innocent: pure because the child was not contaminated by such a dirty thing as sex, and innocent, because the child was not sharing the guilt of adults who committed this sinful activity."
>
> (Brongersma, 1984, p. 81)

During the latter part of the nineteenth century legislation against "indecent" behaviour with children was introduced. The age of consent reveals the arbitrariness of the legislation since it varied from 12 years in one country to over 21 years in another.

There is always a danger in relying on readings of the historical record since these may well be self-serving interpretations that adopt a curiously one-sided perspective. The notion of childhood innocence is a particularly good example. It is inherently the case that if children are construed as innocent then those who despoil them have taken away from them the essence of childhood; if they are regarded as sexual beings then those who engage with them sexually on a consensual basis might be regarded more as benefactors than abusers—or so the paedophile argument goes. But this cuts very little ice with some, and distorts the record too much. Take, for example, Carey's (1993) review of Kincaid's (1993) book broadly sympathetic with paedophiles:

> "Kincaid ... adds that believing children innocent is a silly modern fad anyway—just another bit of our 'cultural myth-making'. Until the late 18th century, nobody thought childish innocence existed, or even noticed that children were different from adults. Kincaid has learned these facts from the somewhat outmoded historian and theorist Phillipe Aries, but he is inclined to shrink the time-scale even more than Aries does. The innocent child is a 'very-late Victorian or, more likely, modern imposition' ... Come again? How about those two men in Shakespeare's *Winter's Tale* who recall their childhood conversations: 'What we changed/Was innocence for innocence. We knew not/The doctrine of ill-doing, nor dream'd/That any did'? How about the founder of Christianity: 'Suffer the little children to come unto me, and forbid them not, for of such is the kingdom of God'? Children may or may not be innocent, but texts like these show that the innocent child is far more ingrained in Western thought than Kincaid realises. How come a professor of literature should be so ill-informed?"
>
> (Carey, 1993, p. 8)

But the issue of childhood innocence is not anything that is meaningful in any absolute terms; it is wholly dependent on conceptions of adults as un-innocents. Revelations about the lack of innocence among children has no real bearing on the issue of adult–child relationships. For example, Freud's claims about the sexuality of children are a remarkable contrast with the notion of innocence, in that they portray children as desiring, in fantasy, incest with their parents (Freud, 1962). This is not construed as a lack of childhood innocence which would warrant sexual intrusion. Similarly, knowledge that quite young children are sexually inquisitive and masturbate is not regarded as a justification for adults to masturbate them. Indeed, during the Victorian period, the "age of childhood innocence", such knowledge spurred attempts to stop masturbation, as we have seen (Haller and Haller, 1974). Knowledge that a recent British survey revealed that one in five women between 16 (the minimum age of consent) and 19 years had had sex under the age of consent would not be seen as good cause for adult sexual interest in underage girls.

The extremes of ideology should be conceived as just that. Just as paedophile activists portray a picture of adult–child sexuality in the phrase "boy–love" as desired by the boy, we have to be a little wary of accepting the reverse of this as being the truth and that the relationship is nothing but exploitative. It probably contributes nothing to the understanding of paedophilia as a social process to strongly hold the view that children never can play a part in child abuse, that they are always to be construed as inadvertent victims. At the very beginning of this book we saw in the childhood of a paedophile a pattern of seeking to be abused which needed to be understood in order to comprehend his adult paedophilia. While his father's abuse of him was responsible for initiating the deviant lifecycle, it would be pointless to attempt to understand this particular case in terms of him being the inadvertent victim of repeated, unconnected, paedophile interest. This in no sense means that the adult men who were sexually involved with him were seduced. To describe him as an innocent or as a seducer almost seems an unnecessary, arbitrary choice.

Research and professional publications on paedophilia contribute their own ideologically based distortion of reality, according to Brongersma (1990):

> "Most papers and books on the subject ... seem to have been born in another world where laboratory and theory remain aloof from living reality."
>
> (Brongersma, 1990, p. 146)

There are a number ways in which such a major "intellectual error" is fabricated:

1. *Using sexual activity as the decisive criterion of paedophilia.* Essentially this is to describe every child molester as a paedophile. But the term "paedophile" ought to be limited to men whose primary erotic interest is children. Among paedophiles are men who never

have physical sexual contact with a child despite their psychosexual orientation, as well as those with extensive contacts with children.

2. *Mingling girl- and boy-orientated sexualities.* This is important in that it encourages the view that adult–child relationships are violent. He suggests that this is more characteristic of girl-orientated men than boy-orientated men.

3. *Biases and distortions in researchers.* Brongersma argues that many researchers draw implications that are based on unproven suppositions. So when sexual activity is invariably labelled "abuse" or "molestation" or when the child is invariably labelled "victim", the grounds in objectivity are confused.

In Brongersma's view, man–boy sex may be normative given that there is some anthropological evidence that there have been cultures in which all adult men were expected to engage in sexual activities with boys. To Brongersma this "suggests that sexual attraction to boys is more or less present in every human male" (p. 153). Furthermore, Brongersma (1984) quotes Stekel as suggesting that "pedophilia constitutes a nearly normal component of the sexual impulse" (p. 84). Paedo*phobia* is based on people's incompletely recognized paedophiliac impulses—we are paedophobic because we are constitutionally paedophile.

He frequently reverses ideas held by others about the nature of offending. Thus, the child may exploit the adult rather than being a victim. Included in his anecdotal evidence for this is the case of an Austrian paedophile in a sexual relationship with a 14-year-old boy. The man was beginning to fall in love with the boy:

> "And so one day he invited him to the movies, to be followed by a good meal at a restaurant. But the boy flatly refused. 'Oh, no. I don't want any of that. I come here to get fucked and nothing else!'"
>
> (Brongersma, 1984, p. 157)

To Brongersma, the problem is not of sex but of violence; he is in favour of legislation to protect children from violence, threats or the abuse of authority. If the child likes the adult and the sexual relationship, the law should not intervene. The offences that might cause the child to feel odd, disgusted or similar negative emotions should be played down by parents and state authorities: much as if the child had witnessed a bad road accident, the events are best passed over.

Sociological Theory

While it may be an appropriate purpose of theory to identify paedophilia's causes, it is not the only objective. Indeed, it is doubtful whether a complete understanding of the origins of paedophilia is possible, and we should not ignore other approaches for one limited quest. For example, paedophilia may be seen usefully as a life "career" choice, albeit one that leads to social condemnation. Furthermore, paedophilia can be regarded as a social movement involving pressure groups akin to the Gay Rights movement, which revolutionized society's response to homosexuality.

Plummer (1981a, 1981b) relates paedophilia to conceptions of deviance in sociology, and, consequently, his views appear less hostile to the paedophile than those of some others. He suggests that these four main arguments need to be considered: (i) that deviance is better seen as a way of life than a sickness, (ii) that stereotypes of sex monsters ought to be debunked and replaced by placing the offender in his full social context, (iii) that deviance is a relative category largely defined by how others seek to describe it rather than an aspect of the act itself, and (iv) rather than focus exclusively on the offender for understanding, the act needs understanding in terms of the society and its institutions.

During the 1970s there had emerged, in Britain, paedophile self-help groups similar to ones established elsewhere at about this time (e.g. the *North American Man–Boy Love Association* founded in 1979). The *Paedophile Information Exchange* (PIE) and the *Paedophile Action for Liberation* (PAL) provided advice, legal help and counselling, as well as an educational and information programme for the general public. They hoped to change society towards greater acceptance of paedophilia. Plummer discusses some of the main arguments put forward by paedophile activists. One of these he refers to as *ageism*, meaning those parts of social structure determined by age criteria. One result of ageist social structures is that members of one age band cannot mix freely with another band. In terms of indicators of social worth, the middle age band is relatively highly valued, but children and the elderly not so:

> "If one can imagine society without these features (and of course they are both heavily contingent upon the importance of a particular kind of family for their existence) ... then one could perhaps imagine a society without 'a paedophiliac problem'."
>
> (Plummer, 1981a, p. 115)

Another argument stressing the sexuality of children is made by people irrespective of their attitude to paedophilia. Adult repression of childhood sexuality is held responsible for malfunctioning, neurotic or perverted adults. While paedophile activists mention psychologists such as Freud and Wilhelm Reich to support this view, broadly speaking, many contemporary experts agree that the repression of childhood sexuality is unhealthy. Revisions of the age of consent have been proposed by paedophile activists to take into account the ability of a child to validly communicate consent to an older person; children of less than four years are presumed unable to communicate consent at all, thus sexual activity with them should remain unlawful. In comparison, 10-year-olds are generally capable of communicating consent, so if a child of this age group has freely consented to sexual activity with an adult, the criminal justice system has no role to play. Only where the child's mental capacities are insufficient should the law prohibit consenting sex. Between the ages of 4 and 10 years the child is also capable of communicating consent. Here the law should not intervene unless the parent or some other responsible person claims that a particular child is incapable of communicating consent. Finally, there would not be any prohibitions against children in the same or adjacent age categories engaging in consensual sex.

For Plummer the issue is a dilemma of liberalism:

> "... we are confronted with the classic problems of liberal theory ... it is largely an asocial theory which does not allow for any drastic structuring of society. While children *may* generally be incapable of consent in *this* society, and likewise may generally be in subordinate roles, we should not see this as inevitable. And if one could envisage a society where children were both equal and able to consent, pedophilia may not be so condemnable."
>
> (Plummer, 1981b, p. 238)

We might contrast this with Kitzinger's (1988) discussion of the ideologies of childhood, in which she sees in the notions of childhood innocence and protecting the weak the means by which children are repressed. Childhood innocence allows adults to repress children's expression of sexuality and to deny them the control of their own bodies. The ideology of protecting the weak she feels ought to be replaced by one of "empowerment" since "... the notion of children's innate vulnerability (as a biological fact unmediated by the world they live in) is an ideology of control which diverts attention away from the socially constructed oppression of children" (Kitzinger, 1988, p. 82). She goes on to suggest:

> "... despite some encouraging individual aspects of the contemporary child protection movement, the mainstream campaigns conspicuously fail to take any overall stand against the structural oppression of children. They are, therefore, not only severely limited in what they can achieve, but they also often reinforce the very ideologies which expose children to exploitation in the first place."
>
> (Kitzinger, 1988, p. 85)

One of the intriguing things about this is that paedophile activists would probably take very little exception to the sentiment of liberating children from structural oppression, which, after all, is partly responsible for taking some choices about sexuality out of the power of the children themselves. Although Kitzinger is broadly with the aims of those who seek to help children to avoid abuse, it is striking that shifts in ideologies of childhood of the sort she describes overlap with what paedophiles themselves might seek.

THE PAEDOPHILE DEMONOLOGY

Paedophiles have a role in modern demonology alongside nefarious others such as joyriders, drug users, illegal immigrants and pornographers. Their creation as such is not new, but only in the latter part of the twentieth century did their evilness significantly enter professional lore. This was not a function of ignorance since there was sufficient data available to establish sexual abuse as a common feature of childhood. Salter (1988) lists seven surveys published between 1929 and 1965 that demonstrate high levels of abuse (Hamilton, 1929; Terman, 1938; Landis, 1940; Terman, 1951; Landis, 1956; Kinsey *et al.*, 1953; Gagnon, 1965), years before sexual abuse became a major issue of social concern. Many professionals must have come across incestuous abuse in their working lives. The rates of reported incest had remained fairly stable until very recent years and there was no explosion of cases sufficient to explain the increasing professional concern about sexual abuse emerging in the 1980s (Howitt, 1992). The real issue lies more in the ways in which abuse is construed than in any other shifts that might have taken place.

It is difficult to assess the extent to which there has been a change in public attitudes towards offenders. The cultural relativistic position which appears in the historical and cross-cultural perspectives on adult–child sexual involvement is extremely sketchy.

It does not really provide convincing evidence of the general acceptability of such contacts even where they are known to have taken place from the historical record. In essence, these are matters about which we will probably never know much. Nevertheless, the public response to adult–child sexual abuse does not follow professional concerns but, in many ways, predates it. In Britain, for example, among the most notorious of criminals are Ian Brady and Myra Hindley, who in the two years ending in 1965 murdered a number of children, whom they buried on Saddleworth Moor. The children were sexually assaulted and tortured before being killed. The prospect of their release produces considerable public outcry whenever it is mooted. Hindley, for example, is portrayed as a scheming, manipulative woman who seeks publicity for her "contrition" to secure her release. In many ways, they are the archetypal child sex offenders in the eyes of the general public: sadistic, evil child killers. At the other end of the scale, the career of singer Jerry Lee Lewis hit the doldrums in 1958 when he was forced to leave Britain after it became public knowledge that his "bride" was just 13 years of age, 9 years younger than himself. Whether or not legally permissible in the southern states at the time, by definitions of abuse that are applied by child protection specialists now, this certainly would be classified as "abuse" because of her age and the age differential between them. At the very least, these examples suggest that the public's potential for outrage was readily aroused by such extremely different episodes.

This thread of public concern about sexual abuse has arisen in a number of contexts, and the response has varied from humour to anger. Recently, the problem has been in connection with media personalities, as in the cases of the allegations against the film comedian and director Woody Allen and the popular singer Michael Jackson. Humour was more often the public response to the case of the Rolling Stone involved with an underage girl. However, more significant are the notorious cases of the misdiagnosis of child sexual abuse based on paedophile groups (e.g. the McMurray case in the USA), satanic abuse (Rochdale, England), ritual abuse (the Orkney Islands, Scotland), and fears of the rampant buggery of children (Cleveland, England). These were more notorious for the embarrassment they caused child protection agencies due to their implications that the system designed to protect children did them great harm because of the dogma adopted by some workers.

There are a number of possible reasons for the increased

willingness to regard paedophiles as devils incarnate. Very few of these can be accounted for by "moral panics", in which, suddenly, critical and concentrated concern is expressed over a certain social phenomenon (Cohen, 1972; Parton, 1985). This concern leads to demands for urgent action to be taken to deal with this now "hot" problem from nebulous groups in society. One of the broader social functions of "moral panics" is to reassert ideologies that are beginning to slip from dominance. Essentially, the process involves the creation of the belief that a particular "folk devil" poses a major threat to society, which may be totally disproportionate to the problem. So, for example, fear of violent crime is far greater than the known risks of victimization would imply. Moral panics are most clearly seen in cases such as the delinquency of young people during the 1950s and 1960s (Cohen, 1972). They are perhaps also to be seen in concerns over the "family" and "family values", which lead to outrage about single parents, divorce and teenage pregnancies. Such ideas seem far less appropriate when discussing many of the issues related to child abuse. The resurgence of interest in child abuse in the 1960s is difficult to explain in terms other than political demands for something to be done about the urban violence of the USA of the 1960s and the willingness of the medical profession to offer a "foolproof" solution to the problem of violence against children by suggesting that child abusers could readily be identified clinically (Kempe and Kempe, 1978). The history of the child abuse movement is more of a web involving the interplay of the needs of state politics with the process of professional development responsible for the "child abuse industry" (Pride, 1987). Similarly, the inclusion of child sexual abuse into the professional debate is more easily seen in terms of the consequence of the work of political activists, especially feminists, highlighting a fistful of issues related to sexual politics, including domestic violence, rape, date rape, sexual harassment, pornography and so forth. In many cases, rather than being a general, public arousal of concern about an issue, the broader public's attitude to some of these issues was sometimes antipathetic to the new message.

Neither can we see the creation of the demonology of the paedophile as a rational process, even where there seems to have been a basis in research evidence. For example, the Cleveland child sexual abuse scandal of 1988 (Butler-Sloss, 1988; Jervis, 1988) involved the local authority taking children into care on the basis of the RAD test, in which there was claimed to be a characteristic response of a child's anus to the separation of his or her buttocks diagnostic of anal abuse (Hanks, Hobbs and Wynne, 1988). The use of this test led to untrustworthy diagnoses of child sexual abuse. The medic largely responsible for the entire episode had attended a professional seminar which promoted the use of the test and proclaimed that such abuse was common. All of the parents alleged to have abused their children in the Cleveland affair were men. This fits in well with the view of the basic paradox of the homophobia of male sexuality, which hides their sexuality's true nature (e.g. Campbell, 1988). But a rational process underlying the creation of a social issue is difficult to square with the research facts from which all of this stemmed. Going back to Hobbs and Wynne's (1986) original publication of the use of the RAD test as a means of diagnosing the anal abuse of children, men were not the only putative perpetrators (Howitt, 1992). Of the 35 cases that they included in their study, six involved a woman. Of these six, two were apparently in collusion with a male partner, one with a female partner, and the remaining three acted alone. Quite simply, the emerging social process of abuse allegations did not reflect the original research data well.

One feature of concern about sexual abuse in recent years has been the creation of the idea that adult–child sexual relations are organized and networked, rather than being individual adult–child contacts. The notions of the paedophile ring, satanic abuse and ritual abuse signal this very strongly. What they have in common is that they present a picture of organized evil, of unfathomable depths. Such imagery of an incarnate devil is readily compatible with fundamentalist Christian theology. In the USA, religious fundamentalism underlies much of the debate over moral issues, and it is clearly compatible with beliefs of the devil's involvement in sexual abuse. Since the 1970s, in Britain for example, there has been a decline in the mainstream religious groups, the Church of England and Roman Catholicism especially, while fundamentalism has gained strength (Jenkins, 1992). In other words, there has been a movement towards religious beliefs conducive to acceptance of incarnate devilry.

The image of paedophilia stems from relatively small coteries of specialists in sexual abuse and other "moral entrepreneurs" who take it on themselves to "expose" paedophiles for "what they are". Moral entrepreneurs may present an image of paedophiles as networked, perhaps at the international scale, as in the case of child pornography (Tate, 1990), permeating through society into the establishment. For example, in the 1980s, one British Member of Parliament, Geoffrey Dickens, exposed a knighted ex-diplomat as a paedophile activist, alleged that such people were working at Buckingham Palace, accused a doctor and a vicar under parliamentary protection from slander and contended that there were child brothels in London. So ingrained was the notion of paedophilia in high places that a damaging smear campaign against a British government minister was effectively perpetrated by intelligence services (Jenkins, 1992).

The conspiratorial view of the paedophile is reinforced by notions of paedophile rings. Thus, rare cases of sexual attack by groups of men on children become construed as part of "an organized criminal threat" (Jenkins, 1992)—this despite no such accusations being made in cases in which adult women are raped by groups of men. While this can be seen as the product of a conspiratorial view of society, it ensures that the extent of paedophilia is unfathomable and that rare examples of paedophile networking can be construed as merely the tip of the iceberg, hidden by the conspiracy. The "bogus social worker" scare of 1990 is perhaps typical of the high profile given to cases that seemed to indicate a possible epidemic of linked attempts to abduct children for sexual purposes in the guise of a visit by social workers. Myth is difficult to separate from reality: parents were known to attribute such motives to innocent visitors to the door (Howitt, 1992).

The murky depths of satanism has been another rich vein in the imagery of sexual abuse, actively promoted by individuals, charities, social services agencies and others (Howitt, 1992; Jenkins, 1992). While the belief may be widely held, equally strongly felt is the rejection of satanism as a social fact:

> "Studies of the satanism panic in the United States have repeatedly emphasized how occult charges arose from flaws in the investigative techniques employed both by prosecutors and therapists who are employed to interrogate the children (Eberle and Eberle, 1986; Hicks, 1991; Jenkins and Maier-Katkin, 1988; Richardson and Bacon, 1991). It is disputed whether small children lie about outrageous sexual abuse, and most authorities suggest that they cannot have the knowledge needed to invent the stories they present. In contrast, skeptics charge that these stories only emerge after lengthy periods, perhaps months, of active interrogation involving the use of leading questions. In order to understand the outcome of such an inquiry, it is necessary to appreciate both the nature of the investigation and the beliefs of the interrogators."
>
> (Jenkins, 1992, p. 182)

There has been a certain wildness in aspects of professionals' response to child abuse which has woven a web of mystery around matters that need cool reflection rather than high drama. In particular, outlandish claims about the nature of offenders has its backlash in the public's response to the treatment of offenders in the community. Hostility to treatment facilities may be encouraged by the responses of the professionals themselves to abuse. By portraying offenders as devious, lying, manipulative, persistent, addicted, violent and organized recidivists, it is not surprising that they are viewed accordingly by the public.

The recent rapid oscillation of ideology surrounding sex offending against children contrasts markedly with anything that had previously occurred in the long history of adult–child sexual contacts. The image of the paedophile is infinitely malleable and will remain so while we are told what they are rather than finding out about them:

> "To express empathy and understanding for sexual abusers often provokes strong irrational and angry responses amongst the public and professionals alike. This response originates from a confusion in which people feel that understanding abusers and showing empathy means making apologies for them and blaming the child. The distinction between interactional and structural elements of responsibility, participation and guilt in child sexual abuse allows us to show empathy and to try to understand why fathers and stepfathers and others become sexual abusers. In the process we may learn about traumatic life events in the abuser's own history, including possible severe physical and sexual abuse in their own childhood ... Showing empathy and understanding towards sexual abusers does not take away one iota from their full responsibility for the abuse they have committed."
>
> (Furniss, 1991, p. 14)

This is probably idle rhetoric. If the traumatizers were themselves traumatized in childhood, what does it mean to suggest that they are fully responsible for their abusing? If we do not hold children responsible for their own abuse, then how can we hold the victim, when he grows adult, responsible for what he then does? Would we hold the girl victim responsible for her resultant adult psychosis and the harm that it might do her child? Underlying the rhetoric of responsibility are the practicalities of the tough treatment of offenders, not the luxury of empathy. Would any of us, faced with these traumas in our own childhoods, have been able to exercise this responsibility in another way? In truth, there are huge gaps in our knowledge of offenders, which will not be filled effectively by the mottoes that too often pass for understanding in this field. Sadness rather than outrage might be the appropriate professional response to the stories of such men.

In the life stories of abusers are to be found somewhat surreal childhood worlds of abuse and sexuality far removed from notions of an age of innocence. But these are their normal worlds, not something created by their innate evil or wickedness. In these cases, not all cognitive distortions are easily seen as self-serving since they might equally be accounted for as deviations from "normal" life experiences—the product of curious childhoods. Assessing the past is difficult, even with complete cooperation from the offender, and one cannot expect crystal bright memories from childhood, especially about things preferred forgotten. In this sense, there may be limitations to our potential to understand paedophilia fully since our glimpses into the origins of paedophile desires and fantasies are subject to the failings of memory.

Knowledge about paedophilia is also layered with incompletely acknowledged ideologies. Just how can disbelief be suspended long enough to absorb what the paedophile has to tell about himself? Whatever means we use to understand paedophilia carries baggage of its own. Even simple pieces of the jigsaw are missing, such as the prevalence of paedophilia. That we can know so little is only partly to do with the sensitivity of the issue—after all, research has been carried out on all sorts of matters sexual and criminal. The distancing of "decent" society from the sex offender is matched by distancing in research. That so much of the research base comes from the managers of offenders, particularly therapists in state institutions, has its own influence on the nature of the knowledge obtained. Thus, we find that research is more likely to concern itself with the intimacies of the offender's penis than the intricacies of his mind. But this is a paradoxical intimacy in that it is largely carried out by the man himself and communicated through electrical cable to a technician in another room. Where the knowledge is obtained in a more directly face-to-face setting, it is almost exclusively in the context of a treatment regime that normally needs to "deliver the goods" of non-recidivism. So instead of a client-orientated ethos, psychotherapy is turned on its head when applied to sex offenders. They are expected to toe the line as a precondition of treatment. Their confession to abuse might be an early requirement; they may be led to see themselves according to the therapist's view of them;

they may be taught to control themselves rather than understand themselves; they may be required to offer themselves for research as a precondition of therapy; they may be humiliated by fellow offenders and, in general, treated in ways that would cause outrage if they were applied to their victims. And while this might be the best thing for them and society, too often we have virtually no evidence that this is the case.

The creation of the paedophile as a "folk devil", the embodiment of evil, is probably as complete as ever could be. What shifts that could happen in society to change this are difficult to imagine and impossible to predict. The rapid change in our understanding of the paedophile is characteristic of the modern period but largely tied to the ascendency of wider ideologies than to psychological or social scientific developments. One can see shifts to the political right in the emphasis on personal responsibility in the treatment of paedophilia, and the power of fundamentalism in the satanist connection. Further shifts could take us in many directions. Why not towards compulsory medicine and surgery? Why not towards the lowering of the age of consent, which would decriminalize aspects of paedophilia but at what expense for the children? Why not back to blaming the victim? Even the latter is not so ridiculous as might at first appear in the light of recent suggestions that negligent victims of other crimes might be fined, for example. In eighteenth century Britain buggery seems to have been treated more severely by the courts than rape (Trumbach, 1987); nowadays the situation seems reversed.

So what is the future of paedophilia? The major question has to be whether it is possible to eliminate adult–child contacts. If we had a certain knowledge of what leads to paedophilia then we might be on firm ground. Unfortunately, there has been a fairly long-standing consensus that offending against children has multiple determinants, none of which is held to be essential. The consequence of this view is that it implies that the supply of criminogenic antecedents is varied and to a degree unpredictable. If, on the other hand, we could accept that there are cycles of sexual abuse, in which abused children themselves become abusers, it would be a different matter. Cycles of abuse can be broken. The main means of achieving this are initiatives to protect children from abuse by education, training and environmental considerations, and effective therapeutic work with individuals damaged by abuse, whether victim or victimizer. If we need to look wider than this direct cycle, the difficulties are immense. What, for example, is the social intervention necessary to ensure that problems relating to adults do not become diverted to relationships with children? What is a mentally healthy society?

Will adults stop having sexual interests in children? It is paradoxical to think that they are expected not to be aroused by the young but sexually mature. The age of sexual consent is tied to the age of permissible marriage for reasons that do not altogether unite the sexual and social functions of marriage. This disparity between sexual maturity and the age of consent leaves a grey ink-blot into which anything can be read. Although not tied to marriageability at this point in time, the age of homosexual consent poses similar problems. As biological maturity occurs at younger ages, the age of social sexual maturity has increased. There is inevitably room for considerable disagreement as to what the age of consent should be. In this lies the potential for new ideological battles. Sexual activity prior to the age of sexual maturity might be the next ideological battleground. What could sexually immature people consent to? The activities they initiate themselves? These are troubling questions. Historical and social relativism do not make the dilemmas less troubling. Twelve-year-old girls marrying may be history's norm, but modern Western societies regard late teenage marriage with trepidation and as a problem. Other age/gender/sexuality bondings which, although legal, were frowned upon, have also become less restricted. So, for example, women with a much younger sexual partner are now likely to be regarded with a gung-ho spirit rather than as "cradle-snatchers".

Our knowledge of paedophilia has been created largely during a wafer-thin slice of history, which is subject to rapid changes in the ways in which such behaviour is understood within wider society. Much as it is comforting to distance oneself from such people, this does little to enhance understanding. While it may be preferable to understand the victim rather than the victimizer, there are no victims without victimizers.

References

Abel, G.G. and Becker, J.V. (1985). Sexual interest card sort. Unpublished.

Abel, G.G., Blanchard, E.B. and Barlow, D.H. (1981). Measurement of sexual arousal in several paraphilias: the effects of stimulus modality, instructional set and stimulus content on the objective. *Behavioral Research and Therapy*, **19**, 25–33.

Abel, G.G., Barlow, D.H., Blanchard, E.B. and Guild, D. (1977). The components of rapists' sexual arousal. *Archives of General Psychiatry*, **34**, 895–903.

Abel, G.G., Mittelman, M., Becker, J.V., Cunningham-Rathner, M.S. and Lucas, L. (1983). Characteristics of men who molest young children. Paper presented at the World Congress of Behavior Therapy, Washington, DC.

Abel, G.G., Becker, J.V., Cunningham-Rathner, M.S., Rouleau, J.L., Kaplan, M. and Reich, J. (1984). The treatment of child molesters. Available from SBC-TM, 722 West 168th Street, Box 17, NY 10032, USA.

Abel, G.G., Becker, J.V., Mittelman, M., Cunningham-Rathner, M.S., Rouleau, J.L. and Murphy, W.D. (1987). Self-reported sex crimes of non-incarcerated paraphiliacs. *Journal of Interpersonal Violence*, **2**(1), 3–25.

Abel, G.G., Mittelman, M., Becker, J.V., Rathner, J. and Rouleau, J.L. (1988). Predicting child molesters' response to treatment. *Annals of the New York Academy of Sciences*, **528**, 223–234.

Alexander, P.C. and Lupfer, S.L. (1987). Family characteristics and long-term consequences associated with sexual abuse. *Archives of Sexual Behavior*, **16**(3), 235–245.

American Psychiatric Association (1952). *Diagnostic and Statistical Manual of Mental Disorders*, (DSM-I). Washington, DC: American Psychiatric Association.

American Psychiatric Association (1968). *Diagnostic and Statistical Manual of Mental Disorders*, 2nd Edn (DSM-II). Washington, DC: American Psychiatric Association.

American Psychiatric Association (1980). *Diagnostic and Statistical Manual of Mental Disorders*, 3rd Edn (DSM-III). Washington, DC: American Psychiatric Association.

American Psychiatric Association (1987). *Diagnostic and Statistical Manual of Mental Disorders*, Revised 3rd Edn (DSM-III-R). Washington, DC: American Psychiatric Association.

Ames, M.A. and Houston, D.A. (1990). Legal, social, and biological definitions of pedophilia. *Archives of Sexual Behavior*, **19**(4), 333–342.

Araji, S. and Finkelhor, D. (1985). Explanations of pedophilia: review of empirical research. *Bulletin of the American Academy of Psychiatry and the Law*, **13**(1), 17–37.

Araji, S. and Finkelhor, D. (1986). Abusers: a review of the research. In D. Finkelhor (Ed.). *A Sourcebook on Child Sexual Abuse*. Beverly Hills: Sage, pp. 89–118.

Armentrout, J.A. and Hauer, A.L. (1978). MMPIs of rapists of adults, rapists of children, and non-rapist sex offenders. *Journal of Clinical Psychology*, **34**(2), 330–332.

Attwood, R.W. and Howell, R.J. (1971). Pupillometric and personality test score differences of female aggressive pedophiliacs and normals. *Psychonomic Science*, **22**(2), 115–116.

Avery-Clark, C.A. and Laws, D.R. (1984). Differential erection response patterns of sexual child abusers to stimuli describing activities with children. *Behavior Therapy*, **15**, 71–83.

Baartman, H.E.M. (1992). The credibility of children as witnesses and the social denial of the incestuous abuse of children. In F. Losel, D. Bender and T. Bliesner (Eds). *Psychology and Law: International Perspectives*. Berlin: Walter de Gruyter, pp. 345–351.

Bachy, V. (1976). Danish permissiveness revisited. *Journal of Communication*, **26**(1), 40–43.

Barbaree, H.E., Marshall, W.L. and Lanthier, R.K. (1979). Deviant sexual arousal in rapists. *Behavior Research and Therapy*, **17**, 215–222.

Barnard, G.W., Fuller, A.K., Robbins, L. and Shaw, T. (1989). *The Child Molester: An Integrated Approach to Evaluation and Treatment*. New York: Brunner/Mazel.

Baron, L. and Straus, M. (1987). Four theories of rape: a macrosociological analysis. *Social Problems*, **34**, 467–489.

Baron, L. and Straus, M. (1989). *Four Theories of Rape: A State-level Analysis*. New Haven, CT: Yale University Press.

Bass, B.A. and Levant, M.D. (1992). Family perception of rapists and pedophiles. *Psychological Reports*, **71**, 211–214.

Baxter, D.J., Barbaree, H.E. and Marshall, W.L. (1986). Sexual responses to consenting and forced sex in a large sample of rapists and non-rapists. *Behavioural Research and Therapy*, **24**, 513–520.

Baxter, D.J., Marshall, W.L., Barbaree, H.E., Davidson, P.R. and Malcolm, P.B. (1984). Deviant sexual behaviour. *Criminal Justice and Behavior*, **11**, 477–501.

Baxter, M. (1990). Flesh and blood. *New Scientist*, 5 May, 37–41.

Bayer, T. and Connors, R. (1988). The emergence of child sexual abuse from the shadow of sexism. *Response*, **11**(4), 12–15.

Beck, A.T. (1967). *Depression: Causes and Treatment*. Philadelphia, PA: University of Pennsylvania Press.

Becker, J. and Stein, R. (1991). Does pornography play a role in the aetiology of sexual deviance in adolescent males? *International Journal of Law and Psychiatry*, **14**(1/2), 85–95.

Becker, J.V. and Coleman, E.M. (1988). Incest. In V.B. Hasselt, R.L.

Morrison, A.S. Bellack and M. Hersen (Eds). *Handbook of Family Violence*. New York: Plenum Press.

Beech, H.R., Watts, F. and Poole, A.D. (1971). Classical conditioning of a sexual deviation: a preliminary note. *Behavior Therapy*, **2**, 400–402.

Berlin, F.S. and Malin, H.M. (1991). Media distortion of the public's perception of recidivism and psychiatric rehabilitation. *American Journal of Psychiatry*, **148**(11), 1572–1576.

Berliner, L. and Conte, J.R. (1990). The process of victimization: the victims' perspective. *Child Abuse and Neglect*, **14**, 29–40.

Bernard, F. (1979). Paedophilia: the consequence for the child. In M. Cook and G. Wilson (Eds). *Love and Attraction: An International Conference*. Oxford: Pergamon Press.

Bernard, F. (1985). *Paedophilia: A Factual Report*. Enclave: Rotterdam.

Bixler, R.H. (1982). Sibling incest in the royal families of Egypt, Peru, and Hawaii. *The Journal of Sex Research*, **18**(3), 264–281.

Bleibtreu-Ehrenberg, G. (1991). Pederasty among primitives: institutionalized initiation and cultic prostitution. *Journal of Homosexuality*, **20**(1/2), 13–30.

Boswell, J. (1980). *Christianity, Social Tolerance and Homosexuality*. Chicago, IL: University of Chicago Press.

Bradford, J.M.W. (1988). Organic treatment for the male sexual offender. In R.A. Prentky and V.L. Quinsey (Eds). *Human Sexual Aggression: Current Perspectives*, Annals of the New York Academy of Science, Vol. 528, 12 August. New York: New York Academy of Science, pp. 193–202.

Bradford, J.M.W., Bloomberg, D. and Boulet, J.R. (1988). The heterogeneity/homogeneity of pedophilia. *Psychiatric Journal of the University of Ottawa*, **13**(4), 217–226.

Brannigan, A. (1987). Sex and aggression in the lab: implications for public policy? *Canadian Journal of Law and Society*, **2**, 177–185.

Brannigan, A. and Goldenberg, S. (1987). The study of aggressive pornography: the vicissitudes of relevance. *Critical Studies in Mass Communication*, **4**(3), 262–283.

Breer, W. (1987). *The Adolescent Molester*. Springfield, IL: Charles C. Thomas.

Brongersma, E. (1984). Aggression against pedophiles. *International Journal of Law and Psychiatry*, **7**, 79–87.

Brongersma, E. (1990). Boy-lovers and their influence on boys: distorted research and anecdotal observation. *Journal of Homosexuality*, **20**(1/2), 145–173.

Brownmiller, S. (1975). *Against Our Will: Men, Women and Rape*. New York: Simon and Schuster.

Budin, L.E. and Johnson, C.F. (1989). Sex abuse prevention programs: offenders' attitudes about their efficacy. *Child Abuse and Neglect*, **13**, 77–87.

Burgess, A.W. and Hartman, C.R. (1987). Child abuse aspects of child pornography. *Psychiatric Annals*, **17**(4), 248–253.

Burgess, A.W. and Holmstrom, L. (1979). *Rape: Crisis and Recovery*. Bowie, MD: Robert J. Brody.

Burgess, A.W., Hazelwood, R.R., Rokous, F.E., Hartman, C.R. and Burgess,

A.G. (1988). Serial rapists and their victims: reenactment and repetition. In R.A. Prentky and V.L. Quinsey (Eds). *Human Sexual Aggression: Current Perspectives*, Annals of the New York Academy of Science, Vol. 528, 12 August. New York: New York Academy of Science, pp. 277–295.

Burt, M.R. (1980). Cultural myths and supports for rape. *Journal of Personality and Social Psychology*, **38**(2), 217–230

Buss, A.H. and Durkee, A. (1957). An inventory for assessing different kinds of hostility. *Journal of Consulting Psychology*, **21**(4), 343–349.

Butler-Sloss, E. (1988). *Report of the Inquiry into Child Abuse in Cleveland 1987*, Cm 412. London: HMSO.

Campbell, B. (1988). *Unofficial Secrets*. London: Virago.

Campbell, T.W. (1992). The "highest level of psychological certainty": betraying standards of practice in forensic psychology. *American Journal of Forensic Psychology*, **10**(2), 35–48.

Card, R. (1975). Sexual relations with minors. *Criminal Law Review*, July, 370–380.

Carey, J. (1993). The age of innocents. *The Sunday Times*, 7 March, 8–9.

Carlson, S. (1991). The victim/perpetrator. In M. Hunger (Ed.). *The Sexually Abused Male: Prevalence, Impact, and Treatment*, Vol. 2. Lexington, MA: Lexington Books, pp. 249–266.

Carter, D.L. and Prentky, R.A. (1990). Overview of the program at the Massachussetts Treatment Center. In D. Weisstub (Ed.). *Law and Mental Health: International Perspectives*. New York: Pergamon Press.

Carter, D.L., Prentky, R.A., Knight, R.A., Vanderveer, P.L. and Boucher, R.J. (1987). Use of pornography in the criminal and developmental histories of sexual offenders. *Journal of Interpersonal Violence*, **2**(2), 196–211.

Cautela, J.R. (1966). Treatment of compulsive behavior by covert sensitization. *Psychological Records*, **16**, 33–41.

Chaney, E.F., O'Leary, M.R. and Marlatt, G.A. (1978). Skill training with alcoholics. *Journal of Consulting and Clinical Psychology*, **46**, 1092–1104.

Clark, A. (1987). *Women's Silence, Men's Violence*. London: Pandora.

Cline, V. (Ed.) (1974). *Where Do You Draw the Line?* Provo, UT: Brigham Young University Press.

Cohen, S. (1972). *Folk Devils and Moral Panics*. London: McGibbon and Kee.

Commission on Obscenity and Pornography (1970). *The Report of the Commission on Obscenity and Pornography*. New York: Bantam.

Condron, M.K. and Nutter, D.E. (1988). A preliminary examination of the pornography experience of sex offenders, paraphiliac sexual dysfunction and controls. *Journal of Sex and Marital Therapy*, **14**(4), 285–298.

Conrad, S.R. and Wincze, J.P. (1976). Orgasmic reconditioning: a controlled study of its effects upon the sexual arousal and behavior of adult male homosexuals. *Behavior Therapy*, **7**(2), 155–166.

Constantine, L.L. (1979). The sexual rights of children: implications of a radical perspective. In M. Cook and G. Wilson (Eds). *Love and Attraction: An International Conference*. Oxford: Pergamon Press.

Conte, J.R. (1985). Clinical dimensions of adult sexual abuse of children. *Behavioral Sciences and the Law*, **3**(4), 341–344.

Conte, J.R., Wolf, S. and Smith, T. (1989). What sexual offenders tell us about prevention strategies. *Child Abuse and Neglect*, **13**, 293–301.

Cook, M. and Wilson, G. (Eds) (1979). *Love and Attraction: An International Conference*. Oxford: Pergamon Press.

Cook, R.F. and Fosen, R.H. (1970). Pornography and the sex offender. In *Technical Reports of the Commission on Obscenity and Pornography*, Vol. 7. Washington, DC: US Government Printing Office.

Cooper, A.J. and Cernovovsky, Z. (1992). The effects of cyproterone acetate on sleeping and waking penile erections in pedophiles: possible implications for treatment. *Canadian Journal of Psychiatry*, **37**, 33–39.

Cooper, A.J., Swaminath, S., Baxter, D. and Poulin, C. (1990). A female sex offender with multiple paraphilias: a psychologic, physiologic (laboratory sexual arousal) and endocrine case study. *Canadian Journal of Psychiatry*, **35**, 334–337.

Court, J.H. (1977). Pornography and sex-crimes: a re-evaluation in the light of recent trends around the world. *International Journal of Criminality and Penology*, **5**, 129–157.

Court, J.H. (1984). Sex and violence: a ripple effect. In N.M. Malamuth and E. Donnerstein (Eds). *Pornography and Sexual Aggression*. Orlando, FL: Academic Press, pp. 143–172.

Cowan, G., Chase, C.J. and Stahly, G.B. (1989). Feminist and fundamentalist attitudes toward pornography control. *Psychology of Woman Quarterly*, **13**, 97–112.

Crawford, D.A. (1981). Treatment approaches to paedophiles. In M. Cook and K. Howells (Eds). *Adult Sexual Interest in Children*. London: Academic Press, pp. 181–217.

Cumberbatch, G. and Howitt, D. (1989). *A Measure of Uncertainty*. London: John Libby.

Cupoli, J.M. and Sewell, P.M. (1988). One thousand fifty-nine children with a chief complaint of sexual abuse. *Child Abuse and Neglect*, **12**, 151–162.

Davenport, W.H. (1992). Adult–child sexual relations in cross-cultural perspective. In W. O'Donohue and J.H. Geer (Eds). *The Sexual Abuse of Children: Clinical Issues*, Vol. 1. Hillsdale, NJ: Lawrence Erlbaum, pp. 73–80.

Davis, M.H. (1980). A multidimensional approach to individual differences in empathy. *JSAS Catalog of Selected Documents in Psychology*, **10**, 85.

Day, D.M., Miner, M.H., Sturgeon, V. H. and Murphy, J. (1989). Assessment of sexual arousal by means of physiological and self-report measures. In D.R. Laws (Ed.). *Relapse Prevention with Sex Offenders*. New York: Guilford Press, pp. 115–123.

De Mause, L. (1976). *The History of Childhood: The Evolution of Parent–Child Relationships as a Factor in History*. London: Souvenir, pp. 1–74.

Dominelli, L. (1989). Betrayal of trust: a feminist analysis of power relationships in incest abuse and its relevance for social work practice. *British Journal of Social Work*, **19**, 291–301.

Donnerstein, E. and Linz, D. (1986). Mass media sexual violence and male viewers: current theory and research. *American Behavioral Scientist*, **29**, 601–618.

Dwyer, S.M. and Myers, S. (1990). Sex offender treatment: a six-month to ten-year follow-up study. *Annals of Sex Research*, **3**(3), 305–318.

Eberle, F. and Eberle, S. (1986). *The Politics of Child Abuse*. Secaucus, NY: Lyle Stuart.

Edwards, N.B. (1972). Case conference: assertive training in a case of homosexual pedophilia. *Journal of Behavior Therapy and Experimental Psychiatry*, **3**, 55–63.

Elliott, M. (1992). Images of children in the media: “soft kiddie porn”. In C. Itzin (Ed.). *Pornography: Women, Violence and Civil Liberties: A Radical New View*. Oxford: Oxford University Press, pp. 217–221.

Ellis, A. and Grieger, R. (Eds) (1977). *Handbook of Rational–Emotive Therapy*. New York: Springer-Verlag.

Ellis, L. (1989). *Theories of Rape: Inquiries into the Causes of Sexual Aggression*. New York: Hemisphere.

Erickson, W.D., Walbek, N.H. and Seely, R.K. (1988). Behavior patterns of child molesters. *Archives of Sexual Behavior*, **17**(1), 77–86.

Evans, S. and Schaefer, S. (1987). Incest and chemically dependent women: treatment implications. *Journal of Chemical Dependency Treatment*, **1**(1), 131–173.

Eysenck, H.J. and Nias, D. (1978). *Sex, Violence, and the Media*. London: Maurice Temple Smith.

Farrall, W.R. (1992). Instrumentation and methodological issues in the assessment of sexual arousal. In W. O’Donohue and J.H. Geer (Eds). *The Sexual Abuse of Children: Clinical Issues*, Vol. 2. Hillsdale, NJ: Lawrence Erlbaum, pp. 188–229.

Farrall, W.R. and Card, R.D. (1988). Advancements in physiological evaluation of assessment and treatment of the sexual aggressor. In R.A. Prentky and V.L. Quinsey (Eds). *Human Sexual Aggression: Current Perspectives*, Annals of the New York Academy of Science, Vol. 528, 12 August. New York: New York Academy of Science, pp. 261–273.

Fehrenbach, P.A., Smith, W., Monstersky, C. and Deisher, R.W. (1986). Adolescent sexual offenders: offenders and offense characteristics. *American Journal of Orthopsychiatry*, **56**, 255–263.

Field, J., Johnson, A., Wadworth, J. and Wellings, K. (1994). The facts of homosexual life. *Independent on Sunday Magazine*, 23 January, 9–11.

Finkelhor, D. (1979). *Sexually Victimised Children*. New York: Free Press.

Finkelhor, D. (Ed.) (1984). *Child Sexual Abuse: New Theory and Research*. New York: Free Press.

Finkelhor, D. (1986). *A Sourcebook on Child Sexual Abuse*. Beverly Hills, CA: Sage.

Finkelhor, D. (1991). Response to Bauserman. *Journal of Homosexuality*, **20**(1/2), 313–315.

Finkelhor, D. and Lewis, I.A. (1988). An epidemiologic approach to the study of child molestation. In R.A. Prentky and V.L. Quinsey (Eds). *Human Sexual Aggression: Current Perspectives*, Annals of the New York Academy of Science, Vol. 528, 12 August. New York: New York Academy of Science, pp. 64–78.

Finkelhor, D. and Williams, L.M. (1988). *Nursery Crimes: Sexual Abuse in Day Care*. Newbury Park, CA: Sage.

Finkelhor, D., Hotaling, G.T., Lewis, I.A. and Smith, C. (1989). Sexual abuse and its relationship to later sexual satisfaction, marital status, religion, and attitudes. *Journal of Interpersonal Violence*, **4**(4), 379–399.

Fisher, C., Gross, J. and Zuck, J. (1965). Cycle of penile erection synchronous with dreaming (REM) sleep. *Archives of General Psychiatry*, **12**, 29–45.

FitzHerbert, C. (1993). Inside the mind of the sex beast. *The Sunday Telegraph*, 27 June, 17.

Flor-Henry, P., Lang, R.A., Koles, Z.J. and Frenzel, R.R. (1991). Quantitative EEG studies of pedophilia. *International Journal of Psychophysiology*, **10**(3), 252–258.

Freud, S. (1905/1977). *On Sexuality: Three Essays on the Theory of Sexuality and Other Works*, compiled and edited by Angela Richards. Harmondsworth: Penguin.

Freud, S. (1962). *Two Short Accounts of Psychoanalysis*. Harmondsworth: Penguin.

Freund, K. (1963). A laboratory method for diagnosing predominance of homo- or hetero-erotic interest in the male. *Behaviour Research and Therapy*, **5**, 209–228.

Freund, K. (1981). Assessment of pedophilia. In M. Cook and K. Howells (Eds). *Adult Sexual Interest in Children*. London: Academic Press, pp. 139–179.

Freund, K. and Blanchard, R. (1989). Phallometric diagnosis of pedophilia. *Journal of Consulting and Clinical Psychology*, **57**, 100–105.

Freund, K. and Kuban, M. (1993). Toward a testable developmental model of pedophilia: the development of erotic age preference. *Child Abuse and Neglect*, **17**, 315–324.

Freund, K. and Watson, R.J. (1991). Assessment of the sensitivity and specificity of a phallometric test: an update of phallometric diagnosis of paedophilia. *Journal of Consulting and Clinical Psychology*, **3**(2), 254–260.

Freund, K., Watson, R. and Dickey, R. (1990). Does sexual abuse in childhood cause pedophilia? an exploratory study. *Archives of Sexual Behavior*, **19**(6), 557–568.

Freund, K., Watson, R. and Dickey, R. (1991). Sex offenses against female children perpetrated by men who are not pedophiles. *Journal of Sex Research*, **28**(3), 409–423.

Freund, K., Watson, R. and Rienzo, D. (1987). A comparison of sex offenders against female and male minors. *Journal of Sex and Marital Therapy*, **13**(4), 260–264.

Freund, K., Heasman, G., Racansky, I.G. and Glancy, G. (1984). Pedophilia and heterosexuality vs. homosexuality. *Journal of Sex and Marital Therapy*, **10**(3), 193–200.

Freund, K., Watson, R., Dickey, R. and Rienzo, D. (1991). Erotic gender differentiation in pedophilia. *Archives of Sexual Behaviour*, **20**(6), 555–566.

Friday, N. (1976). *My Secret Garden: Women's Sexual Fantasies*. London: Quartet.

Friedrich, W.N. and Luecke, W.J. (1988). Young school-age sexually aggressive children. *Professional Psychology: Research and Practice*, **19**(2), 155–164.

Frisbie, L. (1969). Another look at sex offenders in California. Research Monograph no. 12. Sacramento, CA: Department of Mental Hygiene.

Frosh, S. (1993). The seeds of masculine sexuality. In J.A. Ussher and C.D. Baker (Eds). *Psychological Perspectives on Sexual Problems: New Directions in Theory and Practice*. London: Routledge, pp. 41–55.

Froula, C. (1985). The daughter's seduction: sexual violence and literary history. *Signs: Journal of Women in Culture and Society*, **11**(4), 621–644.

Furby, L., Weinrott, M.R. and Blackshaw, L. (1989). Sex offender recidivism: a review. *Psychological Bulletin*, **105**(1), 3–30.

Furniss, T. (1991). *The Multi-Professional Handbook of Child Sexual Abuse*. London: Routledge.

Gaffney, G.R., Lurie, S.F. and Berlin, F.S. (1984). Is there familial transmission of pedophilia? *Journal of Nervous and Mental Disease*, **172**(9), 546–548.

Gagnon, J.H. (1965). Female child victims of sex offenses. *Social Problems*, **13**(2), 176–192.

Gebhard, P.H. and Gagnon, J.H. (1964). Male sex offenders against very young children. *American Journal of Psychiatry*, **121**, 576–579.

Gebhard, P.H., Gagnon, J.H., Pomeroy, W.B. and Christenson, C.V. (1965). *Sex Offenders: An Analysis of Types*. New York: Harper and Row.

Gergen, K. (1985). The social constructionist movement in modern psychology. *American Psychologist*, **40**(3), 266–275.

Glasser, M. (1988). Psychodynamic aspects of paedophilia. *Psychoanalytic Psychotherapy*, **3**(2), 121–135.

Glasser, M. (1989). The psychodynamic approach to understanding and working with the paedophile. In M. Farrell (Ed.). *Understanding the Paedophile*. London: ISTD/The Portman Clinic, pp. 1–11.

Goldstein, M.J. (1973). Exposure to erotic stimuli and sexual deviance. *Journal of Social Issues*, **29**(3), 197–219.

Goldstein, M.M. and Kant, H.S. (1973). *Pornography and Sexual Deviance: A Report of the Legal and Behavioral Institute*. Berkeley, CA: University of California Press.

Goldstein, M.J., Kant, H.S., Judd, L.L., Rice, C.J. and Green, R. (1970). Exposure to pornography and sexual behavior in deviant and normal groups. In *Technical Reports of the Commission on Obscenity and Pornography*, Vol. 7. Washington, DC: US Government Printing Office.

Goodwin, J.M., Cheeves, K. and Connell, V. (1990). Borderline and other severe symptoms in adult survivors of incestuous abuse. *Psychiatric Annals*, **20**(1), 22–23.

Gordon, R. (1976). Paedophilia: normal and abnormal. In W. Kraemer (Ed.). *The Forbidden Love: The Normal and Abnormal Love of Children*. London: Sheldon Press, pp. 36–79.

Green, F.C. (1988). Human sexual aggression: social policy perspective. In R.A. Prentky and V.L. Quinsey (Eds). *Human Sexual Aggression: Current Perspectives*, Annals of the New York Academy of Science, Vol. 528, 12 August. New York: New York Academy of Science, pp. 400–403.

Greenberg, D.M., Bradford, J.M.W. and Curry, C. (1993). A comparison of sexual victimization in the childhoods of pedophiles and hebephiles. *Journal of Forensic Sciences*, **38**(2), 432–436.

Greenland, C. (1988). The treatment and maltreatment of sexual offenders: ethical issues. In R.A. Prentky and V.L. Quinsey (Eds). *Human Sexual*

Aggression: Current Perspectives, Annals of the New York Academy of Science, Vol. 528, 12 August. New York: New York Academy of Science, pp. 373–378.

Groth, A.N. (1979a). *Men who Rape*. New York: Plenum Press.

Groth, A.N. (1979b). Sexual trauma in the lives of rapists and child molesters. *Victimology*, **4**, 10–16.

Groth, A.N. and Birnbaum, H.J. (1978). Adult sexual orientation and attraction to underage persons. *Archives of Sexual Behavior*, **7**(3), 175–181.

Gudjonsson, G.H. (1990). Cognitive distortion and blame attribution among paedophiles. *Sexual and Marital Therapy*, **5**(2), 183–185.

Hall, G.C.N., Proctor, W.C. and Nelson, G.M. (1988). Validity of physiological measures of pedophilic sexual arousal in a sexual offender population. *Journal of Consulting and Clinical Psychology*, **56**(1), 118–122.

Haller, J.S. and Haller, R.M. (1974). *The Physician and Sexuality in Victorian America*. Urbana, IL: University of Illinois Press.

Hamilton, G.V. (1929). *A Research in Marriage*. New York: Albert and Charles Boni.

Hanks, H., Hobbs, C. and Wynne, J. (1988). Early signs and recognition of sexual abuse in the pre-school child. In K. Browne, C. Davies and P. Stratton (Eds). *Early Prediction and Prevention of Child Abuse*. Chichester: John Wiley.

Hansen, R.K. and Slater, S. (1988). Sexual victimization in the history of sexual abusers: a review. *Annals of Sex Research*, **1**, 485–499.

Harrison, P., Strangeway, P., McCann, J. and Catalan, J. (1989). Paedophilia and hyperprolactinaemia. *British Journal of Psychiatry*, **155**, 847–848.

Haugaard, J.J. and Tilly, C. (1988). Characteristics predicting children's responses to sexual encounters with other children. *Child Abuse and Neglect*, **12**, 209–218.

Henson, D.E. and Rubin, H.B. (1971). Voluntary control of eroticism. *Journal of Applied Behavioral Analysis*, **4**, 37–44.

Hess, E.H. (1965). Attitude and pupil size. *Scientific American*, **212**(4), 46–54.

Hicks, R.R. (1991). *In Pursuit of Satan: The Police and the Occult*. Buffalo, NY: Prometheus.

Hildebran, D. and Pithers, W. (1989). Enhancing offender empathy for sexual-abuse victims. In D.R. Laws (Ed.). *Relapse Prevention with Sex Offenders*. New York: Guilford Press, pp. 236–243.

Hindman, J. (1988). Research disputes assumptions about child molesters. *NDAA Bulletin*, **7**, 1–3.

Hinton, J.W., O'Neill, M.T. and Webster, S. (1980). Psychophysiological assessment of sex offenders in a security hospital. *Archives of Sexual Behavior*, **9**(3), 208–216.

Hobbs, C.J. and Wynne, J.M. (1986). Buggery in childhood: a common syndrome of child abuse. *The Lancet*, 4 October, 792–796.

Hobson, W.F., Boland, C. and Jamieson, D. (1985). Dangerous sexual offenders. *Medical Aspects of Human Sexuality*, **19**(2), 104–119.

Hollin, C.R. and Howells, C. (Eds) (1991). *Clinical Approaches to Sex Offenders and their Victims*. Chichester: John Wiley.

Holmes, R.M. (1991). *Sex Crimes*. Newbury Park. CA: Sage.

Horley, J. (1988). Cognitions of child sexual abusers. *Journal of Sex Research*, **25**(4), 542–545.

Howells, K. (1978). Some meanings of children for paedophiles. In M. Cook and G. Wilson (Eds). *Love and Attraction: An International Conference*. Oxford: Pergamon Press, pp. 519–526.

Howells, K. (1981). Adult sexual interest in children: considerations relevant to theories of aetiology. In M. Cook and K. Howells (Eds). *Adult Sexual Interest in Children*. London: Academic Press, pp. 55–94.

Howells, K. (1991). Child sexual abuse: Finkelhor's precondition model revisited. Paper presented to the First Joint Spanish–British Conference on Psychology, Crime and the Law, Pamplona, June 1991.

Howitt, D. (1982). *Mass Media and Social Problems*. Oxford: Pergamon Press.

Howitt, D. (1991). *Concerning Psychology: Psychology Applied to Social Issues*. Milton Keynes: Open University Press.

Howitt, D. (1992). *Child Abuse Errors*. Hemel Hempstead: Harvester-Wheatsheaf.

Howitt, D. (1994). Pornographic piggy in the middle. In C. Haslam and A. Bryman (Eds). *Social Scientists Meet the Media*. London: Routledge.

Howitt, D. and Cumberbatch, G. (1990). *Pornography: Impacts and Influences*. London: Home Office Research and Planning Unit.

Howitt, D. and Cumberbatch, G. (in press). *Criminogenic Fantasies and the Media*. London: Broadcasting Standards Council.

Howitt, D. and Owusu-Bempah, J. (1994). *The Racism of Psychology: Time for Change*. Hemel Hempstead: Harvester-Wheatsheaf.

Hucker, S., Langevin, R. and Bain, J. (1988). A double blind trial of sex drive reducing medication in pedophiles. *Annals of Sex Research*, **1**, 227–242.

Hurry, A. (1990). Bisexual conflict and paedophilic fantasies in the analysis of a late adolescent. *Journal of Child Psychotherapy*, **16**(1), 5–28.

Ingram, M. (1979). The participating victim: a study of sexual offences against pre-pubertal boys. In M. Cook and G. Wilson (Eds). *Love and Attraction: An International Conference*. Oxford: Pergamon Press.

Innes, J.M. and Zeitz, H. (1988). The public's view of the impact of the mass media: a test of the "third person" effect. *European Journal of Social Psychology*, **18**, 457–463.

Jackson, S. (1990). Western ideas on children's sexuality. In M.E. Perry (Ed.). *Handbook of Sexology*, Vol. 7: *Childhood and Adolescent Sexology*. Amsterdam: Elsevier, pp. 23–49.

Jenkins, P. (1992). *Intimate Enemies: Moral Panics in Contemporary Great Britain*. New York: Aldine De Gruyter.

Jenkins, P. and Maier-Katkin, D. (1988). Protecting the victims of child sexual abuse: a case for caution. *Prison Journal*, **68**(2), 25–35.

Jenkins-Hall, K.D. (1989). Cognitive restructuring. In D.R. Laws (Ed.). *Relapse Prevention with Sex Offenders*. New York: Guilford Press, pp. 207–215.

Jenkins-Hall, K.D. and Marlatt, G.A. (1989). Apparently irrelevant decisions in the relapse process. In D.R. Laws (Ed.). *Relapse Prevention with Sex Offenders*. New York: Guilford Press, pp. 47–55.

Jenkins-Hall, K.D., Osborn, C.A., Anderson, C.S., Anderson, K.A. and Shockley-Smith, C. (1989). The Center for Prevention of Child

Molestation. In D.R. Laws (Ed.). *Relapse Prevention with Sex Offenders*. New York: Guilford Press, pp. 268–291.

Jervis, M. (1988). The Cleveland Inquiry Report. *Social Work Today*, **19**(45), 5–11.

Johnson, E. (1990). Review essay: inscrutable desires. *Philosophy of the Social Sciences*, **20**(2), 208–221.

Johnson, R. and Shrier, D.K. (1985). Sexual victimization of boys. *Journal of Adolescent Health Care*, **6**(5), 372–376.

Johnson, W.T., Kupperstein, L.R. and Petters, J.J. (1970). Sex offenders' experience with erotica. In *Technical Reports of the Commission on Obscenity and Pornography*, Vol. 7. Washington, DC: US Government Printing Office.

Johnston, S.A., French, A.P., Schouweiler, W.F. and Johnston, F.A. (1992). Naivete and need for affection among pedophiles. *Journal of Clinical Psychology*, **48**(5), 621–627.

Karpman, B. (1950). A case of paedophilia (legally rape) cured by psychoanalysis. *Psychoanalytic Review*, **37**, 235–276.

Kasl, C.D. (1990). Female perpetrators of sexual abuse: a feminist view. In M. Hunger (Ed.). *The Sexually Abused Male: Prevalence, Impact, and Treatment*, Vol. 1. Lexington, MA: Lexington Books, pp. 259–274.

Kelly, L. (1988). *Surviving Sexual Violence*. Cambridge: Polity Press.

Kelly, L. (1989). What's in a name? defining child sexual abuse. *Feminist Review*, **28**, 65–73.

Kempe, R.S. and Kempe, C.H. (1978). *Child Abuse*. London: Fontana.

Killias, M. (1991). The historic origins of penal statutes concerning sexual activities involving children and adolescents. *Journal of Homosexuality*, **20**(1/2), 41–46.

Kilmann, P., Sabalis, R., Gearing, M.L., Bukstel, L.H. and Scovern, A.W. (1982). The treatment of sexual paraphilias: a review of the outcome research. *Journal of Sex Research*, **18**(3), 193–152.

Kincaid, J.R. (1993). *Child-Loving: The Erotic Child and Victorian Culture*. London: Routledge.

Kinsey, A.C., Pomeroy, W.B. and Martin, C.E. (1948). *Sexual Behavior in the Human Male*. Philadelphia, PA: Saunders.

Kinsey, A.C., Pomeroy, W.B., Martin, C.E. and Gebhard, P.H. (1953). *Sexual Behavior in the Human Female*. Philadelphia, PA: Saunders.

Kirby, T. (1993). Killers tell all for fame or parole. *The Independent*, 14 July, 5.

Kirkendall, L.A. and McBride, L.G. (1990). Preadolescent and adolescent imagery and sexual fantasies: beliefs and experiences. In M.E. Perry (Ed.). *Handbook of Sexology*, Vol. 7: *Childhood and Adolescent Sexology*. Amsterdam: Elsevier, pp. 263–286.

Kitzinger, J. (1988). Defending innocence: ideologies of childhood. *Feminist Review*, **28**, Spring, 77–87.

Knight, R.A. (1988). A taxonomic analysis of child molesters. In R.A. Prentky and V.L. Quinsey (Eds). *Human Sexual Aggression: Current Perspectives*, Annals of the New York Academy of Science, Vol. 528, 12 August. New York: New York Academy of Science, pp. 2–20.

Knight, R.A. (1992). The generation and corroboration of a taxonomic model for child molesters. In W. O'Donohue and J.H. Geer (Eds). *The Sexual Abuse of Children: Clinical Issues*, Vol. 2. Hillsdale, NJ: Lawrence Erlbaum, pp. 24–70.

Knight, R.A. and Prentky, R.A. (1990). Classifying sexual offenders: the development and corroboration of taxonomic models. In W.L, Marshall, D.R. Laws and H.E. Barber (Eds). *The Handbook of Sexual Assault: Issues, Theories and Treatment of Offenders*. New York: Plenum Press.

Knight, R.A., Rosenberg, R. and Schneider, B. (1985). Classification of sexual offenders: perspectives, methods and validation. In A. Burgess (Ed.). *Rape and Sexual Assault: A Research Handbook*. New York: Garland Publishing, pp. 223–293.

Kraemer, W. (1976). A paradise lost. In W. Kraemer (Ed.). *The Forbidden Love: The Normal and Abnormal Love of Children*. London: Sheldon Press, pp. 1–35.

Krafft-Ebing, R. von (1922). *Psychopathia Sexualis*. Brooklyn: Physicians and Surgeons Press.

Kremsdorf, R.B., Holmen, M.L. and Laws, D.R. (1980). Orgasmic reconditioning without deviant imagery: a case report with a pedophile. *Behavior Research and Therapy*, **18**, 203–207.

Kutchinsky, B. (1973). The effect of easy availability of pornography on the incidence of sex crimes: the Danish experience. *Journal of Social Issues*, **29**(3), 163–191.

Kutchinsky, B. (1976). Deviance and criminality: the case of a voyeur in a peeper's paradise. *Diseases of the Nervous System*, **37**(3), 145–151.

Kutchinsky, B. (1991). Pornography and rape: theory and practice? *International Journal of Law and Psychiatry*, **14**(1/2), 47–64.

La Fontaine, J. (1990). *Child Sexual Abuse*. Cambridge: Polity.

Lambert, K. (1976). The scope and dimensions of paedophilia. In W. Kraemer (Ed.). *The Forbidden Love: The Normal and Abnormal Love of Children*. London: Sheldon Press, pp. 80–128.

Landis, C. (1940). *Sex in Development*. New York: Hoeber.

Landis, J.T. (1956). Experiences of 500 children with adult sexual deviation. *Psychiatric Quarterly Supplement*, **30**(1), 91–109.

Lang, R.A. and Langevin, R. (1991). Parent–child relations in offenders who commit violent sexual crimes against children. *Behavioral Sciences and the Law*, **9**, 61–71.

Lang, R.A., Flor-Henry, P. and Frenzel, R.R. (1990). Sex hormone profiles in pedophilic and incestuous men. *Annals of Sex Research*, **3**, 59–74.

Lang, R., Rouget, A.C. and van Santen, V. (1988). The role of victim age and sexual maturity in child sexual abuse. *Annals of Sex Research*, **1**, 467–484.

Langevin, R. (1983). *Sexual Strands: Understanding and Treating Sexual Anomalies in Men*. London: Lawrence Erlbaum Associates.

Langevin, R.M., Paitich, D., Freeman, R., Mann, K. and Handy, L. (1978). Personality characteristics and sexual anomalies in males. *Canadian Journal of Behavioral Science*, **10**, 222–238.

Langevin, R., Lang, R.A., Wright, P. and Hardy, L. (1988). Pornography and sexual offenses. *Annals of Sex Research*, **1**(3), 355–362.

Lanyon, R.I. (1986). Theory and treatment in child molestation. *Journal of Consulting and Clinical Psychology*, **54**(2), 176–182.

Laws, D.R. (1985). Sexual fantasy alternation: procedural considerations. *Journal of Behavior Therapy and Experimental Psychiatry*, **16**(1), 39–44.

Laws, D.R. and Rubin, H.B. (1969). Instructional control of an autonomic sexual response. *Journal of Applied Behavioral Analysis*, **2**, 93–99.

Lebegue, B.J. (1985). Paraphilias in pornography: a study of perversions inherent in titles. *Australian Journal of Sex, Marriage and the Family*, **6**, 133–136.

Lebegue, B.J. (1991). Paraphilias in US pornography titles: "Pornography made me do it" (Ted Bundy). *Bulletin of the American Academy of Psychiatry Law*, **19**(1), 43.

Lederer, L. (Ed.) (1980). *Take Back the Night: Women and Pornography*. New York: William Morrow.

Levin, S.M. and Stava, L. (1987). Personality characteristics of sex offenders: a review. *Archives of Sexual Behavior*, **16**(1), 57–79.

Levine, S.B., Risen, C.B. and Althof, S.E. (1990). Essay on the diagnosis and nature of paraphilia. *Journal of Sex and Marital Therapy*, **16**(2), 89–102.

Li, C.-K. (1991). "The main thing is being wanted": some case studies on adult sexual experiences with children. *Journal of Homosexuality*, **20**(1/2), 129–143.

Licht, H. (1953). *Sexual Life in Ancient Greece*. Westport, CT: Greenwood Press.

Longo, R.E. (1982). Sexual learning and experience among adolescent sexual offenders. *International Journal of Offender Therapy and Comparative Criminology*, **26**, 235–241.

MacCulloch, M.J., Snowden, P.R., Wood, P.J.W. and Mills, H.E. (1983). Sadistic fantasy, sadistic behaviours and offending. *British Journal of Psychiatry*, **143**, 20–29.

MacLeod, M. and Saraga, E. (1988). Challenging the orthodoxy: towards a feminist theory and practice. *Feminist Review*, **28**, 17–55.

Marlatt, G.A. and Gordon, J.R. (Eds). (1985). *Relapse Prevention*. New York: Guilford Press.

Marques, J.C., Day, D.M., Nelson, C. and Miner, M.H. (1989). The sex offender treatment and evaluation project: California's relapse prevention program. In D.R. Laws (Ed.). *Relapse Prevention with Sex Offenders*. New York: Guilford Press, pp. 247–267.

Marshall, W.L. (1973). The modification of sexual fantasies: a combined treatment approach to the reduction of deviant sexual behavior. *Behavioral Research and Therapy*, **11**, 557–564.

Marshall, W.L. (1979). Satiation therapy: a procedure for reducing deviant sexual arousal. *Journal of Applied Behavior Analysis*, **12**(3), 377–389.

Marshall, W.L. (1988). The use of sexually explicit stimuli by rapists, child molesters and non-offenders. *Journal of Sex Research*, **25**(2), 267–288.

Marshall, W.L. and Barbaree, H.E. (1988). An outpatient treatment program for child molesters. In R.A. Prentky and V.L. Quinsey (Eds). *Human Sexual Aggression: Current Perspectives*, Annals of the New York Academy of Science, Vol. 528, 12 August. New York: New York Academy of Science, pp. 205–214.

Marshall, W.L., Barbaree, H.E. and Christophe, D. (1986). Sexual offenders against female children: Sexual preferences for age of victims and type of behavior. *Canadian Journal of Behavioural Science*, **18**, 424–439.

Marshall, W.L., Hudson, S.M. and Ward, T. (1992). Sexual deviance. In P.H. Wilson (Ed.). *Principles and Practice of Relapse Prevention*. New York: Guilford Press, pp. 235–254.

Masson, J.M. (1985). *An Assault on Truth*. New York: Penguin.

Mathews, R., Mathews, J. and Speltz, K. (1990). Female sexual offenders. In M. Hunger (Ed.). *The Sexually Abused Male: Prevalence, Impact, and Treatment*, Vol. 1. Lexington, MA: Lexington Books, pp. 275–293.

McAnulty, R.D. and Adams, H.E. (1990). Patterns of sexual arousal of accused child molesters involved in custody disputes. *Archives of Sexual Behavior*, **19**(6), 541–555.

McCauley, E., Burke, P.M., Furukawa, J. and Urquiza, A.J. (1983). Sexual behavior problems in pre-pubertal children. University of Washington, unpublished manuscript.

McConaghy, N. (1989). Review of *Relapse Prevention with Sex Offenders*. D. Richard Laws (ed.), Guilford Press, New York, 1989. *Archives of Sexual Behavior*, **19**(6), 617–621.

McConaghy, N. (1991). Validity and ethics of penile circumference measures of sexual arousal: a critical review. *Archives of Sexual Behavior*, **19**(4), 357–369.

McCormack, T. (1988). The censorship of pornography: catharsis or learning? *American Journal of Orthopsychiatry*, **58**, 492–504.

McIntosh, M. (1988). Introduction to an issue: family secrets as public drama. *Feminist Review*, **28**, 6–15.

Menard, J.L. and Johnson, G.M. (1992). Incest: family dysfunction or sexual preference? *Family Therapy*, **19**(2), 115–122.

Meyer, W.J. (1992). Depo provera treatment for sex offending behavior: an evaluation of outcome. *Bulletin of the American Academy of Psychiatry and the Law*, **20**(3), 249–259.

Mian, M., Wehrspann, W., Klajner-Diamond, H., LeBaron, D. and Winder, C. (1986). Review of 125 children 6 years of age and under who were sexually abused. *Child Abuse and Neglect*, **10**, 223–229.

Mohr, J.W. (1981). Age structures in pedophilia. In M. Cook and K. Howells (Eds). *Adult Sexual Interest in Children*. London: Academic Press, pp. 41–54.

Money, J. (1972). The therapeutic use of androgen-depleting hormone. In H.L.P. Resnick and M.E. Wolfgang (Eds). *Sexual Behaviors: Social, Clinical, and Legal Aspects*. Boston, MA: Little, Brown, pp. 351–360.

Morgan, R. (1978). Theory and practice: pornography and rape. In R. Morgan (Ed.). *Going Too Far: The Personal Chronicle of a Feminist*. New York: Random House, pp. 163–169.

Murphy, W.D., Haynes, M.R., Stalgaitis, S.J. and Flanagan, B. (1986). *Journal of Psychopathology and Behavioral Assessment*, **8**(4), 339–353.

Nash, C.L. and West, D.J. (1985). Sexual molestation of young girls: a retrospective survey. In D.J. West (Ed.). *Sexual Victimisation: Two Recent Researches into Sex Problems and their Social Effects*. London: Gower, pp. 1–94.

Nelson, C. and Jackson, P. (1989). High-risk recognition: the cognitive–

behavioral chain. In D.R. Laws (Ed.). *Relapse Prevention with Sex Offenders*. New York: Guilford Press, pp. 167–177.

Newton, D.E. (1978). Homosexual behavior and child molestation: a review of the evidence. *Adolescence*, **13**(49), 29–43.

Nichols, H.R. and Molinder, I. (1984). The multiphasic sex inventory manual. Available from: Nichols and Molinder, 437 Bowes Drive, Tacoma, WA 98466, USA.

Nowicki, S. and Strickland, B. (1973). A locus of control scale for children. *Journal of Consulting and Clinical Psychology*, **40**(1), 148–154.

O'Brien, S.J. (1986). *Why They Did It: Stories of Eight Convicted Child Molesters*. Springfield, IL: Charles C. Thomas.

O'Donohue, W. and Letourneau, E. (1993). A brief group treatment for the modification of denial in child sexual abusers: outcome and follow-up. *Child Abuse and Neglect*, **17**, 299–304.

Okami, P. and Goldberg, S. (1992). Personality correlates of pedophilia. *Journal of Sex Research*, **29**(3), 297–328.

Olson, P.E. (1990). The sexual abuse of boys: a study of the long-term psychological effects. In M. Hunter (Ed.). *The Sexually Abused Male: Prevalence, Impact, and Treatment*, Vol. 1. Lexington, MA: Lexington Books, pp. 137–152.

Panton, J.H. (1979). MMPI profile configurations associated with incestuous and non-incestuous child molesting. *Psychological Reports*, **45**, 335–338.

Parton, N. (1985). *The Politics of Child Abuse*. London: Macmillan.

Pawlak, A.E., Boulet, J.R. and Bradford, J.M.W. (1991). Discriminant analysis of a sexual-functioning inventory with intrafamilial and extrafamilial child molesters. *Archives of Sexual Behavior*, **20**(1), 27–34.

Perkins, D. (1991). Clinical work with sex offenders in secure settings. In C.R. Hollin and K. Howells (Eds). *Clinical Work with Sex Offenders in Secure Settings*. Chichester: John Wiley, pp. 151–177.

Peters, J.J. (1976). Children who are victims of sexual assault and the psychology of offenders. *American Journal of Psychotherapy*, **30**(3), 398–421.

Pithers, W.D. and Laws, D.R. (1989). The penile plethysmograph: uses and abuses in assessment and treatment of sexual aggressors. In B. Schwartz (Ed.). *A Practitioner's Guide to Treatment of the Incarcerated Male Sex Offender*. Washington, DC: National Institute of Corrections, pp. 83–91.

Pithers, W.D., Martin, G.R. and Cumming, G.F. (1989). Vermont Treatment Program for sexual aggressors. In D.R. Laws (Ed.). *Relapse Prevention with Sex Offenders*. New York: Guilford Press, pp. 292–310.

Pithers, W.D., Kashima, K.M., Cumming, G.F. and Beal, L.S. (1988). Relapse prevention: a method of enhancing maintenance of change in sex offenders. In A.C. Salter (Ed.). *Treating Child Sex Offenders and Victims: A Practical Guide*. Newbury Park, CA: Sage, pp. 131–170.

Pithers, W.D., Beal, L.S., Armstrong, J. and Petty, J. (1989). Identification of risk factors through clinical interviews and analysis of records. In D.R. Laws (Ed.). *Relapse Prevention with Sex Offenders*. New York: Guilford Press, pp. 77–87.

Plummer, K. (1981a). "The paedophile's progress": a view from below. In Taylor, B. (Ed.). *Perspectives on Paedophilia*. London: Batsford, pp. 113–132.

Plummer, K. (1981b). Pedophilia: constructing a sociological baseline. In M. Cook and K. Howells (Eds). *Adult Sexual Interest in Children*. London: Academic Press, pp. 221–250.

Plummer, K. (1991). Review of "Loving Boys: A Multidisciplinary Study of Sexual Relations between Adult and Minor Males", vol. 1, Dr Edward Brongersma. *Journal of Homosexuality*, **20**(1/2), 320–323.

Pontius, A.A. (1988). Introduction to biological issues, with neuropathological case illustrations. In R.A. Prentky and V.L. Quinsey (Eds). *Human Sexual Aggression: Current Perspectives*, Annals of the New York Academy of Science, Vol. 528, 12 August. New York: New York Academy of Science, pp. 148–153.

Powell, G.E. and Chalkley, A.J. (1981). The effects of paedophile attention on the child. In B. Taylor (Ed.). *Perspectives on Paedophilia*. London: Batsford.

Prendergast, W.E. (1991). *Treating Sex Offenders in Correctional Institutions and Outpatient Clinics: A Guide to Clinical Practice*. New York: Haworth.

Prentky, R. and Burgess, A.W. (1990). Rehabilitation of child molesters: a cost–benefit analysis. *American Journal of Orthopsychiatry*, **60**(1), 108–117.

Pride, M. (1987). *The Child Abuse Industry*. Winchester, IL: Crossway.

Protter, B. and Travin, S. (1987). Sexual fantasies in the treatment of paraphiliac disorders: a bimodal approach. *Psychiatric Quarterly*, **58**(4), 279–297.

Quinsey, V.L. (1983). Prediction of recidivism and the evaluation of treatment programs for sex offenders. In S.N. Verdun-Jones and A.A. Keltner (Eds). *Sexual Aggression and the Law*. Vancouver, Canada: Simon Fraser University Criminology Research Center, pp. 27–40.

Quinsey, V.L. and Carrigan, W.F. (1978). Penile responses to visual stimuli: instructional control with and without auditory sexual fantasy correlates. *Criminal Justice and Behavior*, **5**(4), 333–342.

Quinsey, V.L. and Chaplin, T.C. (1988). Preventing faking in phallometric assessments of sexual preference. *Annals of the New York Academy of Sciences*, **528**, 49–58.

Quinsey, V.L., Arnold, L.S. and Pruesse, M.G. (1980). MMPI profiles of men referred for a pretrial assessment as a function of offense type. *Journal of Clinical Psychology*, **36**(2), 410–417.

Quinsey, V.L., Chaplin, T.C. and Upton, D. (1984). Sexual arousal to non-sexual violence and sadomasochistic themes among rapists and non-sex offenders. *Journal of Consulting and Clinical Psychology*, **52**, 651–657.

Quinsey, V.L., Chaplin, T.C. and Varney, G. (1981). A comparison of rapists and non-sex offenders' sexual preferences for mutually consenting sex, rape, and physical abuse of women. *Behavioural Assessment*, **3**, 127–135.

Quinsey, V.L., Steinman, C.M., Bergersen, S.G. and Holmes, T.F. (1975). Penile circumference, skin conductance, and ranking responses of child molesters and "normals" to sexual and nonsexual visual stimuli. *Behavior Therapy*, **6**, 213–219.

Raboch, J. and Raboch, J. (1986). Number of siblings and birth order of sexually dysfunctional males and sexual delinquents. *Journal of Sex and Marital Therapy*, **12**(1), 73–76.

Ressler, R.K., Burgess, A.W. and Douglas, J.E. (1988). *Sexual Homicide: Patterns and Motives*. New York: Lexington.

Revitch, E. and Schlesinger, L.B. (1988). Clinical reflections on sexual aggression. In R.A. Prentky and V.L. Quinsey (Eds). *Human Sexual Aggression: Current Perspectives*, Annals of the New York Academy of Science, Vol. 528, 12 August. New York: New York Academy of Science, pp. 59–61.

Rhue, T.W. and Lynn, S.J. (1987). Fantasy proneness: developmental antecedents. *Journal of Personality*, **55**(1), 121–137.

Richardson, S. and Bacon, H. (Eds) (1991). *Child Sexual Abuse: Whose Problem? Reflections from Cleveland*. London: Venture Press.

Righton, P. (1981). The adult. In B. Taylor (Ed.). *Perspectives on Paedophilia*. London: Batsford, pp. 24–40.

Risin, L.I. and Koss, M.P. (1987). The sexual abuse of boys: prevalence and descriptive characteristics of childhood victimisations. *Journal of Interpersonal Violence*, **2**, 309–323.

Rosenthal, T.L. (1973). Response-contingent versus fixed punishment in aversion conditioning of pedophilia: a case study. *Journal of Nervous and Mental Disease*, **156**, 440–443.

Roth, S., Wayland, K. and Woolsey, M. (1990). Victimization history and victim–assailant relationship as factors in recovery from sexual assault. *Journal of Traumatic Stress*, **3**(1), 169–180.

Rotter, J.B. (1966). Generalized expectancies for internal versus external control of reinforcement. *Psychological Monographs*, **80**(1).

Rowan, E.L. (1988a). Pedophilia. *Journal of Social Work and Human Sexuality*, **7**(1), 91–100.

Rowan, E.L. (1988b). Predicting the effectiveness of treatment for pedophilia. *Journal of Forensic Sciences*, **33**(1), 204–209.

Russell, D.E.H. (1975). Pornography and violence: what does the new research say. In L. Lederer (Ed.). *Take Back the Night: Women and Pornography*. New York: William Morrow, pp. 218–238.

Russell, D.E.H. (1983). The incidence and prevalence of intrafamilial and extra-familial sexual abuse of female children. *Child Abuse and Neglect*, **7**, 133–146.

Russell, D.E.H. (1988). Pornography and rape: a causal model. *Journal of Political Psychology*, **9**(1), 41–73.

Russell, K., Sturgeon, V.H., Miner, M.H. and Nelson, C. (1989). Determinants of the abstinence violation effect on sexual fantasies. In D.R. Laws (Ed.). *Relapse Prevention with Sex Offenders*. New York: Guilford Press, pp. 63–72.

Salter, A.C. (1988). *Treating Child Sex Offenders and Victims: A Practical Guide*. Newbury Park, CA: Sage.

Sanders, W.B. (1980). *Rape and Woman's Identity*. Beverly Hills, CA: Sage.

Sandfort, Th.G.M. (1988). *The Meanings of Experience: On Sexual Contacts in Early Youth, and Sexual Behavior and Experience in Later Life*. Utrecht: Homostudies.

Sandfort, Th.G.M. (1989). Studies into child sexual abuse: an overview and critical appraisal. Paper presented at the 1st European Congress of Psychology. Amsterdam, 2–7 July.

Sandfort Th.G.M. (1992). The argument for adult–child sexual contact: a critical appraisal and new data. In W. O'Donohue and J.H. Geer (Eds). *The Sexual Abuse of Children: Clinical Issues*, Vol. 1. Hillsdale, NJ: Lawrence Erlbaum, pp. 38–48.

Sandfort, Th.G.M. and Everaerd, W.T.A.M. (1990). Male juvenile partners in pedophilia. In M.E. Perry (Ed.). *Handbook of Sexology*, Vol. 7: *Childhood and Adolescent Sexology*. Amsterdam: Elsevier, pp. 361–380.

Sandfort, Th.G.M., Brongersma, E. and van Naerssen, A. (1991). Man–boy relationships: different concepts for a diversity of phenomena. *Journal of Homosexuality*, **20**(1/2), 5–12.

Saphira, M. (1989). Can men who abuse children change? *Medicine and Law*, **8**, 125–129.

Saunders, E., Awad, G.A. and White, G. (1986). Male adolescent sexual offenders: The offender and the offense. *Canadian Journal of Psychiatry*, **31**(6), 542–549.

Schaeffer, M.R., Sobieraj, K. and Hollyfield, R.L. (1988). Prevalence of childhood physical abuse in male veteran alcoholics. *Child Abuse and Neglect*, **12**, 141–149.

Schouten, P.G.W. and Simon, W.T. (1992). Validity of phallometric measures with sex offenders: comments on the Quinsey, Laws, and Hall debate. *Journal of Consulting and Clinical Psychology*, **60**(5), 812–814.

Scott, M.L., Cole, J.K., McKay, S.E., Golden, C.J. and Liggett, K.R. (1984). Neuropsychological performance of sexual assaulters and pedophiles. *Journal of Forensic Sciences*, **29**(4), 1114–1118.

Scruton, R. (1986). *Sexual Desire: A Moral Philosophy of the Erotic*. New York: Free Press.

Seghorn, T.K., Prentky, R.A. and Boucher, R.J. (1987). Childhood sexual abuse in the lives of sexually aggressive offenders. *Journal of the American Academy of Child and Adolescent Psychiatry*, **26**, 262–267.

Seltzer, M.L. (1971). The Michigan Alcoholism Screening Test: the quest for a new diagnostic instrument. *American Journal of Psychiatry*, **127**, 1653–1658.

Serber, M. and Keith, C.G. (1974). The Atascadero project: model of a sexual retraining program for incarcerated homosexual pedophiles. *Journal of Homosexuality*, **1**(1), 87–97.

Shearer, S.L., Peters, C.P., Quaytman, M.S. and Ogden, R.L. (1990). Frequency and correlates of childhood sexual and physical abuse histories in adult female borderline inpatients. *American Journal of Psychiatry*, **147**, 214–216.

Silver, S. (undated). Available from Northwest Treatment Associates, 315 W. Galer, Seattle, WA 98119, USA.

Simpson, A.E. (1987). Vulnerability and the age of female consent: legal innovation and its effect on prosecutions for rape in eighteenth-century London. In R.P. Maccubbin (Ed.). *'Tis Nature's Fault: Unauthorized Sexuality during the Enlightenment*. Cambridge: Cambridge University Press, pp. 181–205.

Socarides, C.W. (1988). *The Preoedipal Origin and Psychoanalytic Therapy of Sexual Perversions*. Madison, CT: International Universities Press.

Socarides, C.W. (1991). Adult–child sexual pair: psychoanalytic findings. *The*

Journal of Psychohistory, **19**(2), 185–189.
Spence, J.T. and Helmreich, R.L. (1978). *Masculinity and Femininity: Their Psychological Dimensions, Correlates and Antecedents*. Austin, TX: University of Texas Press.
Spielberger, C.D., Gorsuch, R.L. and Lushene, R.E. (1970). *Manual for the State–Trait Anxiety Inventory*. Palo Alto, CA: Consulting Psychologists Press.
Steiger, H. and Zanko, M. (1990). Sexual traumata among eating disordered, psychiatric, and normal female groups: comparisons of prevalence and defence styles. *Journal of Interpersonal Violence*, **5**(1), 74–80.
Storr, A. (1964). *Sexual Deviation*. Harmondsworth: Penguin.
Sturup, G.K. (1972). Castration: the total treatment. In H.L.P. Resnick and M.E. Wolfgang (Eds). *Sexual Behaviors: Social, Clinical, and Legal Aspects*. Boston, MA: Little, Brown, pp. 361–382.
Suppe, F. (1991). Classifying sexual disorders: The Diagnostic and Statistical Manual of the American Psychiatric Association. *Journal of Homosexuality*, **9**(4), 9–28.
Tanner, J.M. (1978). *Foetus into Man*. Cambridge, MA: Harvard University Press.
Tate, T. (1990). *Child Pornography: An Investigation*. London: Methuen.
Tate, T. (1992) The child pornography industry: international trade in child sexual abuse. In C. Itzin (Ed.). *Pornography: Women, Violence and Civil Liberties: A Radical New View*. Oxford: Oxford University Press, pp. 203–216.
Taylor, I. (1984). *The Development of Law and Public Debate in the United Kingdom in Respect of Pornography and Obscenity*. Canada: Department of Justice.
Templeman, T.L. and Stinnett, R.D. (1991). Patterns of sexual arousal and history in a "normal" sample of young men. *Archives of Sexual Behavior*, **20**(2), 137–150.
Terman, L.M. (1938). *Psychological Factors in Marital Happiness*. New York: McGraw-Hill.
Terman, L.M. (1951). Correlates of orgasm adequacy in a group of 556 wives. *Journal of Psychology*, **32**, 115–172.
Tingle, D., Barnard, G.W., Robbins, L., Newman, G. and Hutchinson, D. (1986). Childhood and adolescent characteristics of pedophiles and rapists. *International Journal of Law and Psychiatry*, **9**, 103–116.
Toobert, S., Bartelme, K. and Jones, E. (1958). Some factors related to pedophilia. *International Journal of Social Psychiatry*, **4**, 272–279.
Travin, S., Bluestone, H., Coleman, E., Cullen, K. and Melella, J. (1985a). Pedophilia: an update on theory and practice. *Psychiatric Quarterly*, **57**(2), 89–103.
Travin, S., Bluestone, H., Coleman, E., Cullen, K. and Melella, M.S.W. (1985b). Pedophile types and treatment perspectives. *Journal of Forensic Science*, **31**(2), 614–620.
Trumbach, R. (1987). Sodomitical subcultures, sodomitical roles, and the gender revolution of the eighteenth century: the recent historiography. In R.P. Maccubbin (Ed.). *'Tis Nature's Fault: Unauthorized Sexuality during the Enlightenment*. Cambridge: Cambridge University Press, pp. 108–121.

Urquiza, A.J. (1988). The effects of childhood sexual abuse in an adult male population. Unpublished doctoral dissertation, University of Washington, Seattle.

Urquiza, A.J. and Capra, M. (1990). The impact of sexual abuse: initial and long-term effects. In M. Hunter (Ed.). *The Sexually Abused Male: Prevalence, Impact, and Treatment*, Vol. 1. Lexington, MA: Lexington Books, pp. 105–135.

Valcour, F. (1990). The treatment of child sex abusers in the church. In S.J. Rossetti (Ed.). *Slayer of the Soul*. Mystic, CT: Twenty-Third Publications, pp. 45–66.

Van Deventer, A.D. and Laws, D.R. (1978). Orgasmic reconditioning to redirect sexual arousal in pedophiles. *Behavior Therapy*, **9**, 748–765.

van Naerssen, A. (1991). Man–boy lovers: assessment, counseling, and psychotherapy. *Journal of Homosexuality*, **20**(1/2), 175–187.

van Naerssen, A.X., van Dijk, M., Hoogeveen, G., Visser, D. and van Zessen, G. (1987). Gay SM in pornography and reality. *Journal of Homosexuality*, **13**(2/3), 111–119.

van Zessen, G. (1991). A model for group counseling with male pedophiles. *Journal of Homosexuality*, **20**(1/2), 189–198.

Vine, I. (1990). *How Not to Understand Pornography*. University of Bradford, unpublished manuscript.

Virkunnen (1981). The child as participating victim. In M. Cook and K. Howells (Eds). *Adult Sexual Interest in Children*. London: Academic Press, pp. 121–134.

Walker, C.E. (1970). Erotic stimuli and the aggressive sexual offender. In *Technical Reports of the Commission on Obscenity and Pornography*, Vol. 7. Washington, DC: US Government Printing Office.

Wasserman, S. and Rosenfeld, A. (1992). An overview of the history of child sexual abuse and Sigmund Freud's contributions. In W. O'Donohue and J.H. Geer (Eds). *The Sexual Abuse of Children: Clinical Issues*, Vol. 1. Hillsdale, NJ: Lawrence Erlbaum, pp. 49–72.

Watson, D. and Friend, R. (1969). Measurement of social-evaluative anxiety. *Journal of Consulting and Clinical Psychology*, **33**(4), 448–457.

Wechsler, D. (1981). *Manual for the Wechsler Adult Intelligence Scale*. New York: Psychological Corporation.

Wellings, K., Field, J., Johnson, A. and Wadsworth, J. (1994). *Sexual Behaviour in Britain*. Harmondsworth: Penguin.

Westwood, G. (1960). *A Minority: A Report on the Life of the Male Homosexual in Great Britain*. London: Longmans.

Wettstein, R.M., Kelly, J. and Cavanaugh, J.L. (1982). A pharmacological approach to sexually deviant behavior in the community. *International Journal of the Sociology of the Family*, **12**, 155–162.

Wilby, P. (1994). Research team defends 1-in-90 gay sex claim. *Independent on Sunday*, 23 January, 1.

Wilcox, B.L. (1987). Pornography, social science and politics: when research and ideology collide. *American Psychologist*, **42**(10), 941–943.

Williams, B. (1979). *Report of the Committee on Obscenity and Film Censorship*, Cmnd 7772. London: HMSO.

Williams, M. (1976). A struggle for normality. In W. Kraemer (Ed.). *The*

Forbidden Love: The Normal and Abnormal Love of Children. London: Sheldon Press, pp. 129–145.

Wilson, G.D. (1978). *The Secrets of Sexual Fantasy*. London: J.M. Dent.

Wilson, G.D. (1981). *Love and Instinct*. London: Temple Smith.

Wilson, G.D. and Cox, D.N. (1983). Personality of paedophile club members. *Personality and Individual Differences*, **4**(3), 323–329.

Wilson, P.H. (Ed.) (1992). *Principles and Practice of Relapse Prevention*. New York: Guilford Press.

Winfield, I., George, L.K., Swartz, M. and Blazer, D.G. (1990). Sexual assault and psychiatric disorders among a community sample of women. *American Journal of Psychiatry*, **147**(3), 335–341.

Wolters, W.H.G., Zwaan, E.J., Wagebaar-Schwencke, P.M. and Deenen, T.A.M. (1985). A review of cases of sexually exploited children reported to the Netherlands State Police. *Child Abuse and Neglect*, **9**, 571–574.

Wong, S.E., Gaydos, G.R. and Fuqua, R.W. (1982). Operant control of pedophilia: reducing approaches to children. *Behavior Modification*, **6**(1), 73–84.

Wormith, J.A. (1986). Assessing deviant sexual arousal: physiological and cognitive aspects. *Advances in Behaviour Research and Therapy*, **8**(3), 101–137.

Wright, P., Nobrega, J., Langevin, R. and Wortzman, G. (1990). Brain density and symmetry in pedophilic and sexually aggressive offenders. *Annals of Sex Research*, **3**, 319–328.

Wyatt, G.W. (1985). The sexual abuse of Afro-American and white American women in childhood. *Child Abuse and Neglect*, **9**, 507–519.

Wyre, R. (1987). *Working with Sex Offenders*. Oxford: Perry Publications.

Wyre, R. (1989). Working with the paedophile. In M. Farrell (Ed.). *Understanding the Paedophile*. London: ISTD/The Portman Clinic, pp. 17–23.

Wyre, R. (1990). Why do men sexually abuse children? In T. Tate (Ed.). *Child Pornography: An Investigation*. London: Methuen, pp. 281–288.

Wyre, R. (1992). Pornography and sexual violence: working with sex offenders. In C. Itzin (Ed.). *Pornography: Women, Violence and Civil Liberties: A Radical New View*. Oxford: Oxford University Press, pp. 236–247.

Yaffe, M. (1981). The assessment and treatment of paedophilia. In Taylor, B. (Ed.). *Perspectives on Paedophilia*. London: Batsford, pp. 77–91.

Yates, A. (1990). Eroticized children. In M.E. Perry (Ed.). *Handbook of Sexology*, Vol. 7: *Childhood and Adolescent Sexology*. Amsterdam: Elsevier, pp. 325–334.

Author Index

Subject Index